An Accidental Archaeologist

An Accidental Archaeologist

A Personal MEMOIR

Eric M. Meyers

CASCADE *Books* • Eugene, Oregon

AN ACCIDENTAL ARCHAEOLOGIST
A Personal Memoir

Copyright © 2022 Eric M. Meyers. All rights reserved. Except for brief quotations in critical publications or reviews, no part of this book may be reproduced in any manner without prior written permission from the publisher. Write: Permissions, Wipf and Stock Publishers, 199 W. 8th Ave., Suite 3, Eugene, OR 97401.

Cascade Books
An Imprint of Wipf and Stock Publishers
199 W. 8th Ave., Suite 3
Eugene, OR 97401

www.wipfandstock.com

PAPERBACK ISBN: 978-1-6667-4352-4
HARDCOVER ISBN: 978-1-6667-4353-1
EBOOK ISBN: 978-1-6667-4354-8

Cataloguing-in-Publication data:

Names: Meyers, Eric M., author.

Title: An accidental archaeologist : a personal memoir / by Eric M. Meyers.

Description: Eugene, OR: Cascade Books, 2022.

Identifiers: ISBN 978-1-6667-4352-4 (paperback). | ISBN 978-1-6667-4353-1 (hardcover). | ISBN 978-1-6667-4354-8 (ebook).

Subjects: LCSH: Meyers, Eric M. | Archaeologists—Israel—Biography. | Archaeology—Israel. | Israel—Antiquities. | Excavations (Archaeology)—Israel. | American Schools of Oriental Research. | Sepphoris (Extinct city).

Classification: DS115.9 M49 2022 (print) | DS115.9 (epub)

11/29/22

Dedicated to Julie and Dina, Jacob and Zak,
and of course to Carol without whom
most of this would not have been possible.

Contents

Preface | ix
Abbreviations | xiii

Part One: Before Carol

1. Family Background | 3
2. Teen Years | 16
3. College/Dartmouth, 1958–1962 | 25
4. Graduate School/Brandeis, 1962–1964 | 41
5. Carol | 45

Part Two: With Carol

6. Israel/Europe, 1964–1965 | 53
7. Graduate School/Harvard, 1965–1969 | 63
8. Synagogue Survey in Upper Galilee, summer 1969 | 78
9. Duke Years | 82
10. Planning Khirbet Shemaʿ | 85
11. Gary Termite | 87
12. Breaking News: Dina and Early Tenure | 89
13. Meiron | 91
14. Jewish Studies at Duke and UNC: The Uncooperative Program | 94
15. Jerusalem Happenings, 1973–1975 | 96
16. The Albright Institute, Jerusalem, 1975–1976 | 100
17. Dad's Death (1977) and After | 105

CONTENTS

18 Gush Ḥalav, 1977–1978 | 107
19 Back at Duke, 1978–1979 | 109
20 Venosa, Italy, 1980–1981 | 112
21 Nabratein and the Ark, 1980–1981 | 115
22 Oxford, 1982–1983 | 122
23 ASOR and Yigael Yadin (June 27, 1985) | 127
24 Sepphoris, 1985 | 131
25 ASOR Presidency, 1990–1996 | 140
26 Mom's Death (1994) and Philadelphia | 146
27 Frankfurt, Martin Buber Guest Professor, 1995 | 151
28 Rome and the Catacombs, Summer 1995 | 154
29 Leiden and Rome, 2016 and 2017 | 158
30 The Meyer and Heschel Archives at Duke | 162

Part Three: Other Matters

31 Music and Singing | 167
32 The Havurah | 172
33 Health Concerns | 174
34 Israel, Zionism, and the Jewish People | 177
35 The Jewish Heritage (Foundation) of North Carolina (JHNC) | 180
36 The Professoriate: Teaching as a Calling (*Beruf*) | 183
37 Epilogue | 185

Appendix A: The Meyerowitz Family from Königsberg | 187
Appendix B: Dartmouth Phi Beta Kappa Address | 192
Appendix C: ASOR Obituaries/Tributes | 196
*Appendix D: The Rabbi Marshall T. Meyer Archive
     at Duke University* | 200
*Appendix E: The Rabbi Abraham Joshua Heschel Archive
     at Duke University* | 204
Index | 209

Preface

THE IDEA OF THIS memoir has come about for several reasons. First, I have been privileged to live a very full life, albeit some of it on borrowed time (more about my fortuitous recovery from heart disease below), as a youngster growing up in rural Norwich, Connecticut, one time the "Rose of New England," and as an adult with opportunities to teach and write and administer that I could not have envisioned as a child. Second, in finding a career in university teaching and research I have been able to travel extensively in the Middle East over half a century and have made scores of trips to Israel at the time of this writing. Jerusalem and the Galilee have been a home away from home for me, my wife Carol, and daughters Julie and Dina, and we have lived to see enormous changes there in demographics and the very character of the land itself, most for good and some for bad. But that is to get ahead of the story. All this could not have happened were I not to have been fortunate enough to find a willing life partner in Carol who shared my love of the land of Israel and the excitement of discovery in the land itself in the form of archaeology and with a full and thorough engagement with the text of the Hebrew Bible.

Friends and colleagues have also told me often through the years, after hearing various stories of our adventures and anecdotes, that I ought to write these down somewhere for others to see. And as I prepared to undertake the challenge of writing this memoir, I can see that several key aspects of my personal history have influenced me more than others. For example, the experience of anti-Semitism in my early years and in college made me a staunch advocate of human rights and advocate for diversity and tolerance. While I was deeply affected by these experiences, I can say in hindsight that the ultimate effect was to make me more aware of injustices. Perhaps my love of the Jewish tradition from an early age and pride in public in saying so brought some of this on, but in any case whatever the cause, it is seared into my memory bank and has been a part of me all these days.

As I begin this task of recalling so much, I am in my new Duke office in which several of my doctoral students once studied and worked. For the first time in many years I am finally up to date in my writing obligations. And on the day in July 2017 when I began this writing, the outside heat index was three digits and several colleagues, Chad Spigel of Trinity University in San Antonio and Paul Flesher of the University of Wyoming in Laramie, were hard at work on an open-access archive of all our Duke archaeological excavations, four rural sites in Upper Galilee, and the urban site of Sepphoris in Lower Galilee, working at the David M. Rubenstein Rare Book & Manuscript Library on campus. This is a daunting undertaking and we are ever grateful to them for initiating this so that future generations will have access to the database on which we based our conclusions and presented out reports. No doubt in due course others might have the means to revise and/or correct many of them, and this is the way of scholarship and much of life: things change as they should.

But before I begin, let me say a few words about what is included in this memoir. The first part is my personal story of growing up in Norwich, Connecticut, through Dartmouth College and Brandeis, until 1964 BC. I call it "1964 BC" because it means "before Carol," since after that so much changed for both of us. The middle part focuses on my Duke career interspersed with reference to all the excavation projects and my work in ASOR (American Schools of Oriental Research, renamed American Society of Overseas Research in 2021) as president and trustee. The final section notes some of the more important things in my view I did for Duke Library and its archival holdings in human rights and archaeology. An appendix on my father's family is a slightly revised form of its published version, and two obituaries of key ASOR trustees fill out my remarks about my time as president.

Of course, recalling times and events from long ago is selective, and I may have misremembered some things or exaggerated some of them. But this manuscript is the result, and I hope that anyone who reads it understands me better. Hopefully, there are some lessons to be learned. At first I thought that my two grandsons, Jacob and Zak, would most benefit from and enjoy

PREFACE

these recollections, and that is my most ardent hope. But I realize that I am also speaking at times to all my former students, who have meant so much to me and from whom I have learned so much, and hopefully to others.

EMM

Durham, North Carolina
May 2022

Abbreviations

ACOR	American Center of Research
AIA	Archaeological Institute of America
AIAR	Albright Institute of Archaeological Research
AJS	Association of Jewish Studies
ASOR	American School of Oriental Research
ASOR	American Society of Overseas Research (new name)
BA	*Biblical Archaeologist*
BASOR	*Bulletin of the American Schools of Oriental Research*
CAARI	Cyprus American Archaeological Research Institute
HUC	Hebrew Union College
IES	Institute for European Studies
JCC	Jewish Community Center
JHNC	Jewish Heritage (Foundation) North Carolina
JNF	Jewish National Fund
JSP	Joint Sepphoris Project
JTS	Jewish Theological Seminary
MEP	Meiron Excavation Project
NEJS	Near Eastern and Jewish Studies Department, Brandeis
NELL	Near Eastern Languages and Literatures Department, Harvard
NFA	Norwich Free Academy
PBI	Pontifical Biblical Institute
SBL	Society of Biblical Literature
TJC	Triangle Jewish Chorale

Part One
Before Carol

1

Family Background

The Meyer/Meyers Clan

THE CIRCUMSTANCES THAT BROUGHT my mother and father together were cataclysmic and epochal for the United States in the twentieth century. Isaac (Ike) and Anita Meyer, my mother's parents, moved from New York to Norwich, Connecticut, as a result of the stock market crash of 1929 and because of business disasters that followed. My father, Karl David Otto Meyers, came to the United States because of the Holocaust emerging in Germany and Europe after Hitler came to power in January 1933. My mom, Shirlee Miriam, came with her parents from Brooklyn, New York, and my dad came from Königsberg (today Kaliningrad), East Prussia, Germany, all alone except for Uncle Eddie Meyers who met him on Ellis Island and told him to change Meyerowitz to Meyers. Hence the similarity of his surname to my mother's maiden name and occasional attendant name confusion. As my father liked to say when people asked about the two names, he said when he got married all he had to do was put his "s" on "Meyer." To this day people will often wonder which name is correct, especially since Duke Archives now house materials from my late Uncle Marshall, that is, Rabbi Marshall T. Meyer, human rights activist in Argentina and later dynamic rabbi on the Upper West Side of New York. In reality, the confusion is justified since I am a true mixture of both sides of the family, the Germans and the Meyers [sic].

PART ONE: BEFORE CAROL

My parents, Karl and Shirlee, ca. 1950

Isaac and Anita Meyer, maternal grandparents, ca. late 1930s.

FAMILY BACKGROUND

Eric and sister Connie, 1944

The Meyer family, my maternal grandparents, were second generation descendants of Russian immigrants, came from Brooklyn to Connecticut having had a modestly successful business in the men's pants industry, and Isaac started anew in Norwich with a partner, Phillip Gottesfield, some years after the stock market crash in 1929, in 1937. The new company's name was G & M Manufacturing Co. Isaac spent plenty of time on the road selling, while the pants were cut and sewn locally. It provided a solid and steady income for the family, who resided at 16 Goldberg Avenue where they lived from 1937. As it turns out that was just a few minutes away from where we lived, 1 Buckingham Ave., and my sister Connie and I were in and out of 16 Goldberg Ave. almost as much as our own house. Our dog, a German shepherd by the name of Prince, was the same, and he especially was attached to Grandpa Ike who loved to scratch behind his ears while he read the paper or had a drink. Gram and Gramps had three children: Shirlee, the oldest, my mom, born in 1919; John, the middle child, born in 1924; and

Marshall, born in 1930. My sister was born in 1944 when I was four, and I had the good fortune of being the first of any offspring on both sides of the family and hence enjoyed more than my fair share of attention. The truth is I enjoyed every minute of it, and maybe that's why I was able to withstand lots of pressure later in life. The love and attention came from both sides of the family. Since Marshall was only ten years older than me, he was around all the time, or I was around him in either house. Thus he became sort of a mentor and guide, and babysitter of course, to both me and my sister. He also was crazy about Prince and later in life in Argentina had a German shepherd with that very name. He was not yet deep into Judaism, as he was in college and after, but was a real intellectual and an ardent fan of opera.

The love of music came from my father and my father's sister's (Eva) husband, Kurt Oppenheimer, who was also the family physician to both sides of the Meyer/Meyers clan. Uncle Kurt was so deeply involved with music that when the Saturday afternoon Metropolitan Opera broadcast came on, his house became silent except for the radio that blasted forth whatever was on. He told us that before medicine he had studied conducting, but I'm not sure about the details. Whenever I would visit Uncle Kurt, however, if there was time to spare, I was asked to take the baton and conduct whatever music Uncle Kurt thought was appropriate. Over time I learned that Kurt had a much broader appreciation for music than my father, for whom opera meant the standard repertoire, with verismo to be preferred, along of course with schmaltz, especially German operettas like *Gypsy Baron*. And *Fledermaus* was played so much in our house the record wore out and had to be replaced. The other record we wore down was *South Pacific*. Marshall was more in the mold of my dad than Uncle Kurt, and I attribute my more inclusive taste in music to him. But be that as it may, music was a central part of our household, and no family event or holiday could be held or celebrated without some sort of singing and piano playing and even dance, by Connie.

FAMILY BACKGROUND

Dad with his two sisters, Eva Oppenheimer (left), Leni Heaton (right), and Mom off to right of frame. Formal event at Beth Jacob Synagogue, Norwich, Connecticut, early 1950s.

Dad had studied voice in Königsberg, and as a new immigrant to the US got his first job as a singing waiter in New York City at Sardi's. His university studies at Immanuel Kant University ended when his father told him to leave for America until the Nazi era was over. He actually had a lovely rich baritone voice, and his parents, Benno and Käthe, were both musically engaged most of their lives. Benno was in the textile business and was successful enough to offer his services without compensation as intendant or general manager of the Königsberg opera before the war, in the 1920s, and Oma Käthe was an accomplished singer and pianist. Richard Strauss was a regular visitor to their home, and my father told me he remembers sitting on Strauss's lap when Strauss was playing Skat, a complicated card game, with Opa and Ernst Kunwald, conductor of the orchestra. Except for a couple of famous Richard Strauss arias from *Der Rosenkavalier*, my father never liked Strauss as much as Uncle Kurt and I did (see below Appendix A for a more detailed observation on the Meyerowitz family). Actually, *Der Rosenkavalier* is in my top-four list of favorite operas.

PART ONE: BEFORE CAROL

At left, Benno Meyerowitz, my paternal grandfather, director of the Königsberg State Opera; middle, Ernst Kunwald, conductor of the orchestra; at right, Richard Strauss, renowned composer and friend of the family, walking to the opera house, mid-1920s.

How did all this love of classical music and opera play out in our lives? There are several images and events that may help the reader understand how much a part of our lives it was. There was our non-blood relative uncle Walther Lehmann (lovingly called Uncle "Vacky"), who was a real, live classical pianist, and my mother's parents Anita and Ike had a concert grand piano in their living room. We had an upright at home, and I was taking piano lessons. Uncle Kurt and Aunt Eva also had an upright. And Uncle Vacky at every family gathering played for us. When Connie was just a little scrapper, around three or so, and I was seven, when Vacky played the grand piano at 16 Goldberg Ave. Connie and I and Prince would sit under the piano and be absolutely entranced with the sounds coming out from above us. Uncle Marshall had shared in all this as well, and in high school at NFA, the Norwich Free Academy, when I was about five, he started his own radio show featuring his favorite operas. And so on Sunday nights the family would gather round the radio, often at 16 Goldberg Ave., to listen to Marshall opine about his favorite arias and librettos. The musical theme of the show, which opened and closed it, was the triumphal march from *Aida*; and when it played the second time at the end of the show, it was time for me to go to bed, the glorious sounds still reverberating in my ears. Marshall's tapes of this show have not been located, but I can hear them just by remembering them.

Our favorite tenor during this period, and if not for all time, was Jussi Björling from Sweden whose delicate lyric voice could bring any of us to tears when a favorite song or aria would be played on the Victrola. My favorite non-aria that he sang was Foster's "I Dream of Jeanie with the Light Brown Hair," and my favorite male duet was from Bizet's *The Pearl Fishers*, often recorded with Robert Merrill, and was played at Marshall's funeral many years later. I had a security blanket named Jussi that helped put me to sleep. I think when I got a bit older Connie took it.

In addition to piano lessons, I also started voice lessons at an early age and at eight years joined the Beth Jacob Synagogue choir as the only child; I soon had a few solos. When I was post-Bar Mitzvah, I sang in the state Jewish choir that toured around the northeast. Cantor Israel Rabinowitz was my mentor both in Jewish music and in Hebrew school, where I learned the liturgy in Hebrew more or less by rote. And his influence on Marshall's liturgical skills and tastes is unmistakable. I loved Hebrew School and learned easily, and being kind of a pet of the cantor was something I really enjoyed, especially when I joined the choir.

Uncle John was not around much in those years, for he served in the Navy and later attended several colleges; but when he was around, Buddy or Bud as my mom referred to him, and Marshall would torture me by tickling me till I could no longer stand it. They would pin me on the floor and simply have a go at me, and any mere movement toward my body when the other was holding me down would be sufficient to torment me. But I loved them and the way they included me in so many things even as a little boy. And when Uncle John got married the three of us stayed in one room the night before the wedding. That was very special and grownup. They talked about a lot of serious things that do not bear repeating. This Uncle John was the one who, after college, came back to Norwich and turned G & M Manufacturing Co. into John Meyer of Norwich, the ladies clothing operation that brought madras, Bermuda shorts, and the preppy look into vogue in the 50s and 60s. But Buddy was also very good at tickling, and I can still picture him and Marshall doing this to me at 16 Goldberg Ave.

I was awfully short till after my Bar Mitzvah, when I started to climb up the ladder slowly and grew to over six feet. By the time I was about fifteen or sixteen, Ike, John, Marshall, and I were all about the same size, and John or Gramps enjoyed making each of us a special pair of pants every once and a while that each of us could wear; I also started getting hand-me-downs too. My father was only about 5'9" and had a pretty big waist and was often dieting. No sharing of clothing with him.

By the time Marshall went off to Dartmouth in 1948 and I was eight, my parents were into golf, and so I got interested and took up the game and became good at it. I also started to caddy and made lots of money, at least I thought it was a lot at the time. Golf has remained a lifelong hobby even today; I even won the Senior Championship at the Duke Golf Course in 2014. Private golf clubs were all restricted in those days, and the Norwich Inn Golf Club right near us was simply not open to Jewish members, African Americans, or Roman Catholics. Thus, we joined Shennecossett in Groton, over the Thames River from New London; that's where most of the Jews played on the Donald Ross course, designed at the end of the nineteenth century by the legendary Scotsman. I will come back to Shennecossett, named after the local Indian tribe, when I talk about high school.

In addition to loving Hebrew school and singing in the choir, my childhood years are seared with stories of the Holocaust. Kurt and Eva had barely escaped with their two girls, Hanni and Susie, and wound up for almost a year in Cuba until letters of guarantee could be assured and proof of support identified. Anita and Ike, Mom and Dad were among those who worked to get them over to Norwich and ultimately succeeded. My dad's sister Leni Heaton had escaped earlier by marrying a British Petroleum executive and wound up in Persia, ultimately working underground translating for the Allies against the Germans because she had become a British citizen. She was honored for those efforts by the British government posthumously. Walther Lehmann joined the Oppenheimers in Norwich sometime during the war; despite being such a good pianist and having been a public servant in the East Prussian government for many years, he ultimately took employment with G & M in the office, where Anita was bookkeeper and was passing on those skills to him.

Grandma Anita was also treasurer of Beth Jacob and a pillar of the family. Grandpa Ike always took me in those childhood years to synagogue with him on Saturday mornings where he served as a *gabbai* or official when the Torah was read. He always wore a white Stetson hat in *shul*, except when he went up to the *bima* to assist in the Torah reading and call out the honors, and then I could play with his hat in our regular pew, stroking it and just holding it. I loved going with him and after would wind up at 16 Goldberg Ave. for lunch with him and Gram, just the three of us. I guess this started around when I was seven or eight, and the choir never sang on Saturdays. I still like going to *shul* on Saturdays as an adult because of this experience with Gramps, though today the long Torah service is often hard to take and often seems interminable. I don't understand why it didn't bother me as a kid.

Anita Meyer was the rock on which the closeness of both sides of the family was built. She was self-taught. When Connie needed to confide in someone besides Mom or Dad, it was Grandma Anita. And she would have wonderful family affairs, mostly associated with the Jewish holidays or Shabbat. Everyone loved her, and everyone turned to her for guidance. Her steady support for each and everyone one of us made each of us a better person and got us through some tough times.

If you haven't noticed by now my mom, Shirlee, has not figured very prominently into this story. In hindsight and with the distance of years, it now seems she was having the toughest time of all. Dad did not want her to work because that was the way of the old world in his European eyes. Although she was a decent homemaker, with grandma down the street and our housekeeper Frances doing most of the housework at home, there was not much for her to do. Mom was very bright and even had some notion of becoming a writer one day, but Karl was not in the least supportive of those sorts of ambitions. No doubt Mom leaned on her mother a good deal when we were not around. Mom was also not completely happy with her body image if not her sexuality. I didn't realize it at the time, but again in hindsight one could see this. She was 5'10", or a bit taller than Dad, and a really strong and good golfer. When we took a beach rental next to the Goldbergs (Cook and Bev and their three boys) in Niantic in the late 1940s, there apparently was a lot of heaving drinking. My dad could take it, but Mom could not; she got hooked, and alcohol became a huge problem for her the rest of her life. I think this is why she is absent from my memory for a lot of this time, she simply was seeking other outlets to deal with her disappointments. Their marriage too needed lots of attention, which it never got.

But somehow Connie and I managed, not a little of the reason being that Anita was just down the street and we adored one another as brothers and sisters should. Connie and I are very close to this day. I know there were many years when things at home were not all that great, but we had each other and our grandparents and extended family too. Remember, Marshall was there till I was eight, and John got married and returned and started in the business in 1949, and we had him and Arlene his wife. Connie and I even worked at the factory during school breaks, helping with inventory and shipping and stuff. This paid off handsomely later on when the company was all women's clothing and Connie, Mom, and Carol could take whatever they wanted as Uncle John had directed. The Oppenheimers were there for us as well, especially Susie, who was a classmate of Marshall's, and Uncle Kurt for me, often asking me to join him when he made house calls. That's how my love of medicine started.

My dad followed in his father's footsteps and went into textiles, specializing in repurposing wool waste. He often took me out with him on weekends or during my vacations to visit clients from whom he bought wool waste. We would visit one woolen mill after another, quite a few in Worcester, Massachusetts; he even bought one in Hopkinton, Rhode Island, that later burned down, which was a huge setback to his business. I remember vividly jumping on bales of wool waste there and enjoying his company in his beloved Oldsmobile for hours on end. There were no classical music stations in those days, so we just talked father-and-son type of talk, and some of it was quite embarrassing: who wants to talk with a parent about sex, masturbation, and girls. Yugh! But dad insisted on it, and I guess I learned from it, and he did it because his father had told him about such things too. He wanted me to respect girls and never to be too forceful in physical relationships. Great advice way in advance of the #MeToo Movement. Connie had a special relationship with dad as well, and they were as close as a father and daughter could be and Connie often took advantage of that fact. Why not? My younger daughter, Dina, did that to me also, and no one suffered because of it.

Dad never talked about having had to leave home and a life he loved as a very young man. In Königsberg, he could go to the opera and even backstage any time he wanted. Also, his dad Benno, had a boat that had a crew, and he loved to sail. My dad was pretty popular with the ladies, so he told me.

What happened to my grandparents in World War II? Benno, as best as can be inferred from recent archival materials of the German government, died in 1942 or 1943, either from lack of insulin that the Nazis withheld from him or in a death march. The lack of clarity on the issue is because of several stories about the killing of Jews in Königsberg and the attack on mixed marriages. Dad had known about his father's death for quite a while from an obituary in the *Aufbau*, a journal for German-speaking Jews, but the whereabouts of his mother, Käthe, also known as Mutti, was unknown for years. It was only after the war in a DP camp that she was fortunate enough to have met an Army officer from Norwich; he had been a patient of Uncle Kurt and put her in touch with the family. She apparently escaped and went underground after the ban on mixed marriages and Opa's death, though she had converted to Judaism when Hitler came to power in 1933. After escaping from Kőnigsberg she was apparently housed by Polish nuns through the remainder of the war. I recall the sense of relief when she got in touch with Aunt Eva and Uncle Kurt and made arrangements to come to the States. But our joy in having her return and be reunited was short lived, it became apparent very shortly that either she suffered from dementia or early onset Alzheimer's or was so traumatized by events that she simply could not function on her own any longer. She was ultimately admitted to the State Hospital in Norwich where she spent the remainder of her days. I can recall visiting her many times. She could be found at the piano playing Johann Strauss and *Die Fledermaus*, often singing the words in perfect German, and her fellow patients dancing or strumming along. She had no idea where she was and never recognized her own children or grandchildren again. But somehow the music stayed alive in her and gave her some measure of peace. I'll never forget it. In my heart I blame the Nazis, but maybe it was Alzheimer's, at least that's what Connie thinks.

We once made a family fishing trip with the Goldbergs to Camp Woodrest near Waterville, Maine. The problem was that the cabin walls were paper thin and didn't go up to the ceiling. My father had been there with his fishing buddies and thought it would be good for us as a family to go also. But my father snored like a lion; and the sounds that emanated from him literally shook the cabin, and Connie and I could not sleep very well. We also didn't like the other noises we heard. But I went back again some years later with his male friends a couple of times and actually landed a big small-mouth bass that Dad helped me reel in and that set a record. I caught it on an artificial lure called "the darter." Don't know why I remember that but I do. Dad had the fish preserved, stuffed, and mounted, and it hung in our den in Norwich till Mom passed away. Whatever happened to it when we packed up the house nobody seems to recall. However, I can picture it easily in my mind's eye, so it doesn't matter.

My early childhood sort of culminated when my father thought it was time for me to go to New York to the Metropolitan Opera. Marshall was a freshman at Dartmouth, and I was eight years old. Dad had selected

PART ONE: BEFORE CAROL

Carmen because he felt it was easy to listen to and the staging would be fun to view. He also had a soft spot for the famous tenor aria, the "Flower Song." He was right: I loved the opera and it was too bad Björling wasn't singing, but that didn't really matter. We had a ball. The two of us went out to dinner, and it was a real bonding experience, kind of like catching that big fish together.

So we were a really close family when I was growing up, but there were a few warning signs already: Mom's drinking, cracks in the marriage. But there was lots of love from all quarters, and that made the difference. As the first grandchild and the first nephew and all, and Connie coming four years later, she felt a bit slighted and that got worse over time too since I was such a good student and could do no wrong in the eyes of most of the family. But Connie and I never let that interfere with our relationship, which has stayed strong all these years regardless of what was happening then.

My inquisitive side came out in this period in frequent trips to Yantic Falls and the spot where Uncas leaped, that is, Uncas the Mohegan Indian chief of James Fennimore Cooper. I looked for arrowheads and other traces of those "olden times," but I never thought for once that I would become an archaeologist, let alone someone concerned with the more distant past. Must have been an accident. None of my grammar school teachers stand out in my memory, though they were all caring and decent. Ms. Beebe in first grade at Broad Street School, however, stands out a bit. A few years ago a first-grade classmate, Lucius Carroll, called me from Nashville where he now lives to tell me how much I meant to him because he once wet his pants in that class, and I had successfully defended him from humiliation. Ms. Comstock in fourth grade was not too shabby either and was pretty exacting as a teacher. Walking to school twice a day—coming home for lunch—was mostly lots of fun till it wasn't.

I should add that as happy as things were in many ways there were a few clouds gathering. In those days we not only walked to public school without any adults, but we also walked home for lunch and then back to school. Twice a week we walked to Hebrew School directly from school. We had to switch from the Broad Street School to the Broadway School in fifth or sixth grade, but it was about the same distance to walk and much closer to Beth Jacob Hebrew School. While presumably there was little to fear, I can recall any number of street fights when along the way some of our non-Jewish "friends" called us "dirty Jew" or some other anti-Semitic slogan. I usually walked to school with Harold Baker and Michael Adelman, and after one such name-calling the three of us chose to fight the boys who taunted us. We knocked out a couple of teeth of one of the guys, Kevin Buckley; fortunately they were his first teeth, so we must have been pretty young. (I just read in our NFA Newsletter that Kevin died in 2017.)

Another time, going to Hebrew School, we were jumped by a tough guy from our school, Georgie L'Heureux, and I wound up at the doctor's with a concussion. But we continued to walk everywhere despite these run-ins with the anti-Semites, not like today at all when carpooling is a career for many parents. These guys just happened to know my dad had an accent and was an immigrant and assumed that each of us was pretty rich, at least that's what I think today. We were not exactly rich, but we certainly didn't lack for anything either. This was before Uncle John's label became famous, which caused more resentment directed against some members of the Jewish community. (The labels ultimately included the original John Meyer of Norwich, a specialty line Emily M, and Jones of New York, added after the parent company was sold.) Harold's grandparents were immigrants and very well-to-do; they lived in a big house on Washington St., and that might have had something to do with it. The Adelman's were our closest neighbors, and they were pretty much like us, just regular, middle class, and happy.

And there was the unhappy case of Connie at Gallups Hill after school one day when she was approached by a pervert who exposed himself and tried to touch her. I was walking ahead with my buddies, ignorant of it all until later. I kind of missed the boat on this one, and Connie ran home alone to tell Mom. Connie and I loved to sleigh ride there for years; it was only ten minutes or so from our house on 1 Buckingham Ave., and we were always among the first to get there after a decent snowfall. So Norwich, like many other places, had its problems with diversity and crime, and Mom and Dad had lots of follow-up on Connie's awful experience. But I guess it could have been lots worse. I have no recollection of my parents ever becoming involved in the bullying I experienced.

2

Teen Years

My teenage years really begin with my Bar Mitzvah, May 16, 1953, a few weeks before my thirteenth birthday. I was really psyched for it too. By this time Marshall was about to enter rabbinical school after a year in Israel and had been showering me with advice so that the Jewish content of the day would remain central. I'm not sure that's the way it turned out because I loved my party and Leah Safinowitz gave me a special gift that I never forgot: how to really kiss, and she was four years older and really, really knew how to kiss! I was still quite short at the time, and Grandma Anita was still taller than me. But I did the whole service, read from the Torah, gave a silly sermon that began: "As I stand before the Holy Ark on this shabbas of my Bar Mitzvah my heart is filled with pride and gratitude." That's all I can remember today but that's quite enough. All the *davening* (chanting) went just fine; after all, I was the cantor's pet and sang in the choir. We had a great *Kiddush*—luncheon at the synagogue and a successful party at our home on 1 Buckingham Ave. that night where Leah took me out into our car and taught me how to kiss. The party from my point of view was a huge success. I felt quite grownup, like a man. Isn't that what the rabbi said I was supposed to be that day? And thanks to Leah I truly did feel like a man.

This is also about the time that 16 Goldberg Ave. became kosher. Anita realized that having a future rabbi in Marshall meant that the kitchen would have to be totally reorganized, new dishes and utensils purchased, and milk and meat separated, the whole nine yards. As a good New England Jewish family by this time, ca. 1953–1954, most of us had grown accustomed to certain kinds of sea foods with shells on them, and while we all looked upon the move as one of great loyalty and piety, it would also mean that certain foods would be eaten only at our house on Buckingham

Ave. I won't even mention that Gram's move had zero impact on the Germans, whose love of German wurst and such things as pickled pigs' feet and Königsberger Klopse, remained undiminished. Needless to say, I fell in the middle of this and was pulled in several directions.

Eighth grade stood between me and high school. While I was really ready for the Norwich Free Academy (NFA), I still had eighth grade ahead of me. At least the Broadway School was closer to the public library. That was good, and I can remember that one of the requirements for our class was that every student had to deliver a morning message before class started. One classmate, an Asian-American with a strong accent, one day stepped forward and with only a small piece of paper in his hand, went a bit overtime. While he was quite eloquent, his use of such a modest crib note helped me greatly later in public speaking when simply having a piece of paper with a few notes on it helped me get through a talk. The Broadway School, not far from my previous school, the Broad Street School, was close to St. Patrick's Cathedral where a bishop had been recently installed and everyone was excited about it, elevating the status of St. Pat's church to a real cathedral. The Broadway school has since been torn down, and it needed to be. The playground was smaller than a tiny putting green.

Just before high school or during my first year I was getting involved in scouting. Beth Jacob had its own Jewish scout troop (Troop 3), and Mr. Ornstein, a piano tuner, was its leader. Our off-season program always involved a camping trip at Camp Quinibaug, where I had begun summer camp, as did Marshall, years before. In planning the outing our troop master sought chaperones who would sleep with the kids and oversee meals, etc. I was eager to please and really wanted to see camp in fall or winter whenever the trip would happen. It was about an hour from Norwich in Killingly, Connecticut. So, you guessed it, I volunteered my father since I knew from our fishing trips in Maine that he was kind of a trooper. I had forgotten how badly he snored, however, and that did not go over too well when it was time to go to sleep in the assembly room of camp where we all bedded down. After lots of good hotdogs and hamburgers, and beans too for dinner, and lots of fooling around to delay going to sleep, we finally went down despite the buzz saw coming out of my father's nose and mouth that pushed all the campers farther and farther away from him, although that hardly helped. We simply were tired and managed to fall asleep. But to our utter surprise, sometime after midnight, we all heard noises from outside, some in the form of Native American dancing and chanting. Needless to say, we were all awakened and scared to death. We had no idea what was going on. My father was in a complete state of shock. This went on for some time, probably only minutes, but it seemed much longer then. Suddenly two grown men broke into the hall in Indian garb hooting and shouting. By now you must have guessed who they were: John and Marshall. My father was simply nonplussed by all this, and while in hindsight it seems funny, all of us were scared shitless for what seemed like an eternity. My uncles had planned for such a reaction and had brought along some goodies to show that their intent was not hostile. That assuaged the scouts, but all my father really needed was a big stiff drink of whiskey, which he did not get.

Sometime around the end of grammar school and later while I was at NFA, Beth Jacob entered the Church League in basketball and I was ready to join. Beth Jacob had just built an addition to the Hebrew School with a nice gym and basketball court, and the Beth Jacob Bullets were born. I played center; approaching six feet meant one was big in those days. My friend and classmate J. J. Swatzburg was our dynamic point guard whose three pointers and dribbling confused and dazed many an opponent. Even playing center I don't think I ever scored double digits let alone get ten rebounds. The BJ Bullets never went that far in the tournament of the Church League, but we had a great time. My eventual love of Duke basketball surely dates back to those days.

NFA was special, for it allowed me to display some of my talents that had no outlet before: public speaking, acting, study of other cultures, and real academic engagement with teachers and subject matter. I also joined the golf team and ultimately become captain; we won quite a few matches and even a couple of statewide tournaments too. I had some wonderful teachers who opened doors for me that had previously been only partially open. I loved English, and Mr. and Mrs. Reed were among my favorite English teachers. They lived close to my grandparents, and their daughter Anne was among my best friends at NFA; Anne and I even went to one of the proms together because we were close friends and not boyfriend and girlfriend. And we had a great time. Mr. Reed's enunciation of language was special and helped me in public speaking enormously. But Mr. Burnham, my senior-year English teacher, really helped me improve my writing. He regularly would have a contest in class to see who could write about a topic with the fewest number of words. And for the runners-up he would show in class how they could have written the same piece with the same effect in fewer words. It was a terrific learning experience and editing tool I have never forgotten. My classical studies were limited to four years of Latin with Ms. Sharples, which I truly enjoyed. In those days it was all grammar and reading, with no serious attempt to place the language into its larger context of the Roman Empire.

Mrs. Savard, my German language teacher, was also special. My dad had not taught me German at home and often pretended he had no accent though he smoked Winston cigarettes, which he called "Vinstons." Mrs. Savard also was head of the German Club, and I became president after my second year. We were supposed to have one educational trip per year, and I was asked to organize one. The reader probably already senses that I wanted to take the club to the opera in New York and hear and see a German opera. And yes, that was my plan. But I made a great mistake and picked a Wagner opera, *Siegfried* no less, and it was a disaster. I was familiar with a few sections of the opera and really had no idea about how long it was and how boring it could be for someone not at home in the genre. By midnight we were still at the Met and my classmates never forgave me. Mrs. Savard admitted after that she should have been more involved in selecting the opera. I didn't know then that Wagner was a rabid anti-Semite (I still love *Die Meistersinger*, and it's in my top four). In hindsight we should have gone to *Die Fledermaus*!

Back then we high school students did not focus on college admission, as they do today, until we had to take the PSAT in our junior year. So at least we could enjoy a few years without focusing on college. My PSAT scores were a bit underwhelming, especially math, so a good friend's father, Harold Ross, was coaxed into tutoring me a bit before senior year to get my score up a bit, which I did. In addition to golf, I was also active in Playshop, which produced shows, dramas, and musicals. It helped greatly with public speaking, and I was eventually selected to be Ivy Orator at high school graduation in 1958. One of the benefits of being Ivy Orator was that I was invited to recite the Gettysburg Address by heart at a celebration on the Norwich Town Green on July Fourth, and all the family attended. When Grandma Anita heard it, she said to Uncle Kurt: what a beautiful speech. Did Ricky write it? This may be apocryphal, but it shows that as far as Grandma was concerned I could do no wrong and sometimes could even walk on water.

This is getting ahead a bit. After I got my driver's license at sixteen, in 1956, I loved taking Connie to all her appointments. I was always ready to drive her anywhere she wanted. Not only was driving fun but it made me feel very grownup. Though I didn't have a car till Grandpa Ike died, my dad pretty much let me have our family car when I needed it. In my junior year I loved to go to basketball games and regularly went to the Friday or Saturday night dances that often followed. I had a friend on the cheerleader's team, and she was African American. I don't remember her name, but we were really good friends, not boyfriend/girlfriend, just good friends. We kidded around a lot, and one Saturday after a football game, I drove to NFA and went to the dance. No surprise I saw my black friend, and we hung out together and started to dance. We both loved to dance and were not too bad either. Neither of us noticed the stares of some of the bystanders, and when it was time to leave, we hugged and said goodnight. When I left the gym and was heading out to the parking lot, a group of five or six guys were waiting for me and shouting: "N...-loving Jew bastard" and stuff like that, and they grabbed me and hauled me out to the bleachers and beat the living shit out of me. They also said if I ever would dance with a black person again I would pay for it worse than before. Truth be told, I was scared, real scared. And that was not the end of it.

When I got home and Mom and Dad saw what I looked like, I told them what happened. I was not about to lie. But what I can't understand to this day is why we, all of us, didn't go right to the principal, Mr. Shattuck, and tell him what had happened and who did it. Or even to the police? I knew the guys and they were in the anti-Semitic group, but for some reason we did not go to the authorities at school or to the police. That was a real mistake because this was only the beginning. The horror was going to last. First, it was calls to the house in the middle of the night. Then it was harassment on the road when I was driving. And then later it was getting tripped going to class. And then one day, in physiology class where we were dissecting cats in our lab on campus, I was called "dirty Jew," and I just went berserk. I had had just enough. So I leaped over the lab table at this guy and began to hit him. After a few minutes of this we were both taken to the principal's office and asked to explain what this was all about. Mr. Shattuck listened carefully and patiently to each of us. Of course I had to tell him about the previous incidents, which the other guy did not deny. Nothing happened to me, and for the life of me I cannot recall what happened to the anti-Semite who goaded me on that day. It didn't really matter because Mr. Shattuck realized what had occurred and spared me. But this was the last straw in a series of events at NFA that has disproportionally influenced my memories from high school.

Aside from these incidents, I loved high school, if you can believe that. And in my speech at graduation I took the high road and never mentioned what had happened on the dark side. Even though I became Ivy Orator and got into everywhere I applied to college, even early admission to the University of Michigan and University of Chicago, I was more or less destined to go to Dartmouth since Marshall had gone there and I was totally brainwashed. Actually I had visited Dartmouth every year that Marshall was there, and during my first visit I even managed to infect his dorm with the mumps after delivering a whole suitcase of Grandma Anita's cookies to his dorm, Wheeler Hall. During my annual visits there I got to know some of Marshall's favorite professors too: Pat Scott-Craig, Eugen Rosenstock-Huessy, and Fred Berthold. This would come in handy later when I was at Dartmouth.

In those years I was convinced I was going to be a doctor one day. I even used to go out on house calls with Uncle Kurt and loved the way he treated his patients. So I became an orderly the summers before my junior and senior years at NFA and truly loved the job at the William W. Backus Hospital. I even was OK giving enemas and loved helping old people in rehab—that was before you went to a separate place for rehab. And I often went out on the ambulance to render emergency treatment too.

One day we got an emergency call that a car was soon to arrive with a woman who was about to deliver a baby. Since I was on duty, I went down to ER and met the car. The father-to-be was the driver, and his young wife was in the back seat in labor. In my white hospital garb I opened the door and approached the back seat, and the young woman could not move because she was experiencing intense labor pains. With no doctor around I attempted to help and assist in any way, and she directed me how to do so. The husband was a complete wreck and no help at all, and so within minutes I was holding a newborn in my lap, a boy. We screamed and yelled, and finally a doctor came; the mom and I were greatly relieved. The baby was fine, and I hugged the new mom and wished her well. The next day I got a call to go to the room of someone I did not know, and it was she. The mom was so touched by my behavior that she and her husband decided to name their son Eric after me. If Eric is still alive and gets to read this one day, I'd love to meet him.

My teen years ended in a symbolic way with Grandpa Ike's death in my junior year of high school, 1957. He had been diagnosed with lung cancer a while before; he had been a big-time smoker, just like many people in those days. The cancer soon spread and Grams decided that he was not going to die in the hospital. So she ordered a hospital bed and put it in the dining room on the first floor, and there Gramps stayed for months and months. I was often called to watch him, even on weekends, and sometimes I took my date to sit there with me while he moaned or snored. Sometimes he even tried to climb out of the bed and had to be restrained. The most faithful bedside companion besides Gram was Prince, our beloved German shepherd, who somehow knew the end was near and would not leave Grampa's side. Prince stayed and watched, jumped up alongside the bed often managing a lick to his hand or even better, and even though Gramps was not in control of his faculties, I could tell it touched him. When Ike Meyer died in 1957, however, in a real way it was a relief: Gram got the dining room back, and Prince came back to 1 Buckingham Ave. I got Gramps' Pontiac and that helped a lot in the carpooling department. The license plate on my new car was "IKEM," i.e., an abbreviation for Ike Meyer. But going to *shul* was never the same, and I never saw a white Stetson hat in *shul* since then.

Not too long after Grampa's death, Gram took Mom to Europe on a long-delayed mother-daughter vacation, and they had the best time together. It truly helped both Mom and Grams deal with their loss. One awful thing related to that trip was that while she was away Dad invited a couple up from Florida and had a big reception for them at our house—catered by the way. And it was pretty obvious to me that Dad and the woman were having an affair with the full knowledge of her spouse named "Mo." When Mom came home and heard about it, she was not happy to say the least.

Several other anecdotes stand out for these teenage years before college. One probably occurred in 1956 when Marshall was in seminary in New York. By that time he had already fallen under the spell of his renowned teacher and mentor, Rabbi Abraham Joshua Heschel. Even when Marshall went to New York to the Jewish Theological Seminary, I continued my practice of visiting him during my vacations and attended classes too. I got to know Rabbi Heschel pretty well and became so trusted that I even babysat his young daughter, Susannah, when I was there. Marshall and our Norwich rabbi at the time, Marshall Maltzman, somehow arranged for Rabbi Heschel to visit for a Shabbat in 1956. The plan was to have Rabbi Heschel stay at 16 Goldberg Ave. in Uncle John's old room, which he did. I was still in the choir, and we were singing on Friday nights: the choir and the whole congregation were really excited about the visit. Heschel had been asked to preach that Friday night and to give a talk on Saturday morning too. All I can remember is Friday night. Services started around 8:00 PM and moved along pretty efficiently since Rabbi

Heschel's talk was the main focus. He got up on the *bima* around 8:30 and began to talk, and talk he did. As 9:45 or so approached, the congregation began to lose its concentration and patience. Somehow services ended, and the *Kiddush* following was wonderful as was the entire weekend. But Beth Jacob was never the same, on the one hand inspired by this great man but wary of sermons from outsiders.

Golf Team, Norwich Free Academy, 1958, Rick Meyers, captain. The team was 8–1 that year and went on to the state championship held at Farmington Country Club June 9th. Coach Larry Seybolt, top left.

Two other anecdotes are about golf, and both stories occurred in the spring of 1958, my senior year. By this time I was captain of the golf team and was pretty good, playing at scratch or with a handicap of around 2 or 3. The day I got into Dartmouth—it must have been around mid-April—the NFA golf team was playing at Shennecossett in Groton. I was on the first tee and the golf pro, Vic Panciera, comes running out of the pro shop and says to me "your mother just called and said you got into Dartmouth." She had obviously opened my mail. I was pretty darn thrilled and so were members of the rest of the team. But for some reason our coach, Larry Seybolt, a popular and successful French teacher, acted with disdain and said something like this: "You Jews were born with a silver spoon in your mouth, and your family must have . . ." He no doubt thought I was a legacy admit. I was devastated, and my fellow teammates shocked. We were about to play Groton High School, I guess, and everyone on the tee just sort of remained silent for a few long minutes. I had thought the coach and I were pretty close, and he actually had helped a lot with my game and was also the adviser to Playshop in which I was active. I started wondering: where did this come from? Did he know that Uncle Kurt was head of the professional association of the Backus Hospital or that John Meyer was now pretty well known and a big business success and that's what was bugging him? The Jews were taking over Norwich? Or was he just another anti-Semite at heart and it just burst forth? Who knows? For me the rest of the season was pretty tense as you can imagine.

Unbeknownst to me someone from Shennecossett had nominated me for a caddie scholarship to college based on academic achievement and merit and years of caddying at the club. For the last years I was carrying doubles too, and this went a long way in padding my savings account. Later that spring, after the fiasco with my coach, I was notified by the golf club that there would be an awards dinner when I was scheduled to get some sort of award from the caddie association of Connecticut, or something like that. I was quite pleased, and Mom and Dad and Uncle John said they would come to the awards dinner. It turns out that I won the scholarship, though I can't remember the amount. Just before I was to go up and receive the award Uncle John goes up to the head table and talks to the master of ceremony, and the announcement is made that, although I had won the award, the cash prize would go to the runner up. This act of largesse the announcer said was a result of the generosity of John Meyer of Norwich who felt that the runner up was much needier than his nephew. I guess Uncle John had sweetened the pot a bit and obviously my dad and John had worked this out before, but it came as a total surprise and shock to me. While the audience applauded my academic achievements, they were also thrilled with this turn of events and praised Uncle John. I never saw a penny of the award, but my father did pay for Dartmouth though I contributed all my Bar Mitzvah and caddie money, so from that perspective it turned out quite all right. Still, for years after, I was really upset that I had not been told in advance and that the move had stolen this moment from me. I got over it, but it was tough for a long while—that's probably why I am writing this story all these years later. And the certificate of the award has been lost too along with the mounted fish.

3

College/Dartmouth, 1958–1962

I WAS PRETTY DARN happy about the Dartmouth admission, though that day when I heard the news from the golf pro is bitter sweet. But I was so ready to leave NFA behind and get started with being on my own. I signed up for the pre-freshman week Outing Club hiking and orientation at Mt. Moosilauke Ravine Lodge where I got to meet a nice group of rising first-year students. The highlight, however, was the meeting with the president of the college, John Sloan Dickey. He came in hiking gear and boots and was very charismatic. His pep talks to us were full of sage advice that served us well and instilled in us not only a love of the College but of the north woods and outdoors, which today I associate with Dartmouth. He also nurtured within us a love of learning that is at the heart of the undergraduate experience and was a large part of the reason I ultimately entered the professoriate. Not many students today would associate love of learning and the outdoors, but the Dartmouth Outing Club and President Dickey sure did it for me. His fall convocation address to the College was always a highlight of the academic year for me and many of my classmates, especially his concluding words, always the same:

> And now men of Dartmouth, as I have said on this occasion before, as members of the College you have three different but closely intertwined roles to play: First, you are citizens of a community and are expected to act as such. Second, you are the stuff of an institution and what you are it will be. Thirdly, your business here is learning and that is up to you. We'll be with you all the way and Good Luck!

Mom and Dad drove me to Hanover that first semester and part of the deal of being a freshman was that we were supposed to help upper classmen move in. But since this was before most of the freshman had arrived, it was mostly Outing Club types arriving early. While most of the men hugged their moms and kissed them I noticed that most of them shook hands with their dads. You know already that my father was an Eastern European, and they are very big on kissing, men kissing too. I went up to my dad and offered my hand when we were saying goodbye, and he said, "None of that son, we will still kiss as long as I am alive." The idea was that only male non-Jews didn't kiss their fathers. I learned my lesson pretty quickly: our family traditions and ethnicity would be preserved, and they would also help me in some difficult times as well.

I started out pre-med in large part due to the influence of Uncle Kurt, and I had always been pretty good in science class and actually had won the chemistry prize in high school. But one of the first courses I took that first year was a course in Speech taught by Herbert James. It was a logical step for me after what I had done at NFA. In the first weeks of class Professor James had each student prepare a speech and he would comment on our diction and then tell us about the region we came from and/or something about the ethnic background of one or more of our parents. When my turn came and he commented, he told me that one parent was American born and from New York and the other was foreign born, and probably German. He identified a certain pattern in my speech that he said was unmistakable. Needless to say I was dumbfounded, impressed, as were all of my classmates.

I was also very interested in continuing my study of German and did so along with courses in Religion and History. I also enjoyed taking classes in Music and Art History. By the time I got to organic chemistry and heard the speech about how many would flunk, "turn to your left and turn to your right, only one of you will be left at the end of semester." I realized then I was not going into medicine and decided early on to major in Religion.

One of my German professors, James (Jim) Scott was an early favorite; he was gay and had a partner, Roy Lanfer, who was a professor of Classics. To this day I regret not having taken any course in Classical Studies in college since I had taken four years of Latin at NFA. One day Jim Scott asked if I might be interested in making a little money by housekeeping for them a couple of times a month, or maybe once a week. I can't exactly remember. And I agreed. I cleaned and got quite accustomed to it and even can say that I enjoyed it. To this day I can picture the apartment across from the gym with its oriental rugs and homey feeling. And it turned out to be a really nice arrangement for all concerned. Jim never let this familiarity with me interfere with my performance in class where like everyone else I was expected to prepare and translate and comment on the text. I guess this positive experience with house cleaning helped prepare me for marriage and the pandemic when I took hold of house cleaning, for the first time in years and Carol took care of the kitchen, over which she always had complete control.

After taking Religion 1: Introduction to the Study of Religion, a team-taught class, I got to know Fred Berthold on a personal level and got hooked on the study of Religion. The class was team taught in those days, and Fred was a superb lecturer. While Fred had known Marshall pretty well when he was an undergraduate, the Meyer family connection was more to Pat Scott-Craig, and I waited to take his classes till my sophomore year. Pat was in both Religion and Philosophy. But Fred and I soon became very close, and I eventually was asked to babysit for his daughter Marjorie, who had social problems and was being treated for some form of mental illness at the time. Marjorie and I got along just fine, and my involvement with the Bertholds was a major part of my college experience too. Fred was also head of the Religious Life Council and later Dean of the William Jewett Tucker Foundation. I also joined the Glee Club and made the golf team as well. Marshall had been a sensation in The Dartmouth Players, and so of course I joined but only appeared in one production, Aeschylus's *The Persians* as chorus leader. The well-known actress Blanche Yurka made a special guest appearance in the performances.

I also continued my voice studies privately with a faculty wife and was soon drafted by Rabbi Julius Kravetz to lead services, High Holiday and Shabbat, at Hillel, then called the Jewish Life Council, mostly in Rollins Chapel. Rabbi Kravetz was a full-time faculty member at the Reform Seminary (Hebrew Union College–Jewish Institute of Religion) in New York and commuted to Hanover about twice a month. At one Shabbat service after hearing me sing, Rabbi Kravetz realized immediately that I had more than a casual familiarity with the liturgy. When he inquired, I told him I had been singing in a synagogue choir for years. I was drafted immediately into service. High Holiday services were held at a church nearby to accommodate a large attendance from town and gown, for there was no synagogue or rabbi in the surrounding areas of Vermont and New Hampshire. He also had the unusual but compelling idea that we would not use the *bima* since it did not support his idea of egalitarian worship where the leaders held no special place in God's eyes. In the church we were using, the front of it was a raised platform about four feet above the seating level, as is often the case with many synagogues (*bima* is a raised platform on which the Torah is read and services performed). The experience of being cantor in my first year without much notice forced me to prepare over the next summer and to begin the process of converting many of my pieces that were published only in four parts (SATB) to solo and congregational singing. I can't remember how many times Rabbi Kravetz came to campus, but I or someone else had to lead services on his off weekends. I did not know at the time that having so full a plate of extra-curricular activities along with a full academic schedule would be hard to maintain in the next years, so eventually I had to begin dropping a number of extra-curricular things such as Playshop.

My freshman dorm was Butterfield Hall, my roommate was John Blue from suburban Chicago, and we were right next to the communal bathroom. We had bunk beds, and I was in the top bunk. One of the smallest dorms on campus, Butterfield was right behind the Beta Theta Pi fraternity house, which meant on weekends it was pretty noisy on our side of the building. But the dorm had members of all classes, and some of my best friends were upper classmen. We were pretty diverse too, by which I mean there were quite a few Jews in the dorm and in my class. Chuck Hagerman, one of only a few African Americans in my class, was a good friend, and we maintained close contact for several years after graduation—Chuck became a surgeon.

In those days, diversity meant simply Protestants, Catholics, and Jews. One day in the middle of the night I felt someone rubbing my scalp; I awoke startled, and it was John Blue. I asked him, "What the hell are you doing?" He answered that he was looking for my horns and had been too embarrassed to ask me. He had been taught that Jews had horns like Moses, as in Michelangelo's famous sculpture in Rome. I don't think I knew at the time the reason for depicting Jews with devilish horns, which is probably based on a mistranslation into Latin by St. Jerome of the Hebrew *keren* meaning horn or ray, as when Moses came down from Sinai after seeing God face-to-face, his face was "radiant," or wrongly understood as "with horns." Be that as it may, the fact that I was the first Jew John knew close up was pretty eye-popping for me. This did not lead to a close relationship, as you might infer. John was also pretty much of a nerd, always in the library and getting the highest grades in every class. I was in the do-everything mode still and was trying to find my way.

Our neighbor in Butterfield on the other side of our room did not like the fact that there were Jews in the dorm and at Dartmouth. And though there were quite a few, he chose to pick on me early on. Since John was in the library most of every day, I was often in the room alone. The harassment started when I went to shower next door. His name was Gary. Gary would lock me out of my room when I returned wrapped in a towel. As a result I had to call campus police on a special emergency phone, and then they came to open my dorm room. This happened many times, always when John was away from the dorm. But Gary also did other things, often taking the form of threats and name calling; and my friends in the dorm, while supportive of me, thought that it was not that big a deal and that I should ignore it best as I could. I started taking my key to the bathroom. These actions continued all of my first semester, and it became so bad that I was having stomach problems and had to go to the infirmary (Dick's House) several times.

As second term approached, I was excited that my dad would be coming up for Freshman Father's Weekend, around the beginning of February, 1959. We had just been together in Norwich for the passing of Grandma Anita, and I had looked forward to the visit greatly. We had all sorts of plans with friends, dining out, cocktails, and even chess for my dad with my friend Dave Feingold, just down the hall in Butterfield. For some reason my father came by train to White River Junction and by cab to Hanover, where I met him at the Inn. We walked across the big green in front of Dartmouth Row and Baker Library over to Butterfield, and as we approached we saw a big yellow banner hanging over the front entrance on which was written in big letters alongside an even bigger swastika: "Jews Go Home." When my father saw this he screamed and yelled, "What the hell is all this about? I didn't leave Nazi Germany to deliver you to something like this." I then began to tell him about the harassment that I had received from Gary, and he said, "Go pack your bags, we're not going to let you stay in such an environment." I started to cry and protest and say that we have to go to see Pat Scott-Craig, Marshall's beloved teacher and by now family friend. So we left his bag in Butterfield and rushed on down to the Scott-Craig's. Pat and his wife Mary listened attentively and asked why I had not come to them earlier, but seemed to understand why I was just trying to get through the year until Gary graduated. So they called Thaddeus Seymour, Dean of Freshman, who en route to the Scott-Craig's went to Butterfield to confirm the existence of the anti-Semitic banner. Dean Seymour, after very little discussion, informed all of us that Dartmouth does not tolerate this sort of hate speech and that immediate action would be taken to expel the perpetrator.

Well, we were all stunned and of course appreciated his quick response. Within days the perpetrator was gone, and since my father relented on his demands for me to withdraw from the college and transfer, we hung around Butterflied all weekend and had to watch Gary pack and get ready to leave. Before he left, however, he made a terrifying pledge to take revenge one day and kill me. He said I would never graduate. Needless to say my dad and I were totally unnerved by this threat, and it was good that the campus police were watching our dorm that weekend. I am certain this quick action could not have occurred today, but nonetheless we were totally relieved by it as were my dorm mates and friends.

At my fiftieth reunion some years ago, Dean Seymour was the major speaker at our class dinner. I went up to him after dinner and gave him a big hug and told him thank you for saving my academic career if not my life. I told him briefly about what he had done, and while he nodded knowingly I am not sure he remembered the incident. For me, I will never forget it. And at graduation in 1962, with Connie, Mom and Dad, Uncle John and Aunt Arlene in attendance, we all celebrated; though we looked around and briefly feared a possible assassin's bullet, thankfully a joyous weekend was had by all. By retelling this story, which I revealed for the first time in writing in my fiftieth reunion book, I mean no harm to Dartmouth. It is meant only as a cautionary tale about how important it is to accept and respect people of other backgrounds regardless of whether they have horns or not.

The sense of relief after Gary's expulsion was enormous as you might imagine, though things remained tense with my roommate. But I was skiing regularly that winter, and it was a big relief to hit the slopes until one day at Suicide Six I crashed and tore my meniscus on the right knee. I had surgery that month on St. Patrick's Day at Dick's House, the first of many surgeries to come until a total knee replacement around 2000.

By sophomore year, however, I was in a single in Butterfield and was raring to go. My best friends were classmate Dave Feingold, upper classman Russ Brooks, and Mike Fitz, a Fulbright scholar from Vienna. Plus I had Steve and Dick Macht from Mystic. Freed from harassment, I finally began to enjoy campus life to the fullest. I had taken ski lessons the previous year and had enjoyed skiing until that one bad accident. But skiing made it possible to tolerate the long winters. As a member of the golf team, practice in winter term was in very modest facilities at the gym, where we would hit balls into a net for hours on end and putt on an artificial turf in a smallish room. As I recall, we did not travel down south till spring. I learned to watch and enjoy ice hockey in the unheated rink, but I rarely went to basketball games for some reason, even though we had a good team. Football was big on campus and the occasion for road trips and dating, usually with a fix-up.

I believe it was my sophomore year when we drove to the Harvard game in Cambridge with Russ Brooks to meet his girlfriend, Patsy there—they married the next year in Huntington, Long Island, New York, and I was their best man. Though I must have had a date, I have no recollection of who it was. But I do remember some of the events that weekend. A group of us had been convinced to paint the toilet seats of a Harvard dorm green; I—but not Russ—was part of the group that did the deed on Friday night. I had a friend (Perry Molinoff) in that dorm whom I saw the next day, and he told me how his housemates had reacted, and you can imagine: they were not happy. At the game in Harvard Stadium that Saturday afternoon, tension was high since by then everyone on campus knew about what had happened. The halftime show started with the Dartmouth Marching Band and cheerleaders, and then came the Harvard Marching Band in all their regalia. They processed around the field and when they faced the Dartmouth side, the entire band mooned us. For the modern reader this means they dropped their pants and pushed out their big butts at us, and a rousing cheer went up from the other side of the field. Harvard got their revenge, of a sort.

My developing friendship with Mike Fitz meant that he often came to Norwich with me for vacations and an occasional weekend. My father loved it and they chattered away in German; and Mike loved Connie, and they became very close too. In the course of these years with Mike, I decided to study a semester in Vienna, spring of my junior year 1961, where he would be completing his law degree. My parents loved the idea, especially since Mike and I would room together.

In Hanover, as a result of my friendship with Mike and my continuing studies in German language and literature, I became active in Germania, the German Club—but I had no intention of taking the members to any opera. Instead I took a wonderful course on opera in which the teacher, James A. Sykes, sat at the piano and, while he talked about a certain composer or aria, would play parts of it. I found it thrilling. I wrote a paper on Richard Strauss, and Sykes loved it. Another favorite course was a seminar on Goethe in German and taught by Frank Ryder. I wrote a paper on Faust and Ecclesiastes. In Religion, I took Old Testament with James (Jim) Ross, who in later years taught at the Theological School of Drew University and the Episcopal Theological Seminary in Virginia. I did so well he offered to tutor me in Biblical Hebrew one-on-one, and that began my serious encounter with the Hebrew language. My Hebrew school background and cantorial work did not amount to a hill of beans in that setting. Jim Ross subsequently became very involved with archaeology and ASOR and its Jerusalem School, later the Albright Institute of Archaeological Research (AIAR); but at this time, for me and him, it was mainly Hebrew and text. The Religion Department was small and friendly, and it provided a cozy and congenial intellectual home for me as I became more and more drawn to the discipline and range of subjects that it covered. Having Pat Scott-Craig and Fred Berthold there was also just wonderful. I believe it was this sort of atmosphere that I would later want to recreate in my teaching at Duke. Offerings in the History Department also attracted me at this time and especially courses on the modern Middle East. Modern Hebrew and Jewish Studies were totally absent at this time, and I became increasingly disturbed by this fact.

As a result of leading services so often, I became very active in national Hillel and started to participate in occasional weekends in Cambridge, where there was something called the Harvard–Yale–Princeton Hillel Colloquium. As I recall, it was held on a Shabbat weekend with several major talks, one Friday night after dinner and another on Saturday, often with small groups. This is where I first heard Nahum Glatzer talk about Franz Rosenzweig and where I fell in love with modern German-Jewish Studies. I had heard none of this from my German side of the family and was thrilled to learn about the rich intellectual heritage of German Jewry. Marshall was so focused on Heschel that he never helped me to understand or appreciate the many contemporaries or predecessors of Heschel's, and I was just eager to learn more about the German-Jewish intellectual underpinnings of modern Judaism. As a result of meeting Glatzer in Cambridge, I decided to combine my interest in religious studies with German-Jewish studies and to study at Brandeis after Dartmouth. In the spring of 1960 Rabbi Kravetz told me that there would be a National Hillel Summer Institute at Camp B'nai B'rith in Starlight, Pennsylvania, later in the summer and that he would like me to attend, paid for by Dartmouth Hillel. It was for leaders and individuals who would benefit from training sessions in program planning and other aspects of Hillel campus life. In addition, for Shabbat the scholar in residence would be Rabbi Heschel. That was a huge plus, and I heartily agreed.

Before going to the Hillel retreat, since Mike Fitz was leaving Dartmouth to finish his law degree in Vienna, he and I decided to drive across country for a month and see the US. We invited Tommy Gardener from Norwich to join us. Mike had become friends with him as a result of working for Tommy's father, Gus, on and off in a local woolen mill (Yantic Woolen Mill). Somehow we got a Chevy convertible for the trip and managed to visit my relatives on the west coast and Chuck Hagerman in Nevada en route. It was truly an amazing trip. Because of lack of funds we often camped out and even ate road kill once or twice (rabbit as I recall). One night at a bar in San Francisco we met a Japanese guy who took a fancy to us and drove us all around and entertained us as well. I was a bit naïve at the time, but in retrospect it's likely that he was gay and had taken a fancy to one of us, probably Mike, the best looking of the three. At the conclusion of the trip Mike returned to Austria and I got ready for Starlight.

The camp was in the northeastern corner of Pennsylvania and had a lovely lake and creek. The setting was just fantastic, and we were about a hundred or more students from colleges and universities in the US. Obviously it was also a great opportunity to meet members of the opposite sex, and that was certainly a large part of the attraction of going. And I met a lovely girl from Vassar whom I really liked, but the relationship never lasted after that week. Rabbi Heschel's presence at services and dinner Friday night culminated in an inspiring talk, the subject of which I have long forgotten.

Saturday services that summer, however, were memorable for another reason. The Torah service culminates with several honors that require two individuals, *hagbah* and *gelilah*, to lift, process, and wrap the Torah scroll after the weekly reading was completed. Depending on the congregation or setting Torah scrolls can vary in size and weigh a lot. I don't recall how large or heavy the Torah scroll was in Starlight, but the young man who was called upon to hold and march around with it dropped it. Rabbi Heschel was sitting in the first row of the congregation, which was meeting in a large tent, and rose and called for immediate silence and attention in a very dramatic way. He began by asking if we knew what had just happened and how serious it was. He emphasized that dropping a Torah on the ground was not an ordinary event. He said that as the most sacred object in a synagogue, the document in which the word of God was preserved, appropriate action was called for. No one in the congregation except perhaps the other rabbis there had any idea of what was about to happen or be uttered. In any case, Rabbi Heschel said that the only proper response, the one called forth by centuries of tradition, was to declare a half-fast, which meant no lunch. He went on and on, and as the import of the declaration of the fast began to set in, the boy who had dropped the Torah began weeping uncontrollably. He wept and wept and was completely disconsolate and humiliated. No one could console him. After services I went up to Rabbi Heschel and asked him if it was really necessary to declare such a fast and publically humiliate the young person, and I urged him to console the young man. Rabbi Heschel staunchly declined to do so and continued to defend his banning of lunch, our big meal of the day. The Hillel encampment ended on this sour note, and none of the participants could talk about anything else until they left the next day. Till today, I think the reaction was extreme and uncalled for. Rabbi Heschel was not pleased that I questioned his judgment on this, to say the least. While I hold Rabbi Heschel in highest regard to this day, admire his work in human rights and social justice, in this instance I could not bring myself to recognize the appropriateness of his actions that day or their justification since they hurt a human being so much.

Speaking of food, Dartmouth food was pretty awful, and the mystery meat and other nameless dishes did not go unnoticed. Two good friends from Mystic, Connecticut, brothers Richard and Steve Macht (the latter an actor and now rabbi), a French student, Patrick Franchon, who later developed a relationship with my sister, and I—Mike Fitz would not join in such a silly activity—would line up close to one another and march around the dining hall, shouting damning remarks about the food to encourage our fellow classmates to join the protest. Oftentimes it resulted in food fights, but our little group never sanctioned that: we only marched in silly protest. One note about our funny alignment when we marched around: everyone who followed had his jaw on the person in front of him, with hands at our sides, and in perfect unison picking up our stride marching as we circled the Thayer Dining Hall. I can't remember what came out of our mouths while we were protesting.

There were a few other silly things we did; some even had a cost attached to them. One prank was to fill up a student's room to the ceiling with crumpled newspapers after he went home for vacation or a weekend. When he came back and opened his dorm room, he would find it filled to the ceiling with newspaper. I have no idea how we picked the victim or even if I was directly involved, but I do remember the startled face of one person who opened up his door and screamed as the paper rained down on him. A similar custom arose in late spring. When getting ready for graduation, the grounds crew started putting fresh sod down in bare areas where the lawn has disappeared. With the newspaper custom in mind someone got the weird idea of emptying someone's room and putting fresh sod down for carpeting. When that student came back to his room, he went berserk and the perpetrators had to pay for the sod. All in good fun, and I enjoyed seeing this as much as anyone.

My junior year in Hanover was brief since I was headed to Vienna for six months. I was affiliated with the Institute for European Studies (IES) and also registered as a special student at the University of Vienna since my German by this time was pretty good. I did not want to lose any time toward graduation, so I arranged for several of the IES courses and also my work at the university to be transferred. My IES fellow students mostly lived together, but Mike Fitz had arranged for us to live in the Ninth District on Grünertorgasse, which was close to the university and IES.

Our landlady, Frau Kessner, it turns out was Jewish. I had a Hebrew prayer book in our room that she discovered one day, and when I was home alone once she asked me to come visit in her apartment. She then told me what it was like in the apartment house during the war and what the Nazis did. It was after this encounter that I had trouble sleeping for a while.

I did manage to go to services in the old Seitenstettengasse synagogue every once and a while, but this was long before the East European migration to Austria; at that time only a few old-timers attended services, which were not very inspiring. What was inspiring, however, was the knowledge that this was the synagogue where Solomon Sulzer, the great cantor and composer of liturgical music and interpreter of Schubert *Lieder*, had sung and where Franz Schubert had visited to listen to his good friend, the cantor after 1825. Sulzer was also a professor at the imperial conservatory in Vienna.

While I was in Vienna I arranged to study voice with Josef Mashkan, who had sung with the Volksoper (People's Opera) and whose wife was then singing there. He was associated with the Horak Conservatorium (later called the Franz Schubert Conservatory). In a strange coincidence that to this day I do not understand, Jon Marans, a Duke graduate, wrote a play, *Old Wicked Songs*, which featured a music professor named Joseph Mashkan and was nominated for a Pulitzer Prize in 1996. The student

PART ONE: BEFORE CAROL

in the play, Stephen Hoffman, while a pianist, also wanted to study the poems of Heine through the music of Robert Schumann's *Dichterliebe*, a song cycle I started to learn in Vienna with Mashkan. When I read about the play, I called Marans and told him of the coincidence of the music teacher in the play and my voice teacher having the same name; he said that's all it was, a coincidence. The Jewish content of the play also resonated with me, but Marans insisted he had never studied with me at Duke nor had he ever met me. My Viennese voice teacher's name was so unusual I firmly believe Marans must have seen it somewhere, remembered it, and used it. In any case my studies with Josef Mashkan were memorable, and I still use some of his vocal exercises to warm up today. When I had a cold or cough, however, he would give me a raw egg to swallow; he swore that it would help me get through the hour's lesson. I remember only that I could hardly bear it. His students, both private and in the conservatory, did recitals later in the spring, and I met a lovely soprano with whom I became quite enamored for a short while. Meanwhile, I spent every spare night standing at the Staatsoper (State Opera) and often sitting at the Volksoper, which was less expensive.

Part of the IES program was travel, and we did a major tour of Italy for two weeks and other locations in Europe for shorter visits. For the long spring break a number of us traveled by train to Russia, where we were closely monitored in those days by Intourist. I recall vividly being repeatedly approached by college-age students wanting to buy my blue jeans. When I started running out of cash, I broke down one day and sold a pair for what I thought was an exorbitant amount.

Another time, later in the term, I took my first trip to Israel, traveling by train on the Orient Express to Athens and then by boat from Piraeus to Haifa. My traveling companion for this trip was Philip Arnold, who later became an ordained minister and who today is living in Montreat, North Carolina, also known as Presbyterian Heaven. Israel was thirteen years old at the time and still had the feeling of a new state with all the excitement and pioneering spirit. It was then that I first knew that this was only the beginning of a lifelong attachment to the Jewish State. What I did not know then was how complicated the international politics of Israel would become after fifty years of Occupation in 2017 when I began to write this memoir.

A course with Professor Kurt Schubert in Hebrew Bible and Qumran at the University of Vienna proved to be very influential in my future studies. Schubert was a great pedagogue and had very wide interests in biblical and Jewish studies. He also collaborated with his wife Ursula in Jewish Art. Even at this early time in the emerging discipline of Jewish Studies, Schubert was at the forefront of what was happening in Dead Sea Scrolls research just a decade or so after their discovery. His teaching assistant at the university was an Israeli PhD candidate who was very helpful to me in thinking about my studies in Hebrew Bible, and we often ate together in the student Mensa or cafeteria.

In IES my course in European politics and history with Professor Fritz Fellner was memorable and helped me greatly with understanding our travels and appreciating what was happening at the time on the continent. His knowledge of Austrian politics was amazing. I was so enthusiastic about his class that Mike Fitz came one time to listen and introduce himself, but I think Mike really came to meet some of the female students.

I learned later that spring that when I returned to Dartmouth in the fall I would be lacking one required course, which for some reason was not going to be offered that year, for my Religion major. So I had to revise my European travel plans and take a summer course on "world religions" at Columbia University and stay at the home of my grandmother's brother, Uncle George Silberstein, and his wife Aunt Dorothy. The teacher, Anton Sigmund-Cerbu was fantastic, and living with the Silbersteins was fun too.

Being a senior in college (AY 1961–1962) is the best. Being a senior after being abroad with all sorts of stories to tell is even better. That year I lived in Giles and had a roommate, Peter Tuschak, a Hungarian refugee (1956) whom the eminent mathematician John Kemeny, future Dartmouth president, helped come to Dartmouth. We had a good year together, and I did my best academic work, finishing up my major in Religion and having the freedom to take classes simply for the fun of it. That's when school is best, simply having the opportunity to explore important and interesting subjects with great minds.

By this time I was already pretty convinced I was going to apply for graduate school and made a special visit to Brandeis to visit and talk with Professor Glatzer, who was chair of the Near Eastern and Judaic Studies (NEJS) department at the time. I told him that I thought I was interested in modern German-Jewish thought and that I had been inspired by his Rozenzweig talk at Harvard. He then went on to talk about the importance of getting a good general background in Jewish thought first, and if I were to come to Brandeis next year Erwin Goodenough was going to be there, Shemaryahu Talmon would also be there, and I would certainly have to study with them simply because they were great scholars and their subjects important to Jewish Studies: art and archaeology for Goodenough, Hebrew Bible for Talmon. This was advice I took to heart and never forgot since as an undergraduate teacher you often have to teach subjects that are quite removed from your area of specialization. Little did I know that in the course of study I would get totally involved with ancient Jewish studies despite loving modern more, so I thought. Applying to graduate school in 1961 was not as complicated as today, and as I recall I only applied to Brandeis.

Concentrating on my studies more than ever before was dictated by my desire to get into graduate school, and it paid off. I also ended some of my extra-curricular activities so that I would have more time to study and thus get better grades. I quit golf and Glee Club but worked hard with my voice teacher. Religion in those days had comprehensive exams that stretched out over several days and culminated with an oral defense. This was spring term, and while my grades qualified me for distinction, in the major I had to earn a certain grade in comps in order to officially get recognized at graduation. Well, to my dismay only one professor, my New Testament professor, Robin Scroggs, did not like my essay on Paul and held out against my getting honors. In my orals we had a wing dinger of a debate on Paul and Judaism; while it was very exciting and stimulating, the teacher won and I lost. But my deep and abiding interest in the issue of the relationship between early Christianity and early Judaism was kindled and would stay with me for the rest of my life. For the life of me, I cannot remember the nature of our debate, but I would assume it was the issue of to what degree Paul's writings were rooted in the Judaic tradition.

A highlight of my senior year was when I was asked to serve on a named-lecture committee that decided to bring to campus none other than Rabbi Heschel for a whole week. The lectures were intended for the whole campus, as were previous ones, but he would also do certain things just with Jewish students. Since he was to all intents and purposes an Orthodox Jew in his practices, we had to arrange kosher meals for him at the Hanover Inn, which was a bit of a challenge. Our Hillel rabbi was Reform, and there was not yet any kosher facility on or near campus. Moreover, there was no Chabad either to call in for special duties. But the Inn cooperated fully with special dishes and all the requisite requirements, and Rabbi Heschel was quite satisfied with the arrangements. The steering committee had dinner alone with him one night and was most impressed with his cigar smoking after dinner. The cigars appeared to be about a foot long, and we all had a chuckle when he whipped one out and lit it. He asked us why we were laughing, and all we could say was that we had never seen such big cigars! When he and I walked around campus alone several times, there was not a trace of animus in regard as to what had occurred at Starlight. On the contrary, he was concerned about my state of observance of Halacha—keeping kosher, Sabbath observance, etc.—and he, like Chancellor Louis Finkelstein previously, was eager to recruit me to the Jewish Theological Seminary (JTS) in New York for a joint rabbinic/PhD program that the eminent Judaic scholar Jacob Neusner had done some years before. I had told Chancellor Finkelstein that I was not prepared to sign an oath for full observance of Halacha and repeated this to Rabbi Heschel. Neither of them seemed to appreciate the depth of my reservations about taking an oath, and by this time, the fall of 1961, I was pretty set on going to a "regular," secular graduate school, with a strong Judaic Studies program, namely, Brandeis.

One other highlight of my senior year was the Great Issues course. In addition to Rabbi Heschel, there were always wonderful speakers coming to campus, and my other favorite besides Rabbi Heschel was alumnus Robert Frost, the poet. I had attended his readings each year and always managed to get a front-row seat in Webster Hall. But in Great Issues we had a distinguished visitor every week or so and a follow-up seminar with an assigned reading on the topic of the lecture. Coat and tie were required, and so to show our displeasure at this dress code requirement we all put on wild and colorful ties that clashed with everything. A memorable visitor that fall was the presidential candidate John F. Kennedy, whose hand I got to shake. The course was truly unforgettable and made all of us seniors aware of and informed about the main issues facing the US and the world at that time. President Dickey had conceived the idea and it was his pet project. The gravitas that Dickey brought to the course and the quality of the visitors made this a truly special part of the Dartmouth experience.

The absence of Jewish Studies offerings at the College was noticeable, and my Hebrew language study with Jim Ross compensated a good deal for this lack. But there was a lot of rumbling in Hillel and among the Jewish student body, and I was asked to lead a delegation to meet with President Dickey to discuss the situation. I do not remember the names of the two or three students who went with me to see the president, but Rabbi Kravetz must have recommended them. In any case, the meeting lasted an hour or more, and President Dickey was completely receptive to the idea of hiring a Jewish Studies scholar as soon as possible. Fred Berthold got the message and sure enough a search went out that academic year. The result was that Jacob Neusner joined the faculty after my graduation. We were all very proud of that.

Despite the way my Dartmouth career began, by the time graduation rolled along I had been accepted at Brandeis and the family would come up for graduation. Peter and I were planning some nice cocktail parties in our dorm; we invited our favorite professors, and they all came. We smoked and broke the white clay pipe on the stump of the old pine tree at the BEMA in remembrance of the Indian peace pipe and heard about how Dartmouth's origins related to the Native Americans of the north woods. Actually those cheap clay pipes were similar to coach drivers' pipes, which were used by those early drivers who brought students to Hanover from White River Junction to campus. Those coach drivers would, when the nicotine and tar levels around the mouthpiece grew too dark, break off a few inches of the stem to get to a more pristine part. Those clay pipes also were used in taverns where patrons could use a communal pipe by first breaking off a few inches of its stem for sanitary sake. Then in unison we broke our ceramic pipes on the tree—and received wooden canes with a carved Indian head on top as a souvenir of that event, which was the day before graduation. The custom was discontinued in 1993.

My family and I were keeping an eye out for Gary, who had threatened me nearly four years before, but thankfully there was no sign of him. The staged picture of me and my dad holding up his empty wallet with Uncle John, Aunt Arlene, Connie, and my mom looking on, reminds me still of the check I never received the day I won the caddie scholarship four years before. It also reminds me of the exorbitant cost of a bachelor's degree today. But all's well that ends well, and graduation weekend was a ball. After returning to Norwich I went off to a job of painting bunks at Camp Ramah in Connecticut. My roommate was Rabbi Hillel Friedman, Marshall's brother-in-law, who invited me to be his High Holiday cantor in Pelham, New York, the next two years. That was my first real pulpit with a very nice honorarium too.

Lest you think that I held a grudge against my old alma mater, in 2012 for my Fiftieth Reunion at the College I was elected to Phi Beta Kappa and was asked to give a short talk to members of the society. My address can be found in Appendix B.

4

Graduate School/Brandeis 1962–1964

WHEN I MOVED TO Boston later that summer, Marshall was already doing miracles in Buenos Aires with the Jewish community and was absolutely thrilled that I was going into Jewish Studies. He also sent me a check for $400, quite a lot then, to help with all the new expenditures I was facing. Dad had told me I was on my own now, and my car was not in the best condition and I could really use the money to buy a new car. Four of us decided to room together in Newton Corner in a big old house on the Charles River: Peter Tuschak, my Dartmouth senior-year roommate, Mike Coit, a close friend from high school, and Jeremy Zwelling, also a rising PhD student in Jewish Studies at Brandeis and friend from United Synagogue Youth (USY).

Our kitchen duties in our big old house were very much regulated. Each of us was assigned a night to cook, and we each put money into a common fund from which to draw for food and drink. I don't remember what we did for weekends, but I do recall we did have Shabbat dinner and it was always roast chicken. Jeremy only made meatloaf with Campbell's tomato soup poured over it. And we had some good parties too.

I sought out a new voice coach too at this time and was fortunate to find the legendary Cantor Gregor Shelkan from Temple Mishkan Tefilah in Chestnut Hill, who had been featured on the well-known TV show "This Is Your Life," and available on YouTube today.[1] He was born in Libau, Latvia, descendant of a family of rabbis and cantors. He studied for the cantorate in Vienna under Cantor Heinrich Fischer at the famous Seitenstettengasse synagogue, and he also studied opera at a conservatory there. In 1938 he became the leading tenor in Riga, Latvia, where he also

---

1. https://www.youtube.com/watch?v=7oThCpX-1a8.

officiated at his home synagogue. By 1941 he and all the Jews of Riga were rounded up by the Nazis into the ghetto, and subsequently survived three concentration camps. He also became a close friend and mentor in liturgy, and I soon was to become the cantor for the High Holiday overflow services at Mishkan Tefilah.

The NEJS department at Brandeis was bursting with talent in those days. In my first semester I took the Moses Mendelsohn seminar with Alexander Altmann, Goodenough's class in Jewish Art, Talmon's class in the book of 1 Samuel, and Glatzer's "Job and the Problem of Evil." What a start and what a feast of learning! Goodenough taught in the Department of Mediterranean Studies for some reason, and that's where I later met Jack Sasson, who was working with Cyrus Gordon, chair of the Department. Jack, who would become a prominent Assyriologist and biblical scholar, and I became lifelong friends. And next term there was more Glatzer and Goodenough and Talmon and also Benjamin Halperin on Zionism.

Glatzer must have learned somehow that I was a good cantor and that I was studying *hazzanut* (cantorial singing) and voice with Cantor Shelkan; or perhaps I told him about it. One day, late in the second semester, I get a call from Abram Sachar, founding and long-time president of Brandeis. I had no idea what he wanted from me but accepted his invitation and went to his office to meet him. He was very strong and charismatic and spoke with commanding authority, though his voice had a very high pitch. After some chitchat he said to me: "Eric, we have a problem with Hillel on campus. Our Hillel rabbi, Leonard Zion, is unable to continue and has been hospitalized. I have spoken with Dr. Glatzer and he has recommended that you become interim Director of Hillel for one year while you finish your MA and continue your studies for the PhD." He went on to say that of course there would be a small salary and free room and board with an upgrade to a better accommodation and that a search committee would be convened and hopefully they would find a candidate for the job the following year. The person the search committee ultimately came up with was Albert (Al) Axelrod, who was hugely successful over the succeeding years.

I was twenty-three years old at the time and could hardly say no to the president. He said that I would have limited responsibilities on campus with services, which pretty much ran by themselves, all three of them (Orthodox, Reform, and Conservative), but that I would have to lead services at Wellesley College for special holidays and Shabbat at least once a month and also would have to bring over kosher Friday-night meals and give a short talk each time.

Little did I know that in accepting this invitation I would ultimately meet and marry Carol, in her senior year at Wellesley, which would be the most important thing I will ever have done in my entire life.

That summer I moved into my new digs on campus and read all of Josephus in the Loeb Classical Library edition at the suggestion of Dr. Glatzer. Actually I read certain parts over and over, and as a guide to my reading I used Dr. Glatzer's several abridgements of Josephus with commentary. It was a great exercise, and I learned a lot by reading the English and the footnotes. By now it was pretty clear that I was not going to specialize in modern Jewish thought let alone focus on German-Jewish thinkers as I had all I could do to keep up with Goodenough, especially when we turned to Philo along with his magnum opus, *Jewish Symbols in the Greco-Roman Period* (thirteen volumes).

I actually enjoyed the Hillel work, especially going to Wellesley. President Sachar was right about on-campus activities, they pretty much ran by themselves. I checked in at the office daily, met with a few committees but focused that fall term on finishing the MA, which I did with a concentration on Second Temple and Philo and Josephus. My vocal studies and training with Cantor Shelkan were a real source of joy and fulfillment. I also began teaching at Mishkan Tefilah and established a close relationship with Rabbi Israel Kazis. He would in a year ask me to start a Hebrew High School there, which I did and hired all the best PhD candidates in Jewish Studies at Harvard and Brandeis.

I also began to doubt that an academic career was in the cards for me. Sooner or later I guess everyone has doubts if they are on the right path or not, and questioning my career choice at this moment was a healthy exercise for me. Cantor Shelkan wanted me to think about a professional career in singing and/or the cantorate. He even introduced me to Boris Goldovsky, a good friend and impresario in the American operatic community. I could combine the two as he had done, the cantorate and opera, they both said, and have an even bigger role at Mishkan Tefilah as second cantor and possibly as educational director. I also contemplated going to law school and applied to one school—Boston College Law School and was accepted. A high school friend of mine, Margaret Norman, was living in Boston at the time and knew the dean of Boston College Law School, Father Robert Drinan, and arranged for us to meet. In his office, after hearing what I was doing and listening to my enthusiastic summary of my intellectual interests, he said it would be silly to go to law school and give up all I had described to him. And that was that. As for singing, I saw that I could somehow maintain a very serious engagement with it by continuing to work as a part-time cantor. That winter for the first time I actually was asked to co-officiate at a wedding, and Cantor Shelkan gave me some music to learn and helped me prepare.

5

Carol

BUT THE SPRING OF 1964 was most memorable because on April 24th on a Friday night at Wellesley I brought the Brandeis-prepared, regular kosher dinner to Bates Hall. Little did I know when I set up for services and dinner there that the young woman on desk-duty in Bates, one Carol Lyons from Kingston, Pennsylvania, near Wilkes-Barre, would join us for grace after meals or part of it, sit down next to me, and wow, shezam, that was it. She said she heard me singing and came to see who was singing so beautifully in Hebrew. After dinner we decided to drive to Harvard Square and walk around and talk, and we barely got back to campus in time for her curfew.

Among the things we discovered that we had in common was that we were both studying Bible and archaeology and religion. But most astounding of all was the fact that we each had been awarded Hebrew Union College scholarships to study in its Summer Institute in Israel. By this time I had intended to stay the rest of the year and study at Hebrew University. Carol had already accepted a big fellowship to do a PhD at the University of Pennsylvania under the renowned scholars Ephraim Speiser and Moshe Greenberg. But the extraordinary coincidence of this and the fact that we were immediately attracted to one another left a powerful impression on me that night, so much so I couldn't sleep. Carol's exceptional beauty and charm and intellectual savvy just bowled me over.

I had enough foresight to write a letter to her the next day inviting her to a lecture at Harvard by Nahman Avigad from the Hebrew University of Jerusalem on ancient Northwest Semitic seal inscriptions at the Harvard Semitic Museum that week, and the rest is history. As it turned out, she was unable to go with me to that lecture, but she teases me to this day about how romantic our first "date" would have been. We were inseparable after that, and nine weeks later were married on June 25, 1964.

Our courtship was brief, but thankfully it was very rich. We often studied together; Carol was preparing for comprehensive exams in her major (Biblical History, Literature, and Interpretation), and I was winding up the Hillel job and thinking about what I would do for the PhD. My feeling at the time was that I wanted to work with Goodenough on Jewish art and archaeology but had no detailed idea what that meant. Jack Neusner, who was destined for Dartmouth, was actually in residence at Brandeis at this time working on a thorough treatment of Goodenough's *Jewish Symbols the Greco-Roman Period*, so I had an inkling that this field was going to open up in a big way. By the end of the summer and early fall when we were in Israel, it was quite clear that working with Goodenough would not be possible after Goodenough sent me a short note informing me that he would not be there when I returned because he had terminal cancer.

Before Israel and while still at Brandeis, Carol and I would often end up our study time together at Friendly's at the end of the day for ice cream, and my car could find its way pretty easily to Wellesley on its own after a few weeks. Norwich was only a couple hours' drive from Waltham, and soon I was bringing Carol home to meet the family. On one such weekend in May we drove home and Uncle George Silberstein (Grandma Anita's brother) and his wife, Aunt Dorothy, were staying at 18 Briar Hill Rd. at my parents' new house, up from New York for the weekend. It was pretty clear to all that Carol and I were attached at the hip and meant for one another. While we were schmoozing in the kitchen the next afternoon, my mother disappeared for a while, soon reappeared with a ring that was Grandma Käthe's, and said to Carol "why don't you try this on?" Carol did, and Aunt Dorothy exclaimed "I guess you're engaged." And while I was somewhat in shock and actually fell off my chair, things had progressed so fast that it was clear that this was inevitable; we both knew that it was right. The celebration began and at our house and that meant lots of booze and way too many cigarettes, though I never smoked except for a pipe for a couple of years. I thought Carol cried for joy at the time but I later learned her eyes were watering from the cigarette smoke, to which she was allergic, so it seemed.

The next challenge was how to deal with the logistics of it all. First we had to tell Carol's parents. Then we had to decide if we would postpone getting married for a year or get married before we left to Israel. It would be a little awkward for us to live together at the Summer Institute unless we were married, especially with many participants being New Testament professors who were also ministers. Staying on in Israel for the year looked more and more appealing, but it meant Carol would have to cancel or postpone going to Penn. First thing we had to do was go to Kingston and break the news in person to her parents. And that was tough. Carol's mom, Irene, at first thought Carol was pregnant or if she was not why couldn't she wait a year so she could plan a nice wedding at leisure. Her dad, Harry, a dentist, lovingly called no-Novocain Harry by our kids later in life, was also in shock. Ultimately they agreed to let "Cookie" Carol loose, and Carol and I made arrangements for the wedding, which would take place a week later.

Carol did not have time to look for a wedding dress, which was a concern. We were all finally excited about the wedding, but we had one more important visit to make: Carol had to tell Professors Speiser and Greenberg that she was not coming to Penn. She wanted to do that in person, so we drove to Philadelphia so she could meet with Professor Speiser, who was very gracious about her decision to forego a Penn degree. While it was difficult for her, it was the right move, and neither she nor I ever regretted our course of action. As it would turn out, Carol would ultimately get her PhD from Brandeis and I would get mine from Harvard, but that is getting ahead of the story.

There were a number of things we needed to do before the wedding, not the least of which was having two graduations, my MA from Brandeis and Carol's AB from Wellesley. Both of those events were fun, and while we could not get me a ticket to Wellesley's ceremony, I was just pleased to be in the overflow crowd. By that time Carol had been able to introduce me to a couple of her teachers; Ernest Lacheman in ancient Near East and Akkadian was a favorite of hers, and I readily agreed.

The wedding in Wilkes-Barre went off flawlessly. Carol's rabbi, Rabbi Barras, was away, and my rabbi, Marshall Maltzman from Norwich, together with Uncle Marshall's father-in-law, Rabbi Theodore (Ted) Freedman, co-officiated. Marshall and Naomi were already in Argentina and could not attend on such short notice but were there in spirit. Since there was no time for Carol to shop for a wedding dress, she lucked out when her first cousin Sally offered to let her borrow the dress she had worn at her wedding a few years earlier; many years later we learned that it was a high-end Priscilla of Boston gown. Fortunately, it fit pretty well, though the fastenings came slightly apart during a wedding dance and were quickly repaired on site by Uncle Max's (Harry's brother) assistant at his photography studio. Uncle

PART ONE: BEFORE CAROL

Max took our wedding pictures. With other cousins aplenty and a few college friends a wonderful dinner and party followed at the very same venue where Carol's parents had been married decades before. Uncle John chartered a plane and flew his family down too. On such short notice, we could not have envisioned a better outcome. We were happy as clams.

Our wedding picture, Wilkes-Barre, Pennsylvania, June 25, 1964. Max Lyons, photographer, brother of Carol's dad, Harry Lyons, DDS.

We planned a few days in the Hamptons before going to Israel with the Hebrew Union College flight, but first we went via Norwich to attend a reception for us at John and Arlene's and to meet and greet the whole Norwich crowd who never made it to Wilkes-Barre. We got all sorts of presents, most of which were delivered to Carol's parents' house after we had left the country. Carol's mom opened them and sent us a list of what we had received. We sent out thank-you notes from Israel, although we didn't actually see the gifts until a year later.

Part Two
With Carol

6

Israel/Europe 1964–1965

Hebrew Union College Summer Institute, 1964, in Jerusalem

THE SUMMER INSTITUTE WAS populated mainly by professors of Bible at many different Christian colleges and universities in the US and even from Europe. Sponsored by the Smithsonian Institution, we began with an intensive seminar in Hebrew Bible led by Frank Moore Cross, Jr. from Harvard, outgoing Director of the fledgling Hebrew Union College Biblical and Archaeological School in Jerusalem. We were two of a total of three graduate students, and we became very friendly with most of the participants but especially with an Episcopal priest and Navy chaplain, the Rev. William (Bill) Broughton. We lived close to Ramat Rachel in a very modest apartment that we shared with Kent Richards the other graduate student, who would one day become Executive Director of the Society of Biblical Literature (SBL), and his then wife, Christy. We had no fridge, but there was a tiny shop across the street, where every morning we bought a day's worth of milk, eggs, yogurt, and other essentials so we could survive.

Cross was awesome in seminar for those who were really good in biblical Hebrew. We studied among other things the Nash Papyrus and the Ten Commandments in Cross's own unique way, with all the ancient versions at hand. We didn't get very far, but I immediately saw how different this was from what I had done at Brandeis. The touring component of the Summer Institute was in three parts: Jerusalem, Galilee, and the Negev. Exploring Jerusalem was ongoing and ad hoc, and we had many opportunities to meet with dignitaries, public and governmental, and private individuals, like Martin Buber.

Our visit to Buber's home that summer of 1964 was memorable for several reasons. All of our Christian colleagues were most familiar with his theological writings and not his larger oeuvre, which was considerable. When we visited him at his home one evening, most of the questions concerned his well-known interfaith ecumenical writings. But Buber at this time was also a peace activist and spokesman for the Palestinian Arab community. I asked him if his I-Thou treatise had been the underpinning of his recent activism and championing the idea of a single state with Arab and Jew sharing equal rights. After hearing my question he went up to me and pulled me to the front and said: "Now we can begin to talk seriously." This meant that he wanted to talk about how theology could and should serve social causes. The rest of our conversation that evening at his home was about the problem that still confronts the Jewish state and that remains unanswered till today.

Eric with David Ben Gurion at Sde Boker, his home in the Negev, July 1964, discussing the issue of how important it was to live in Israel to maintain one's Jewish identity. Ben Gurion said he only attended synagogue in the Diaspora.

The other memorable meeting that summer was with David Ben Gurion at Sde Boker in the Negev. We had a very engaging discussion, i.e., he and I, about whether it was necessary for a Jew in Israel to attend synagogue and how important it was for Jews in the Diaspora to attend, in his opinion, in order to preserve their Jewish identity. Needless to say we had a heated exchange of ideas and he insisted it was much easier to live a Jewish life in Israel but that it was not necessary to go to synagogue there.

Nelson Glueck, a prominent archaeologist and explorer, was president of HUC at the time and was our guide in the Negev. He was a handsome man and a powerful speaker. Our home base in the Negev with him was the Desert Inn in Beersheba. From there we went out to all the Nabataean sites that he favored, and he told all sorts of stories about his explorations in the Negev and Transjordan. He got all of us hooked on archaeology. He was very kind and warm to Carol and me, probably because we were so young and attentive to his narrative. He was also a very fine scholar of Hebrew Bible, having received his doctorate in Germany at Jena in that area, with a dissertation on the biblical concept of *hesed*. He was very close to Frank Cross and to G. Ernest Wright, who would succeed Cross as Director of the Jerusalem HUC, because of their mutual love of ASOR and W. F. Albright, the father of American biblical archaeology. Glueck had been a major figure in ASOR as head of ASOR's Jerusalem research center for many years while also leading surveys and excavations in Transjordan. Professor Wright, when he came to Jerusalem later that summer to take over from Cross at HUC, was president of ASOR and Parkman Professor of Divinity at Harvard.

In addition to having Glueck as our guide in the Negev, and resident head of HUC in Jerusalem, we also spent a week digging with Yohanan Aharoni, then professor of archaeology at the Hebrew University of Jerusalem, at Tel Arad. Carol and I were fortunate enough to be assigned to the area where we would help uncover the shrine with an altar from the early Iron Age. Our supervisor at the dig was someone younger than we were, apparently the teenage son of Aharoni's family doctor. We are still pretty confident that we did not lose any important data, although we were awfully surprised at the low level of supervision at the time.

Our tour leader and guide in Galilee was the geographer Zev Vilnay, author of the most popular guidebook on Israel for many years. Zev was truly inspirational. He knew every nook and cranny of the region and was also familiar with the many graves and holy sites of Jewish pilgrims through the ages. Vilnay's knowledge of the country on land and in text was unparalleled. To this day I attribute my special love of the Galilee to those days and to Vilnay's stimulating walks through time. As with Glueck, Vilnay seemed to take a special interest in Carol and me, probably because we were so young and enthusiastic at the time but also, I think, he believed we would one day carry forward the unique story of that region, which spawned two world religions, Judaism and Christianity. I don't think we disappointed him.

The HUC experience was formative for both of us, and when Dr. Wright arrived to replace Dr. Cross, we were invited to be affiliated with HUC for the rest of the academic year. Along with our affiliation with Hebrew University, where we were to have the status of "special students" (that is, not degree candidates) for the year, this was not a bad way to begin an academic career.

Ulpan and Hebrew University, 1964–1965

After HUC, Carol and I both began to work on our Modern Hebrew. To do so, we enrolled at Ulpan Etzion, Israel's flagship Hebrew-to-Hebrew intensive language program, in Jerusalem, and since we were at different levels, we were in different classes. Mordecai Kamrat was head of the Ulpan, designed originally to teach new immigrants Hebrew, but there were a few there for other reasons. Two of our classmates became good friends. One was Volkmar Fritz, later to be head of the German Archaeological School on Mt. Scopus and distinguished professor at the University of Mainz. The other was Peter Schäfer, another rising German scholar who later assumed important positions in Jewish Studies at Köln, the Free University in Berlin, Princeton, and then back to Berlin as head of the Jewish Museum. We were all very young so it didn't matter where we were headed; all that mattered was that we learned to read and speak Modern Hebrew. And the learning experience was just great. As I recall we began at 8:00 AM and ended at 1:00 PM, which gave us plenty of time to do both grammar and speaking. With the emphasis on everyday speech, it was truly a blessing for our year to come. Volkmar, whose first wife was American and from Norwich, Connecticut, and Peter remained lifelong friends. In any event, after months at the Ulpan, Carol and I felt ready for the academic year ahead at the Hebrew University, with most of our classes in Hebrew.

In the course of study at Ulpan, Carol and I remained in our HUC apartment, which was not too far from the home of Shemaryahu Talmon, with whom I had studied at Brandeis when he was a visitor there, and his first wife Yonina, a distinguished sociologist. When we walked to Ulpan we passed their house (as well that of the great writer S. Y. Agnon) and often on the way back stopped off for a coffee and chat with the Talmons. When the academic year began, we moved to the JTS (Conservative) dorm, which was then the only building of the Beit Hamidrash LeRabanim of the New York-based JTS, near the Hebrew University campus at Givat Ram. Marshall's father-in-law Ted Freedman, one of the rabbis who married us, was one of the faculty members that year and had urged us to live there. He also invited me to study Talmud with him and my Talmud *ḥaver* (fellow student in rabbinics) that year was Ivan Marcus, who would become a long-term professor at Yale in medieval Jewish studies. So our home base, next to the Givat Ram campus of Hebrew University and also near the Knesset, was with quite a few rabbis and rabbinical students. We loved it because we were blissfully happy and had bought a 404 Peugeot with wedding money and were totally mobile. Carol had to learn to drive a stick shift in Jerusalem and that was a challenge, which with difficulty she managed. Driving in Jerusalem was bad enough even back then, but going up a big hill on Rehov Agron next to Supersol proved to be the worst especially since there was always a red light waiting to stop you on that darn hill.

We did not know, when we moved into the JTS dormitory, that the new Israel Museum would be built that year right next to us, adjacent to what is still called Neve Shananim and Neve Schechter. We heard and saw the pile drivings and site preparations and could not imagine then what was to be built on the site designed by the Russian-born Israeli architect, Alfred Mansfeld. There was a small synagogue near our dorm, and I went there several times after we moved to our small JTS apartment. I had several *aliyot* (honor of being called to the Torah) there and even *davened* (chanted) for them on Shabbat a couple of times as a result of which I was invited to lead their High Holiday services. The head of that *minyan*, who lived in Neve Shechter and was a leader of the president's Bible study group, invited us for a New Year dinner, and that was memorable as well. As guest of honor, I got the fish head (*yugh*). The little synagogue there survived till the Museum tore it down, and then services were moved to another *shul* nearby. We understood that the chief rabbinate would not allow the old one to be torn down till another synagogue or *minyan* was declared to replace it.

Fall semester Carol and I enrolled in Yigael Yadin's biblical archaeology class, and that was truly influential in every respect for both of us. Yadin was a close friend of Cross and Wright and had probably been tipped off by one of them that we would be heading his way that fall and to keep an eye on us. Perhaps Nelson Glueck was in on this as well. The fact of the matter is we loved his class and were riveted by his lectures and totally taken in by his charisma and charm. Shortly into the term he announced that he would be taking volunteers for his winter dig at Masada. Carol and I signed on immediately. Meanwhile I was taking a number of other courses in Hebrew philology with Chaim Rabin, a new course with Shemaryahu Talmon in Bible, a course in Septuagint that I dropped, and several other courses mainly for Hebrew fluency. Carol and I also took Aharoni's course in historical geography. Yadin's course on biblical archaeology was everything it was cracked up to be, and we were excited to be going to Masada during the long winter break.

That fall was also fateful for us because Dr. Wright and Dr. Glueck had announced the beginning of a new joint excavation of Tel Gezer sponsored by the Harvard Semitic Museum and HUC. While Wright and Glueck were listed at co-directors, it was to be the launching pad for two of Wrights' PhD students, William (Bill) Dever and H. Darrell Lance, who really ran the dig. Wright asked me and Carol to join the staff, and the fall was to be the first season. The plan was to commute from Jerusalem each day, which was fine with us, and Wright asked us to ride in his car. That was a huge treat as we heard all sorts of stories from him about Albright, Shechem, and members of his former excavation teams. Carol was assigned to Wright's area to keep the field book, and I was assigned to Bill Dever's adjacent square to keep his field book. But Wright had never kept a field book before, and Dever had other responsibilities, so we were soon designated area supervisors. These were the first areas opened, and we stayed in these areas for the next five years and seasons to come.

There were no great discoveries that fall, but for me the big discovery was pottery reading, which I absolutely loved. Watching Dever and Wright identify the sherds after they had been carefully washed and dried was truly exciting, and I can remember Dr. Wright exclaiming when he didn't recognize something, "It's a different world from Shechem!" Actually, in those first seasons when a sherd was not like anything found at Shechem that meant that it was an everyday ware that would go misidentified until the ceramic typology would be better understood at Gezer. My love of ceramics started that first season, and pottery reading always remained a highlight of the digging day in all my own excavations. After a day digging in the dirt, it was really nice to get back to our cozy little apartment in Neve Schechter and take a hot shower and get clean again for supper which we had in our tiny flat.

We also made some good friends that year away from JTS. As a result of our studies with Yadin, a very lovely German couple (the Weingartens) invited us regularly to their Rehavia apartment for Shabbat meals, which were truly memorable as were some of the melodies that came direct from Germany! Ludwig Mayer's bookstore on Jaffa Rd. was a regular stopping place for us too; the shop manager, Aya Sapir, was very welcoming, and we often visited her home. We spent a fortune on books too at the store and soon became very good friends. We also purchased several prints at the store including the painting of an open sardine can that has hung in our dining room all these years. And that year we established close ties with Sidra and Yaron Ezrahi who were living on Metudela Street in those days. Sidra, a college classmate of Carol's, became a prominent scholar of literature, and Yaron would be a leading Israeli political theorist.

Masada, 1964–1965

Working at Masada that winter of 1964–1965 was magical. With hundreds of volunteers from all over the world, we lived in tents, had stand-up toilets a good trek from our tents, a bar with beer and peanuts for afternoon and evening entertainment, and food driven in from Arad by the army. The food was awful, but the excitement of the dig was thrilling, punctuated with announcements of discoveries by Yadin on the loudspeaker every once in a while to keep us interested in the details. It was freezing when we climbed the hill to start work at 5:00 AM, but by second breakfast, which was around 8:00 or 8:15, we were usually stripped down to shorts and short sleeves, though it did rain a couple of times, including on our first New Year's together, which we spent shivering in a cave.

The excavation staff knew we were newly married and still placed us in separate work crews, and we were not happy about that since men and women were segregated in separate tents in camp. But we managed for a while and tried to meet up for second breakfast. The staff relented after about a week and let us join up on the same work crew, and that meant we could relax a bit and not have to complain about how hard it was to meet up for second breakfast. After all we were newlyweds.

Some of the staff were to become good friends: Ehud Netzer, Gideon Foerster, Amnon Ben Tor, and others. Professor Yadin also was to become a big supporter through the years until his untimely death in 1984, especially because of our ASOR connection and leadership roles in it.

Eric and Carol at Masada excavations, January 2, 1965.

During our time at the dig, I guess the biggest discovery was the cache of scrolls in the synagogue. Cameras were strictly forbidden on site, and Yadin was the enforcer. He and the *London Observer* had made an agreement that all new discoveries were to be announced and featured first in that paper—not sure about the Hebrew press, which probably could write about them. One day a volunteer was discovered taking pictures on site, and that afternoon Yadin publicly shamed him by announcing to all what had happened. He then destroyed the camera and all the film. To dramatize this and to show how seriously he took the offense, Yadin did this in full view of everyone, and the volunteer was ushered into a cab and sent packing. That was that, and that's why we don't have any photos of the dig except for one of us in the camp below, which someone sent us.

Finishing in Jerusalem and Returning Travels, 1965

By the beginning of second semester Carol and I had already been on three digs, Arad with Aharoni and the HUC Summer Institute, the fall and spring Tel Gezer expeditions, and the winter season at Masada. Carol had already excavated in Wyoming at a Harvard-sponsored prehistoric dig at

Hell Gap, and the previous year at Ashdod and Tel Beit Yerah on the southwestern shore of the Sea of Galilee. I actually felt I was catching up a bit to her, and it was pretty darn clear by now that I had caught the archaeology bug and could not any longer be considered an accidental archaeologist. Dr. Wright had already asked me to consider transferring to Harvard, and by this time I had already applied and Carol was applying to Brandeis; we did not think we should each be in the same doctoral program at the same time. We also wanted to concentrate on separate fields of research though largely under the umbrella of what might be called biblical archaeology. Carol would be more Iron Age (ca. 1200–586 BCE) oriented and I would be more Persian through Roman periods oriented. This was a good decision, and between us we covered a lot of ground.

While we were in Israel, each of us wrote lots of letters to parents, relatives, and close friends. Everything went slowly by snail mail and mostly was handwritten. I preferred those green foldable aerograms. We rarely if ever called home, it was almost unthinkable.

When I got my letter of acceptance from Harvard, I was informed that I had been awarded the National Defense Foreign Language (NDFL) Fellowship in Hebrew and that a government contract to be signed would arrive soon. Dr. Wright was thrilled, Carol was thrilled and got into Brandeis with significant financial support, and we were on our way. At least so I thought. When my NDFL contract arrived, however, the date for signing had long ago passed, and Dr. Wright called back to his office to see what had happened. It turned out that the contract had been sent in error by sea mail instead of by airmail. The money—tuition and fellowship—in the form of a federal grant could not be recovered and was lost to the department. Dr. Wright was furious and assured me that my tuition would somehow be covered and not to worry and that he would also arrange for a TA position for some additional monies for which I would not have to work.

However, the sum of that was not nearly equal to what I had been awarded, so Carol and I had to come up with a plan. It was at this point that Carol's dad promised a gift of $1,000 to help—a nice chunk of change in those days. That plan would involve us at Brandeis as housemasters in Hamilton (later Massell) Quadrangle near the kosher kitchen that had brought us together in the first place when I took kosher meals to Wellesley once a month. Also, after returning to live on the Brandeis campus, I agreed to start a new Hebrew high school program at Mishkan Tefilah, and I continued on there as High Holiday overflow cantor and head of the new post-Bar

Mitzvah school. The new package worked just fine, and as a result we would incur no debt in graduate school as is so often the case today.

After finishing up in Jerusalem, we rode our new Peugeot 404 to Haifa and traveled with it by boat to Turkey and drove all around Europe for about six weeks. We often slept in the car since the front seats could lie flat and were pretty comfortable. We combined archaeological site touring with regular touristy things and dozens of museums. We had an absolutely fabulous time and felt attached to Europe in a way that has brought us back dozens of times as tourists, teachers, and just plain curious and inveterate travelers. Carol's family was all of Hungarian background, in fact all four grandparents emigrated from Hungary in the early twentieth century. We succeeded in visiting some cousins in Budapest on that trip; they were struggling financially, and we gave them our heavy winter coats. I believe it was on this trip that the two of us first visited my father's other sister, Leni Heaton, who at this time was living in Blonay, Switzerland, near Vevey, where she had retired with her dear friend, Ada Schweitzer, niece of Albert. In later years we returned frequently to Blonay, usually on returning from Israel to the States.

7

Graduate School/Harvard, 1965–1969

WE SETTLED DOWN IN Boston that summer of 1965 and moved into a small basement apartment on Marlborough Street, where my sister had lived. Since I had dropped out of Greek in Jerusalem, I had to take a special course in Classical Greek to satisfy a requirement for my department at Harvard. In that class I met Steve Molinsky from Slavic Studies with whom I have recently reestablished contact. Turns out he ultimately switched to teaching English as a second language and wound up in the School of Education at Boston University for fifty-five years. Today it's called the Wheelock College of Education and Human Development. His textbook, *Side by Side*, has sold more than 30 million copies. The Greek course was tough and boring, and the highlight came when our young professor came to class one day with his fly open. After giggles and smiles I received a note from Steve to just get up and tell the professor to button up his fly so we could concentrate. I did and not surprisingly our teacher was mortified.

Carol had a temporary job in a furniture store in Boston Harbor, and we roasted in our airless, un-air-conditioned apartment in a summer of soaring temperatures, a precursor of global warming. In addition to that, I was teaching a course for foreign students who were matriculating in local colleges and universities in a program called BASIS, Boston Area Seminar for International Students. The BASIS courses were meant to introduce international students to academic work in American institutions of higher learning before the fall semester began. It was a bit of a challenge, but one I enjoyed; and we made a good friend from Nigeria. He was an Ibo whose first name was the unlikely Kingsley, last name Ipke-Awujor. We invited Kingsley to join us for a long holiday weekend with Carol's parents in Kingston, Pennsylvania; her parents were gracious and pretty surprised.

When Kingsley said he needed a haircut after we got there, Harry's barber was nonplussed since he had never cut a black person's hair before. That summer we also met a Jewish girl from Iraq, Jamilla Lavi, with whom we maintained contact for years. We also became friends with a young German, Michael Bodemann, today emeritus Professor of Sociology at the University of Toronto, and supported him in his desire to convert to Judaism, including adult circumcision. His father, a prominent artist, sent us a gorgeous oil painting in honor of the Six Day War and our friendship, which hangs in our living room today.

And after the BASIS seminar concluded, we moved into Renfield Hall in Hamilton Quad at Brandeis. While we had a bit of training before school started, neither Carol nor I were prepared for the next two years and the kinds of situations with which we were confronted weekly as housemasters. Of course there was the noise factor: the guys lifting weights upstairs from us and the noise outside. In the Quad the real challenge was the drug situation. This was the year of Timothy Leary and LSD, and many of our students seemed to have easy access to the drug. One student cut her wrists on several occasions and knocked on our door one afternoon with blood dripping everywhere, and somehow Carol managed to get locked out of the room with a towel wrapped around her but did succeed in getting her to counseling right away. There were multiple suicide attempts including one of our students climbing high up on a construction rig and refusing to come down while threatening to jump. We wound up in ERs numerous times, and yet were advised by the deans not to call parents even when things got very bad. Needless to say it was difficult to study at home in the evening, and the job was taking both of us away from our studies quite a bit. In our second year on the job after a couple of hectic days and sleepless nights, I fell asleep in a class at Harvard. When I awoke alone with my professor, he simply asked me what was going on and I told him. Needless to say we did not continue a third year on campus.

Connie in those days was living nearby in Framingham with her first husband, Pat Westfeldt at this time, and after her first daughter, Amy, was born her apartment became a new destination for us and my parents. God forbid anyone but us would babysit for Amy, and when our first daughter Julie was born, who else but Connie could take care of her?

I had an inkling about what Harvard would be like from my seminar with Professor Cross in Jerusalem. I had no idea how competitive it was going to be though, at least as far as most of my classmates were concerned. Those who were Catholic priests were not nearly as competitive as their Protestant counterparts, and I became very close friends with Dan Harrington, a Jesuit. We each had expressed a preference for specializing in Second Temple literature and languages. The department's usual track at the time for anyone in Hebrew Bible or Old Testament was to have at least four semesters of Akkadian, and Dan and I thought we might substitute other more relevant courses for Akkadian to be better prepared for the study of later periods. We would do all the other Old Testament requirements, including Ugaritic, which Carol and I had studied at the Pontifical Biblical Institute in Jerusalem, a Jesuit institution. Since Dan and I petitioned to do this together, our unusual request was approved and we had most of our classes together.

What did Dan and I substitute for Assyriology and Akkadian? Instead we took Qumran and Dead Sea Scrolls with Cross and John Strugnell and rabbinics with Isadore Twersky, who was chair of our department at the time, then called Near Eastern Languages and Literatures or NELL. (Twersky was the one in whose class I had fallen asleep.) That meant that Dan and I would often be the only two people in a class with Twersky studying a rabbinic text that we had prepared together at the Jesuit House, just a short walk from the Semitic Museum. Professor Twersky, a devout Jew and rabbi, did not like that I did not wear a skull cap to study with him and often stared at my uncovered head but did not say anything out loud. I talked to Dan about it and said, "for God's sake this is Harvard and not a *yeshiva*." But Dan finally convinced me that it was better to cover my head than to annoy him. So I relented, and Twersky smiled and did not say a word. The tension was gone. Dan and I also did Aramaic dialects together, mostly with Thomas Lambdin, and also Syriac with Robert Thompson.

While I loved Dr. Wright, he was not the best lecturer, and he felt most at home when he took Larry Stager and me down to the storerooms of the Semitic Museum and talked about pottery or another interesting artifact while holding a potsherd gently in his hand. He often insisted that we take hold of the object and feel it and get a sense of what it was. And there in the bowels of the Semitic Museum it was like the pottery reading at Gezer all over again. The only great teacher in NELL at that time was Tom Lambdin, Semitist par excellence, who taught every Semitic language and historical Hebrew grammar. He also ate lunch with the students every day in the Divinity School refectory, where I enjoyed my regular tuna fish sandwich.

The Old Testament seminar was huge, looming over all of us like a dark cloud. We were told that each student would be assigned a topic or choose from a list of suggested topics and that papers were to be handed in at a certain date and time before the weekend so that they could be reproduced and distributed to faculty and all students in the program. Let me remind you that in those days we had no Xerox and had to type our papers on mimeograph sheets. The secretary of NELL, Carol Cross, would then help us run them off. We all got high on doing this from the excessive use of correct-o-tape that the process required. If this weren't bad enough, we were also assigned a student and faculty critic to evaluate our paper and then anyone attending the seminar that day could offer criticism. I had no idea what was coming. Most of the student critics saw this as an opportunity to get in good with their adviser, so they went out of their way to nitpick and posture. The seminar was a key component of the program, and few of us liked it. Others, just a few, seemed to relish the opportunity to trash a fellow student.

In my first seminar I was assigned the topic of "Messianism in the Exile and Early Postexilic Period." I was very pleased with the topic, which became a lifelong interest. But no one warned me that certain scholars, like Yehezkel Kaufmann from Israel, were off limits or that I had to know everything that the senior faculty had written on the topic or anything that was remotely close to it. I also used some Modern Hebrew articles, and that did not go over well at this time. The result was that my student critic, who was a couple of years ahead of me, trashed my paper, ripped it to shreds. The faculty was no less kind, and I got some sort of B, my lowest grade at Harvard. I was crushed, and my old doubts about academic life resurfaced; but Carol helped me get through it, as did Dan and Tom Lambdin. Thank God for them. I sure got the message, and next time my seminar experience was lots easier. Another fellow student handed in his paper late, and he was brought to tears in seminar with a tongue-lashing I'll never forget.

When a major snowstorm hit on seminar day, one would not think for a moment of cutting class; you had to get there—by hook or by crook, by foot or by taxi. Once when we were living in Belmont I walked to school in the snow, and it took a good couple of hours. In my subsequent years as a teacher of graduate students, I never once considered replicating this sort of "learning" experience. In speaking recently with my old friend from Slavics, Steve Molinsky, he asked me what my biggest takeaway from the Harvard PhD program was, and I said I learned what sort of teacher I did not want to become but aspired to be as great a scholar as they all were. Steve fully concurred, and his choice to leave Slavics is not unrelated to his similar experiences.

After two years of classes I was ready to prepare for preliminary exams in my third year. I had to do the normal Hebrew Bible exam, which meant being prepared to translate and annotate sight passages from anywhere in the whole Hebrew Bible; I had been preparing for this since we had been married, reading with Carol regularly when we were in Israel. There was also a sight exam in Qumran texts and Mishnah, the latter limited to the order of Moed. There was also an exam on Aramaic dialects and, of course, an archaeology exam, with a focus on Qumran, Samaria/Sebaste, and with a surprise question on pottery. There was lots to do and of course including getting back to the Gezer excavations every summer, which was one of the most important things to do.

Being away for a couple of months each summer meant that not a heck of a lot was accomplished by way of study in those months. Add to that jet lag and visiting both sides of the family, fall semester came around pretty quickly. And I was second cantor for the high holidays at Mishkan Tefilah too! I had been studying at Harvard on a 2S (student) deferment from the draft. Sometime in the spring of 1966 I lost that and at the height of the Vietnam War stood to be drafted at any moment. I elected to apply for conscientious objector (CO) status. As a result I was called to appear before the Norwich draft board one day that spring and drove home from Boston and went with my father. The first question addressed to me was whether I would have served in World War II to oppose Hitler, and I answered yes. That meant I was a selective CO and not a true CO, and my case was dismissed quickly. So I went home and wrote out my appeal and was called back to Hartford the next time to appeal to the state draft board. My dad accompanied me on this trip as well; the same Hitler question was asked, and I repeated my answer. Then they asked if my wife were being attacked or raped would I fight to defend her, and I responded affirmatively that of course I would defend her. My appeal was rejected again, and I was totally dejected and feared that I would now be called up right away.

So Carol and I had to think of an emergency, alternative strategy. I had known that clergy could get a deferment, but that would mean going to seminary, and I had declined a very generous offer to go to JTS in New York when I was at Dartmouth. So we decided I should explore possibilities at HUC; I could perhaps do rabbinic school and come back and then finish my PhD degree. Rabbi Martin Katzenstein in Harvard Divinity School recommended I contact Harry Orlinsky at the Reform Seminary (HUC-JIR) in New York and I did. Carol and I traveled there to meet him. We had a most engaging talk with him, and he was very understanding; but in the end he said I would be foolish to give up my academic aspirations—he felt it would be impossible to be a pulpit rabbi and scholar at the same time. So I went back to the drawing board and back to the library to figure out something else. And we did. We discovered that by getting Carol pregnant and having a child one could defer for a limited while, and we thought that would give me enough time to finish and then maybe the lottery would be implemented and I might be set free. And we were successful. So that summer is when Carol got pregnant and I got deferred. Happy days, so we thought.

So fall consisted of regular prelim study, auditing a few courses including the Old Testament seminar and New Testament, and of course teaching Hebrew High School. As head of the program I also taught Modern Hebrew to a small class on Wednesdays. Sundays we started with a short worship service at 9:15 and began classes at 10:00. Our faculty consisted of Jeremy Zwelling, Sidra and Yaron Ezrahi, Larry Silberstein, and Carol. The pay was very good, and we had a bagels and lox luncheon once a month at noon. There had been some parental grumbling with a few classes, where we talked about Islam and Christianity, but I was not prepared for the pushback at one of our best programs.

Cantor Shelkan had survived the ghetto in Riga, Latvia, prisoner and slave labor camps, and several concentration camps, and also survived a 300-mile death march with the retreating German army. But he was first and foremost my beloved voice teacher. He was finally liberated by the Russian army on March 10, 1945. I asked him if he would like to be our luncheon speaker one day and talk about his experiences during the war. He said yes. He had never talked about his life from his first incarceration in 1938 until his release in 1945 at the synagogue, though his TV appearance on "This Is Your Life" in 1954 made him a very prominent figure in the community.

On the day he came to speak he was dressed in his black-and-white-striped concentration camp outfit, which he had saved. He got up to the podium, talked and talked about his horrific experiences during those years of suffering and survival. After he concluded there was not a dry eye in the room, faculty and students went up to hug him and thank him for such a meaningful and moving presentation. By the time I got home in Belmont there was a call from Rabbi Kazis to come to his house immediately. He told me that his phone had been ringing off the hook regarding the day's program with Cantor Shelkan. I drove over and sat with him, and he told me that a significant number of parents had complained about the program; they did not like that their kids had been exposed to the Holocaust in such a direct way. I described the program to Rabbi Kazis and reminded him that Cantor Shelkan was his right-hand man and had been with him for years and finally had the courage to come out and tell his story to his congregants, albeit youngsters, and that it was as tough for him to tell it as it was for us to hear it. Rabbi Kazis told me he would inform all the parents of his support for the program and support my continuation as head of the high school program. Such a reaction did not reflect well on his wealthy congregation in Chestnut Hill, though I would say the rabbi did the right thing; as for Cantor Shelkan, God bless him. The same sort of reaction repeated when I invited a Harvard classmate of mine to talk to the students, Ephraim Isaac, an Ethiopian Jew who came in traditional African garb and gave an inspirational talk on African Jewry. Parents complained again, and Rabbi Kazis did not call this time.

That winter, 1966–1967, was the time for my prelims, also known as qualification exams, which advanced you to the status of PhD candidacy. Carol had a relatively easy pregnancy at the beginning but as of late had not been feeling well. The exam schedule was Monday to Thursday for the written exams, one each day with a break, and oral defense on the next Monday. I think the length was four hours each. I took the exams on the first two days, and suddenly Carol was told to go to the hospital, where treatment brought her into premature labor. After an awful delivery, we were told that the infant, a girl, was in a precarious situation and that Carol had a huge non-malignant tumor, a placental hemangioma that had caused the problems, and while she was recovering she had a long way to come back. I was a wreck to say the least, and then we got word the baby had died. We were both devastated.

I called Dr. Wright and told him that I could not appear the next day for an exam and would appreciate some sort of delay due to the unprecedented nature of these circumstances. I also called home; Mom and Dad were at John and Arlene's, and Mom was sent up right away to Boston, driven by John's private driver. It was a stormy and icy night, and when she got out of the car at the hospital, she fell and hurt her knee.

Nonetheless, she came right to Carol's room and was of immense support immediately. A bit later she got crutches so she could move around on her own a little better. The nightmare continued. Dr. Wright had asked me to call back that evening, and I did. What he told me was that he had consulted with the committee and they had agreed to give me Wednesday off but I would have to finish prelims on Thursday and Friday and take the oral on Monday. At the time I could not believe my ears. I had asked for a delay of a couple of weeks so that I could take care of Carol and get our heads back in place. But it was a firm no. I had been studying all these months, and with Carol's support I decided to tough it out so long as Mom stayed, which she did, crutches and all. Somehow we made it through that fateful week and my orals went just fine except that Professor Twersky wanted me to come back in a couple of months to read and translate another passage from Moed—he did not particularly like my translation of whatever passage he had assigned for the prelim. I was still recorded as a pass and admitted to candidacy, and the appointment with Twersky later in the term was uneventful and a complete success.

There was one issue that required immediate resolution. What to do about burial. We consulted Rabbi Kazis, who said that we would have to name the baby first in order for it to have a proper Jewish burial. Our close friend Larry Silberstein, also a Conservative rabbi, said he did not agree with that opinion and that he would take care of the burial, including going to the cemetery with the body. We agreed with him and were spared the trauma of naming and having a kind of funeral for a child who had lived only hours. Larry's compassionate understanding of Jewish law resonates with me to this day, and Carol and I are forever grateful to him for his decisive actions at that time.

After all this trauma, Uncle John suggested we go up to his ski lodge in Bondville, Vermont, to recuperate and get into a better mindset. Carol and I were close to all three of Arlene and John's kids: Lisa, Robbie, and Emily. We asked if Robbie (John's only son) were free and could we take him along—I guess it must have been intersession or something for him. Robbie eagerly agreed to join us. He was pre-Bar Mitzvah at the time, and I would study with him when we weren't skiing. For some reason I decided to study Pirkei Avot, Ethics of the Fathers, from the Mishnah, with him with Carol alongside, and it was truly therapeutic for me. Not sure about Robbie, though he still recalls that week with warm feelings. The down time we had to recover in the Green Mountains really helped us through that hard period, and when we returned to Boston, we got back to our work without delay.

In another trip to Norwich, Carol and I visited with Uncle Kurt to talk about getting pregnant again. The doctors in Boston had told us to wait a good while to start trying again. We were not sure what exactly that meant, and Uncle Kurt said after Carol had healed there was no need to wait but that going forward right away would be the best medicine for all ailments, mental and physical, and that we should not fear reoccurrence of a similar tumor, which he said was very rare. His advice greatly relieved us, and to our delight Julie was born a little over a year later, on December 16, 1968, a real "jewel."

Later that spring of 1967 we began to worry more and more about the future of Israel as the threats from the Arab League and especially from Egypt became more alarming. By the end of May we feared the worst, and with the closing of the Straits of Hormuz in the Red Sea it was clear to us that war was inevitable. When we woke up on Monday morning June 5th, my birthday, we were not surprised to learn that war had started and that Israel had launched a preemptive strike against its enemies. Even though we soon learned that the Egyptian air force had been wiped out, the fear that something akin to the Holocaust was about to happen was palpable, not only in the Jewish community, but also in the Gentile community. Christian neighbors called their Jewish friends and the synagogue non-stop, and on Friday night our synagogue, Mishkan Tefilah on Hammond Pond Parkway, was filled to overflowing with Jews and non-Jews in a Sabbath service everyone there will always remember. The war would end the next day, but the concerns expressed about the survival of the State of Israel were very real.

Many of us in Boston headed to Federation, today Combined Jewish Philanthropies of Greater Boston, the next day on Sunday to offer assistance of any kind. Carol and I were asked to interview volunteers who wanted to go and pick crops since there was hardly anyone to do it because so many Israelis had been mobilized into active IDF service. I also remember interviewing truck drivers and struggling with how to identify someone who would really be able to help. We had been prepared to dig at Gezer again, and to our delight and surprise we heard that the excavation would go forward but with an abbreviated schedule in the field for only one month. We were especially excited to see the Old City of Jerusalem and places in the West Bank we had only heard of. It was a bold move for HUC, and we were psyched to go.

Within a few weeks we were walking in the Old City, where flattened cars run over by tanks still littered the streets. My old high school buddy Harold Baker had immigrated to Israel and was a lawyer—he was working in behalf of Arabs who had lost cars and wanted repayment. After the 1973 Yom Kippur War he was so disenchanted he no longer took Arab clients. The Arabs were still in shock in 1967, and Israelis were flooding in to see the sights they had only dreamed of and couldn't go shopping in the *souk* (market) in the Old City fast enough. The area in front of the Western Wall had been cleared, but the main access road to the Wall was not ready for the onslaught that would come in the months and years to come. There was a plan to build a plaza there, and bulldozers were hard at work clearing.

Back at HUC on 13 King David Street, Nelson Glueck, who had been director of ASOR in East Jerusalem (soon to be renamed the Albright Institute of Archaeological Research [AIAR]) years before, was eager to visit his old house and renew ties with Omar the cook, who had accompanied him on many journeys in Transjordan. No one was thinking yet of how the two American institutions would coexist when the Glueck School of Archaeology in West Jerusalem had been conceived to replace ASOR in East Jerusalem. In any event, seeing Israel at this moment in time was exciting to say the least. There was no imagining in our minds the challenges that lay ahead. There was rather a kind of naïve optimism that it would all work out over time. When we returned home via Norwich I became sick as a dog, apparently from the poor water quality in Jerusalem after the merger of the two systems. I spent a day or so in the hospital for dehydration and then we went back to Boston.

1967–1968 was a fateful year for me. That fall Dr. Wright informed me that ASOR wanted to launch several new excavation projects in Israel and that ASOR had been assured of Smithsonian backing and funding. In those days, some of Israel's USAID (United States Agency for International Development) monies were funneled back into American projects in Israel in the form of US counterpart funds, some of which the Smithsonian administered. One of the ASOR projects was to have a focus on the early periods and the other on the later periods, Greco-Roman and Byzantine. Dr. Wright was going to organize them through ASOR. The one focusing on early periods was to become the Tel el-Hesi Expedition. The one for the later periods he wanted me to organize and direct. I was totally taken aback, and while I did not fall over in my seat in his office, I could have. I was just shy of twenty-eight years old at the time and had still not completed my dissertation, didn't have a job, and Carol was going to get pregnant again. But Dr. Wright had apparently thought all this through and no doubt had consulted with Nelson Glueck, who had never had a PhD student. I was pretty sure that Wright wanted there to be a project with a Jewish director and with Jewish content. In addition, the stratigraphic refinements that had been introduced at Shechem and Gezer had never been introduced to a "late" site. Having trained there, I was poised to do that. Indeed Wright spoke eloquently of the need for there to be new archaeological material so that the study of early Judaism and early Christianity could be brought up to speed in the maturing field of biblical archaeology. He told me that Robert Jehu Bull of Drew University would be a kind of senior advisor for a year and that he was looking for someone in Helmut Koester's New Testament Program in the Divinity School to be an assistant to me. To this day when people think of "biblical archaeology" they rarely think of anything later than the Persian period, and many end it in the Iron Age. Wright's idea was to get New Testament and late Second Temple and early rabbinic periods involved and in the end succeeded, a field that he aptly labeled "the archaeology of early Judaism and early Christianity."

Koester at this time was already taking New Testament students to survey and photograph archaeological sites in Greece and Turkey. Wright wanted me to get started right away. He hoped we could begin digging in 1970 and survey potential sites no later than the summer of 1969, preferably after the Gezer dig season. In one of those far-ranging talks about organizing an excavation team, Dr. Wright gave me some sage advice that has served me well through all these years. He said: "Never be afraid to appoint the best people who might even be smarter or better than you. If you do this, you will succeed."

It was in this context and mindset that I turned to Tom (A. Thomas) Kraabel in the ThD program in the Divinity School to become my Associate Field Director, and later Associate Director in 1971. Tom had worked at Sardis and was interested in ancient synagogues, and we had already become good friends. It was the best possible choice. Dr. Wright took a recommendation from the New Testament committee to have another person from Divinity join the staff and that was Dean Moe, a person with no field experience to speak of; his involvement with the dig did not work out. In my last season with the Gezer dig, I had met Jim (James F.) Strange and invited him to join the staff, and after one season it was clear to Tom and me that Jim should be the other Associate Director replacing Dean Moe who had served as Field Supervisor that first year, 1970. Carol joined the field staff but was not yet ready to have a larger role till after Dina was born and her PhD was nearly completed.

Having the guarantee of a major Smithsonian grant, while it relieved a great deal of pressure in the area of fundraising, there was an awful lot of paper work to do because of government regulations and accounting procedures. ASOR and its Executive Director, Tom Newman, would help with keeping track of all expenditures since a government-worthy audit was required for every penny. But a consortium of academic institutions had to be lined up in advance that would provide other funds for the expedition and additional staff and students. Even our volunteers had to sign up to take one course in those days. The Masada/Gezer student volunteer model was widely adopted from this time forward, but our model, after all these years, which stressed the academic side of things more, seems to be the dominant one today. All this had to be incorporated into proposals and statements for the Smithsonian.

I was still without an academic appointment, but Tom Kraabel had already accepted a position at the University of Minnesota and successfully brought them into the consortium. He also sought support from his alma mater, Luther College, and succeeded in bringing them in with Simon Hanson as epigrapher. Dr. Wright told me that we would have Harvard support as well. He also had close ties to Dropsie University and assured me they would also join the consortium as well. Along with Dropsie came Baruch Kanael as our first numismatist. John Gager had been a close friend of Tom and me at Harvard; he had accepted a job at Princeton and got them to join as well in 1971. All I had to do next was find a job and get that institution to support the project and we'd be all set.

Getting a job was easier than I had thought. In light of the dramatic downturn in humanities placements as I write this, when I entered my last year at Harvard with my MA from Brandeis in hand and about to finish my PhD, I actually was called by a number of institutions to apply for an opening. Two of those institutions actually offered me a position after a phone interview (University of Florida and Indiana University). John Gager, who had already committed Princeton to our project, invited me to apply there. But one day an opening at Duke was announced, and Dr. Wright and Dr. Cross literally told me that this was the ideal job for me.

Cross had been recruited there some years before for the position in the Divinity School that was eventually filled by John Strugnell, who was now at Harvard. My good friend Shelly Isenberg from Harvard was at Duke, and he encouraged me to come down. I accepted an invitation for an on-campus interview in the fall of 1968.

To the best of my knowledge, I had never been in North Carolina except to drive through en route to Florida with my parents one year when I was a kid. I had heard about it of course and was excited to visit, though the Princeton opening was pretty much in my mind as well. My interview and meetings with faculty members all went well, and I was very taken in by the Gothic beauty of Duke's West Campus and the natural beauty of Durham and nearby Chapel Hill then when its population was a fraction of what it is today. I also loved the climate. The road connecting Durham and Chapel Hill at that time was two lanes with trees separating them and the only building on the boulevard was an old colonial type building that was a restaurant. I was nervous about the so-called racial restrictions on campus, but I was assured that it was dramatically changing that very year, and it did. I was also told about the courage of some of my future colleagues (Robert Osborn, Harmon Smith, and Fred Herzog), who had been imprisoned after heroically challenging lunch-counter laws and segregation.

The biggest shock of my meetings in Durham was that my good friend Shelly, at the time he was urging me to accept the job at Duke, was interviewing at Princeton and kept that from me. Thomas (Tommy) Langford was chair of Religion at the time and was my gracious host—he later became dean of Divinity and then provost. The search committee had wisely organized meetings with key members of the Jewish community who were on the Duke faculty, and that made a huge impression on me. But Wright had counselled me to be sure to meet with the Provost or equivalent when I was there so that, should I accept the job, I would be assured of institutional support for the dig.

My meeting with Marcus Hobbs, acting Provost, was the key to my accepting Duke. In explaining to him that I was directing a new project in Israel under the aegis of the Smithsonian Institution and ASOR and that among the academic sponsors were Harvard, I got his attention pretty quickly. He informed me that Duke had been sponsoring a dig at Winchester Cathedral in England for some time and that is was just winding down and that students had loved it. He asked how much joining the consortium would cost, and I think I said $5,000 a season and he committed to it on the spot from his budget for the foreseeable future. All that remained was to bring Carol down and get her reaction and to explore future possibilities for her.

The next trip for both of us followed, and by this time we heard that Shelly Isenberg was leaving to go to Princeton. Carol and I met Martin Lakin of the Psychology Department along with a number of very distinguished future colleagues from all sorts of fields, many of whom had worked in Israel and spoke Hebrew. I had talked with Tommy Langford on my first visit about Carol's future employment, and he had assured me that when she had her PhD in hand and was ready to begin teaching that he was certain something could be arranged. After this visit I accepted the job.

Back in Cambridge, as on many campuses including Duke that year, there was great unrest, even malaise. While I had always worn a coat and tie, albeit with khakis, to seminar or when I met with a professor, now graduate students started wearing jeans and t-shirts. By spring and after the Massachusetts Hall takeover at Harvard, various units of the university joined hands in protest and marched together in support of change. NELL joined with the Divinity School. We were not absolutely sure of what that change might look like, but we the students wanted to have more influence on the shape of our education and to participate in the decision-making process. At Duke it had meant a more open policy for African-American admissions and recruitment of black faculty. At Harvard in our corner of campus students really wanted a much higher degree of participation in all university matters. And the dramatic march to the Harvard football stadium that glorious day in the spring of 1969 actually led to significant change not only at Harvard and Duke but around college campuses all across America. I felt this acutely, namely that this was a new time in higher education, and I was about to get on the bandwagon since I was graduating and a starting the next phase of my life.

Mom and Dad and Carol came to my graduation, and Dad bought my crimson academic robe for me. John Lindsay, mayor of New York, was our speaker, and Mom thought he was gorgeous. We left Julie with cousins Cecile and Morris Adler, who had a private reception for us after. Morris was a psychiatrist at Harvard, and we were related on the Meyer side via Cecile who was a Padal. Morris introduced me to martinis that day using bitters, which I ditched many years ago.

Next was to move to Durham after first getting a new car, switching from our old Peugeot 404 to a new Chevy wagon. We decided to rent that first year and had found a three-bedroom apartment with an outside pool in the Lakewood section not far from campus. Carol's brother Charlie drove her and Julie to Durham and dropped them off at the apartment.

I left for Israel and my last season at Gezer, eagerly anticipating a two-week survey of sites in Galilee following the dig. David Noel Freedman was director of the AIAR in Jerusalem at this time. He was my chief liaison with ASOR and would join me for the end of the survey after narrowing it down to three possible sites. The Department of Antiquities, later renamed the Israel Antiquities Authority (IAA), had assigned me a regional inspector, Nathaniel Tfilinski, to be my guide, and I would be the driver. The other person along with me was Dean Moe of Harvard Divinity School. He was completely unhelpful; he never finished his PhD, and he seemed more interested in his constant smoking, which annoyed the hell out of me and Tfilinski. Moe barely lasted our first season in 1970.

8

Synagogue Survey in Upper Galilee, Summer 1969

TFILINSKI, OR TIFFY AS we lovingly called him through the years, kind of looked like a Jewish Santa Claus, He was born and raised in the Old City of Jerusalem and had only attended *yeshivas* but was a devoted lover and student of the land and archaeology. He was especially knowledgeable about the Galilee and Upper Galilee in particular. He barely spoke English and was strictly Orthodox and always wore a kippah or skullcap. We absolutely hit it off together, and when he learned that I was a part-time cantor he was just thrilled. I had to offer up a few melodies for him every once and a while of his most beloved parts of the liturgy. It was clear to me and him pretty quickly that the best sites were ones that had ancient synagogues partially preserved on them. Since we were starting a new team it was pretty clear that we also did not want a very large site either. So I focused on small village sites that had hints or traces of a public structure or synagogue. We did this for two weeks, except for Shabbat, and in the second week before we met Noel Freedman to visit our final three, we had narrowed the list down as best we could.

    I was very taken by the Upper Galilee and with its lack of serious excavation decided we would begin there. The wild scrub oak bushes, the rolling hills and Mt. Meiron towering over them, and Tsefat its jewel in the crown, just won me over. Tfilinski lived in Moshav Meiron, an Orthodox *moshav*, where ten new A-frame cottages had just been built as holiday bungalows. In planning a dig, logistics were key and I had to think of where we would house the group and how we would feed them. Meiron was a real possibility. The final site list included Khirbet Shema', Gush Ḥalav, and 'Umm el-Ammed. It was time for Noel to come up and spend a few days with us and

SYNAGOGUE SURVEY IN UPPER GALILEE, SUMMER 1969

talk about each site and logistics. He decided we would stay at the Galei Kinneret Hotel on the Sea of Galilee, a gem of a spot and gorgeous place that was top of the line. Noel assured me he would handle all the payments and not to worry. Dean Moe was absolutely orgasmic about the choice. As it turns out, the hotel was owned and managed by a childhood classmate and close friend of my father from Königsberg, Lotta Eisenberg, with whom Carol and I maintained contact till her death years later. The food and accommodation were in the best of the old world traditions.

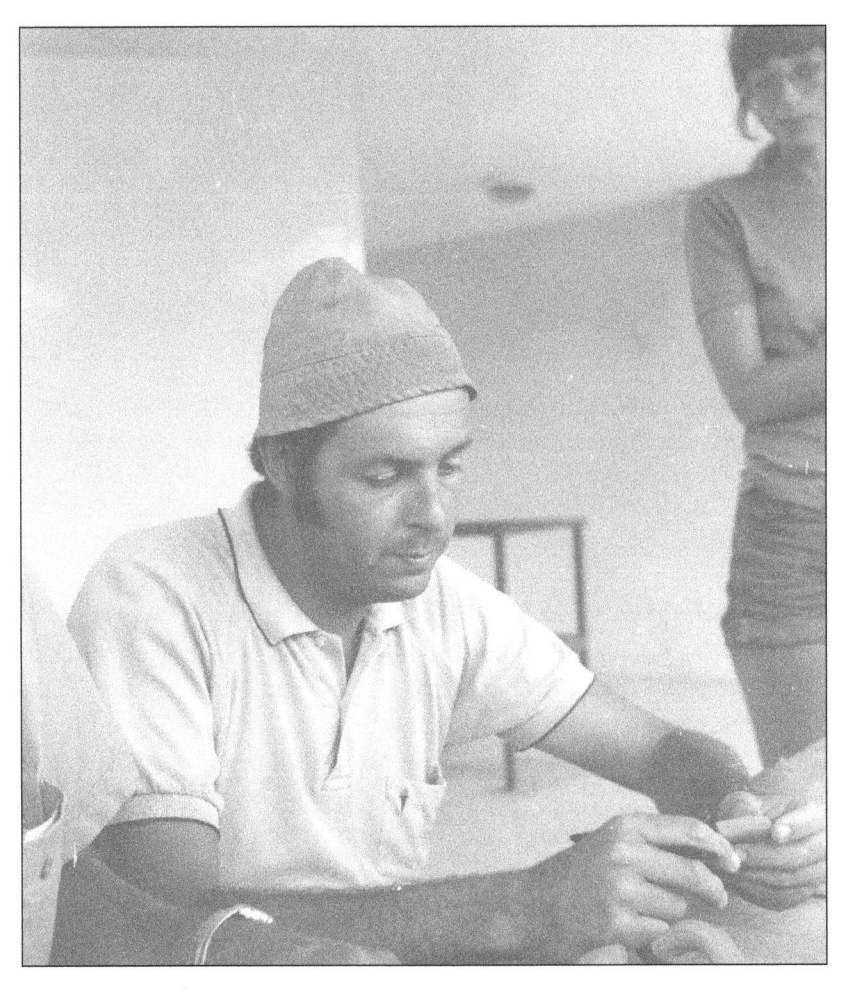

Eric reading pottery, Meiron, early 1970s.

PART TWO: WITH CAROL

Staff for 2011 Study Season at Sepphoris on tour in the Golan at Umm el-Qanatir, a Byzantine-period synagogue. On the *bima* far left to right on bottom, Jessica Vahl, Elizabeth Baltes, Carol, Eric, Ben Gordon, Dave Hendin. Top, Sean Burrus, Emanuel Fiano, Alan Todd.

We visited each of the sites and the top two by far were Gush Ḥalav and Khirbet Shemaʿ and with Meiron in between them, it was not hard to narrow it down. Gush Ḥalav was in the Arab village of el-Jish and the challenge of finding appropriate accommodation there seemed insurmountable. Umm el-ʿAmmed was alongside a major N–S highway, and I was afraid that we would be bothered by passersby. Khirbet Shemaʿ had traces of a synagogue, I was pretty sure, a large tomb monument named after the rabbinic sage Shammai, and other tombs close by, and what seemed to be a very accessible and excavatable village that was not too large. Its major shortcoming was that there was no road or track to the site, and it was a big climb up the hill. Having worked at Masada and climbed to the site each day, I did not think this was a prohibitive challenge as long as we could get our supplies up to the top of the hill by vehicle. And I was twenty-nine years old. Noel was happy and promised the Institute's Jeep and old Chevy wagon for the first season. Tfilinski was overjoyed and promised we could find a suitable cook and kitchen staff and take over the A-frames in Meiron for the dig, Moe was indifferent, and I couldn't wait till next year.

Eric working on an olive press at Qatzrein,
Golan Heights, October 2017

9

Duke Years

Needless to say, upon returning to Durham and our new home I was raring to go. Carol and Julie had survived my two months absence with the help of the pool and wonderful neighbors, Jackie and Joe Denk and little Jeremy, today a world-famous pianist. For some reason we were still on a wait list for a phone, and I had to go to the shopping lot to use a pay phone unless I was on campus. At my office one day, I had an urgent message to call home that evening. When I called, I learned that Uncle John had been diagnosed with cancer of the kidney and was to have surgery right away. The news was of course devastating to all of us, and while the surgery was successful, he died five years later at age fifty.

While we loved our apartment and became close to the Denks, it soon became apparent to Carol and me that there was a lot of nighttime activity in one of the apartments below us. It turns out that it was a drug house or brothel, and we did not think this was the kind of atmosphere for raising a child. So we soon began looking for a house and were hopeful that by the end of fall semester we could move in somewhere nice and convenient. In looking for a suitable neighborhood we knew we wanted to be between Durham and Chapel Hill and not too far from campus. Duke Forest houses close to campus on university-owned land were too expensive at the time, and we soon found a neighborhood not too far away and a house that was being completed on Waterbury Drive. The subdivision was called Whitehall and was being developed by Wilson Garrett, who was to become our future neighbor in the house next door. Coming up with a down-payment was the next challenge, and it was Uncle John who came through with a loan and a pledge from us to repay it as soon as possible. Actually in the next couple of years we paid half of it back; and when he died a few years later Aunt Arlene forgave the remainder of the debt. This greatly assisted us in our financial planning for those early years.

The neighborhood was a perfect mix of people. Our closest friends were to be the Scotts, David and Judy, in the house behind us and their sons Jason and Joshua, and Pepper, their dog. Up the street a bit were Dan and Christa Johns and Sheridan, where we watched them light Christmas candles on their tree every year and once had roast goose there for Christmas dinner. The kids did everything together, and when there was snow sledded down the street together. After Uncle John's death in 1974 we inherited Abette, his beloved golden retriever dog. I guess Arlene had enough of the dog, and her kids were pretty much out of the house by then. Apparently I flew back with Abette to North Carolina after *Shiva* without ever telling Carol and the kids before I arrived! But she became a much-loved member of the family until her untimely passing some years later after being fed too many bad leftovers from the new neighbors.

In my first year at Duke I had to share my office on East Campus with another new professor by the name of James (Jim) Charlesworth, though he was not new to Duke since his MDiv and PhD were from Duke. Fortunately, it was a very large office, and sharing it lasted only one year. We both moved over to West the next fall, 1970.

One of the preconditions I had set for my acceptance to come to Duke was that I would become a member of the graduate faculty immediately. Dr. Wright or Dr. Cross had told me to do this, since often one had to wait till promotion with tenure. Thus my department had numerous people on faculty who had nothing to do with graduate students. The majority of graduate faculty came from Divinity. At my first graduate faculty meeting that fall, about October, we assembled and the acting director of the Graduate Program, Corky Lacy, began by asking us to bow our heads in prayer and went on to give a really pious and Christocentric prayer. By the time he finished, I was truly upset and stood up in a quiet anger and said something to the effect that if the program would continue its practice of opening with such a prayer, I would resign from the graduate faculty immediately. Several colleagues rose in support of me—Hans Hillerbrand and W. D. Davies were two of them—and my complaint was taken to heart. As the first non-Christian member of the graduate faculty in Religion at Duke since the early 1940s, when Judah Goldin was there, albeit for only a few years, apparently no one had thought about it before. There were no more prayers at graduate faculty meetings after that. Years later I learned that some Divinity professors said prayers at the beginning of their graduate classes, but there was no protesting their right to do that since the courses originated within the Divinity faculty.

My undergraduate teaching in those first years was pretty well defined: I was to teach three courses in the fall and three in the spring, but in the fall I did back-to-back sections of the introductory OT course, Introduction to Old Testament (Hebrew Bible), and Modern Jewish Thought. I would ultimately swap out modern thought for Varieties of Ancient Judaism. At the graduate level I taught Aramaic and Syriac on and off, and a course in rabbinics (Pirkei Avot in Hebrew) with some additional mishnaic texts. After E. P. (Ed) Sanders arrived in 1990, he also taught some rabbinics, and I offered seminars in Dead Sea Scrolls. Every year or so I did readings in archaeology for a selected few. And after the first Anchor Bible commentary was published (more below), I started doing a seminar on Late Hebrew Prophecy.

The dig in Israel had a field school and credit program; both undergraduates and graduate students could earn academic credit for their work in the field. In those first years we had wonderful students at both levels: Oli Jenkins, Karen Dubilier, Tricia Dykers, and Louise Upchurch to mention only a few coming from undergraduate courses. Two courses were offered on the dig. One focused on archaeology and methods gleaned from the fieldwork, and the second was largely based on the content of our lecture and travel program. The materials of both courses were integrated into a required daily journal that ended with a written exam. The exam consisted of a visit to a site unknown to them; the students had to collect pottery sherds and then plan how they would excavate the site and predict expected outcomes. The lecture program at the dig was organized by our dear friend and colleague, Richard Simon Hanson, Frank Cross's first PhD at Harvard, who took over numismatics from Kanael the next years. Simon taught at Luther College, and his work in behalf of our student academic program all those years in Upper Galilee proved a model for our work later at Sepphoris. The field school is the heart of the academic program for all excavations that depend on students.

10

Planning Khirbet Shema'

As many dig directors can attest, getting ready for a new project halfway across the globe can be a big distraction from regular teaching. On the Duke campus in those days, the 1970s, classes were fully enrolled with eager students, and Duke was paying my salary. I had to learn pretty quickly how to divide up my day between teaching and other departmental and university responsibilities, let alone keeping up with my research agenda. One of those university roles was serving for several years as secretary of the Undergraduate Faculty Council, a job I truly enjoyed because it got me involved in the wider university and its diverse faculty and subject areas. And with a beautiful little girl and a supportive and loving wife at home, life was very full to say the least. How to balance all these things had not been part of my graduate training for sure. Also it was pretty clear from first attempts to get a working excavation budget that more money would be required, though between Smithsonian and the consortium we were pretty close. Learning how to raise money was something no one had taught me either.

Sometime that year, 1971, Sara and Emanuel (Mutt) Evans approached me about starting a campaign to raise money for a Jewish Studies program that would serve both Duke and UNC Chapel Hill. They would be my mentors in this area for years to come, and I was a quick learner; and soon enough learned how hard it was to raise funds and equally hard to ask prospective donors. I also had to separate fundraising for the dig from fundraising for Jewish Studies. In addition I had to find a suitable mechanism for gaining academic credit for the dig, and the Duke Summer School was a willing and helpful partner in this under the direction of Olan Petty, and years later Christa Johns. Duke would serve not only as the main academic sponsoring institution of the dig but also would offer summer course credits to anyone who would pay tuition. While academic credit was always advocated if not required, we rarely accepted non-students into the program as well. The missing and necessary funds were most always made up by a tuition remission plan that Duke pioneered, which meant that tuition monies collected for the dig courses were redirected to cover excavation expenses. In later years the amount was greatly reduced and was only a small percentage of what it had been in the past.

11

Gary Termite

ONE EXAMPLE OF A non-credit student will suffice. Shortly after the dig was approved by the Department of Antiquities in Israel in the fall of 1969 and a permit issued, I received a letter from one Gary Lindstrom of Oakland, California. A high school graduate, he had always been a history buff and wanted to do field archaeology. He had just started a termite exterminating company that was doing all right, and he could get off in the summer for about six weeks. The tone of the letter was very warm, and after showing the letter to Carol, who agreed that he was special, I sent Gary a letter of acceptance. He was thrilled and stayed with us the next decade or so; he became a valued staff member as conservator and cement specialist. Gary ultimately joined up with Jim Strange's excavations in later years and with Douglas Edwards's project at Cana. The nickname he earned with us at Khirbet Shemaʿ, Gary Termite, remained with him till his dying days.

Toward the end of his life Gary was very generous to ASOR and funded any number of interns, rising graduate students, to assist at the Annual Meeting or participate in excavations overseas. The small foundation he established for such purposes and on whose board Jim Strange and I served, did not survive his passing in 2009. This quote is taken from his obituary: "Aside from his termite business, he had many varied interests, but foremost and dear to his heart was the Lindstrom Foundation for Archaeological Research and Development, which helps professors and college students to make it possible to travel to the Middle East every year to experience and partake in the archaeological digs; and temporarily live in an entirely different culture. He loved the Middle East, and went there every summer for over 30 years. As per his wishes, he will be cremated and his ashes laid to rest in Barʿam, Israel." At the ASOR convention in

New Orleans in 2009, Gary had come to say goodbye, and there on his deathbed, all his excavation friends joined hands and recited the Twenty-third Psalm as he passed away.

That is the power of archaeology and what it can do outside the sheer academic, classroom component of it. Somehow most of our students saw in the soil and stones of Galilee something they could not see at home, and it had to do with the discovery of the past made real and tangible. It was so for Jews and Christians alike. The experience of working in Galilee where long ago early Judaism and Christianity took root often made a difference that was life changing, as it did for Gary Termite. Bringing students from their classrooms on campus to a field school in Israel, therefore, was a huge privilege and even larger responsibility.

In those years in the Upper Galilee not only did we hear the cannon fire that was intended to scare away the wild boar on Mt. Meiron, but we often heard the border fighting and planes heading toward Lebanon. We changed the title of the popular African-American spiritual accordingly: "There is a bomb in Lebanon . . ." (from "There Is a Balm in Gilead"). The rapport one can establish with students in a 24/7 living and learning environment is something impossible to replicate on campus. And recalling the dig experience many years later, I often think back to those heady first days and weeks in the Upper Galilee. I can still taste the sweet Galilean onions that we enjoyed at second breakfast with canned tuna and fresh rolls brought out from the Beit Am, the large assembly hall where we had our meals.

The dig was a huge success in every way. We could hardly accommodate all who wanted to participate. Dr. Wright had been upset by what he heard had happened at Gezer between male senior staff members and young women volunteers and the numbers of divorces that had resulted. He gave me this long talk when I was still at Harvard that I should go out of my way to see to it that any married staff who wanted to bring their spouse and kids would be accommodated. As for that first season, to show how important this was to him, he awarded our toddler daughter, Julie, a Harvard Semitic Museum scholarship to cover her $50.00 plane fare. By our second season the Strange family, the Kraabel family, and the Hanson family, not to mention the Meyerses, joined the dig. We had run out of space in the A-frames cottages and had to rent tents, which we put on the lawn alongside the ten A-frames, for all the kids. Julie's scholarship and Ernest Wright's vision inspired a movement. Thanks Jules!

12

Breaking News: Dina and Early Tenure

Back at Duke a couple of big things happened. In 1971 I began to get several overtures to leave Duke, two of them quite strong: the University of Wisconsin at Madison, and Wellesley College, Carol's alma mater. When my department chair, William (Bill) Poteat heard about it, and not from me, he marched me up to see the Dean, who would have none of it; I was awarded tenure and got a little bump in salary. In truth, neither institution was at that time prepared to think about adding Carol to the package, so I was not inclined to leave nor was I about to let Tommy Langford's promise of a future job for her at Duke be forgotten. In any case, the pressure was off, and archaeology became more and more central to our lives.

But another huge change was in the offing in late 1971 and that was Carol became pregnant again and on April 14, 1972, in Duke Hospital South, Dina was born. We were thrilled to welcome her as was Pat Westfeldt, Connie's first husband, who of all people had coincidentally come to pick up a used car from Hertz at the airport the day Dina was born. Even in the hospital if not before, Carol declared that Dina was coming on the dig that summer even while she was breastfeeding. So Dina, while she did not get a Harvard scholarship that summer like her big sister, became the youngest member of the Meiron Excavation Project. Dina would stay with the project till later years, and all those experiences would come in handy later in life in the entertainment industry. In order for Carol to stay fully engaged in the fieldwork and remain on staff we brought a babysitter with us to stay with the girls each morning until lunch, while Carol was in the field, and so the pressure was off.

PART TWO: WITH CAROL

My favorite picture of Carol. In her office at Duke,
going through slides, remember them?

13

Meiron

LIVING IN AN ORTHODOX *moshav* had its challenges. Our cook, Yudah Itzkowitz and his wife ran the kosher kitchen. They were both eastern European immigrants. Some of their meals that I thought were awesome did not go over well with some of our students who were unaccustomed to eastern European fare. Also, not having meat with milk was tough for many of them until one day we started getting ice cream for dessert on really hot days. You can imagine their surprise when they heard that the ice cream was made from soybeans. The *moshav* also locked up the entrances to the village for Shabbat, which meant if we stayed in the A-frames but wanted to go somewhere on Friday night or Saturday, we needed to park outside the gates. We learned to live with that and often we traveled on Friday to Tsefat for dinner at the Galilee Hotel with Moshe and Sara Pearl, the owners.

One area of constant tension between us and the local people was the matter of female attire. As you can imagine in the heat of summer we all dressed accordingly; for college-age women it meant tank tops and shorts. The Orthodox Jewish women in the village were pretty much covered and wore long skirts. Our women's attire was not a great problem till we started the rescue dig in Meiron in 1972. One day without warning I was told to appear before a Beit Din (rabbinic court) at such and such a time and place. The issue was women's attire in the village. After doing my level best to defend the women's prerogatives, I saw it was a losing battle. The compromise we worked out was this: they could wear what they wanted at the dig site and at lectures, meals, and pottery washing and reading. But when walking from our A-frames through the village to the dig site or to the grocery store, they had to put on gray ankle-length smocks. The smocks—we called them by the Yiddish term *schmatte*—were provided by the *moshav* and they looked like what a grocery-store salesperson would have worn, only these went down to the ankles. In subsequent years another issue other than modesty was added to the criticism of our women: some of them wore crosses on chains around their necks. This was offensive to many ultra-Orthodox whom I would call *haredim*, the extremely zealous. A real war was ultimately waged over this issue in the trenches of the dig itself at Nabratein in 1980–1981.

At the dig in those years we had a team of Druze workers from nearby Mughar; they helped with the heavy work, especially breaking rock with a sledgehammer, getting the site prepared, cutting shrubs, etc. We had about two carloads. The senior member of the crew was a man named Fatfut, and he presented a striking picture in his black jalabiya and white keffiyeh. But it was his wonderful huge mustache and easy smile that got everyone's attention pretty quickly. As the senior member of the team he also made coffee for our senior staff each day, which was greatly appreciated. Our *moshav* host, Eli Meironi, often came to the site with a glass of walnut brandy, locally made, and even an occasional arak. Jim Strange and I readily agreed to all of the above; Tom Kraabel only preferred the coffee. We loved the Druze and they loved us back.

But there was another nasty fight brewing that had nothing to do with women but with tombs. In the 1970s it was quite legal to dig ancient tombs though with Jewish tombs one could have expected to have some pushback from certain Orthodox quarters. We began our tomb survey at Khirbet Shemaʿ the first season, and I remind the reader that the big tomb monument there and several underground tomb chambers were right next to the synagogue. Pious Jews would come up to the so-called Tomb of Shammai and kiss it and pray in front of it. It was on the regular sacred tomb tour of the very pious. We had a few tombs on the eastern slope to clean and mostly they had been robbed in antiquity. Several times we were threatened with demonstrations and occasionally a group of *haredim* showed up in Mercedes limos to express their displeasure but without any bones there was not much to complain about. And so we completed the work at Khirbet Shemaʿ without many problems. Jim Strange and Carol's brother Charlie did a great job on the tomb survey at Khirbet Shemaʿ.

Our work at the site of Meiron progressed up the hill, closer and closer to the synagogue, on the western side of the ancient synagogue but quite close to the several *yeshivas* that lined the hilltop, the most famous one named after Shimon Bar Yochai. We discovered the mouth of a cave that turned out to be a large untouched ancient burial chamber. The expedition had been encouraged to forge ahead with tomb excavation by Avraham Biran, then director of the Department of Antiquities. The underground chamber was pretty much hidden from sight by the large outcrop of rock that was the western wall of the ancient synagogue; nonetheless we decided we would excavate it by night so as not to invite demonstrators who would oppose the excavation. We estimated that the work would take about two weeks. Jim Strange volunteered to head this operation, and we found students who were willing to join him and sleep late in the morning. The amount of human remains recovered was astounding, and we managed to get them to Hadassah Hospital where forensic pathologists could examine them and publish them. Their report appears in our final publication on Meiron and is one of the last and best reports on Jewish skeletal remains from Roman antiquity in Israel. Some of our most important insights regarding the people who lived in Meiron in antiquity have been inferred from the report by Patricia Smith, our bioanthropologist. One of those concerned body size or gigantism and mortality, another related to endogamy and inbreeding. Interested? Read the report. The *haredim* missed this one thanks to our nocturnal excavation.

14

Jewish Studies at Duke and UNC

The Uncooperative Program

THE EVANS'S PUSH TO get an official program in Jewish Studies started on our two campuses was successful soon after it began. A number of donors had committed early on and had already paid their pledges. They were alumni of both schools, just as were Sara and Mutt, Mutt from UNC and Sara from Duke. Duke consequently gave the green light to hire another full-time Jewish Studies scholar in 1972, and I had my sights on one person I knew was right for the job: brilliant, dynamic, a great teacher, and Brandeis PhD. That was Kalman Bland, z"l. Kal was at Indiana University, and with a little bit of coaxing and a successful interview he came in 1973. The Jewish Studies Program at Duke was officially recognized the year before, in 1972. Getting tickets to Duke basketball games was a major consideration for Kal, a true basketball enthusiast, and in those days it was not a problem to buy a season ticket.

It was then that we founded the Cooperative Program in Judaic Studies at Duke and UNC. The plan was for us to split our teaching between the two campuses, offering at least one course per term at UNC for the foreseeable future. At UNC we did Introduction to Judaic Civilization at least once a year and then a course of our choosing for the other. We each loved the arrangement and thought it might be a model for other institutions that were close to one another. We enjoyed having different kinds of students as well. One of the biggest challenges at UNC was getting a parking place, and Hillel allowed us to park at its house. The other challenge was having our voice heard in the UNC Department of Religious Studies. As it turned out, they sort of took us for granted, though we continued to love teaching there. We did this for five years when finally, through the intervention of Governor Jim Hunt, Chancellor Ferebee Taylor approved a new tenure-track positon in Jewish Studies for Chapel Hill. This had happened in 1977 as a result of my lobbying the governor at a private fundraising event at the home of the Cassell family in Greensboro. The Cassells were big supporters of the governor and major donors to Duke. Mutt Evans, former mayor of Durham and UNC grad, had coached me on what he thought I should say to the governor. I was introduced to Governor Hunt and everyone left us alone together in the Cassell study for about twenty minutes or so. It was a success. At least so I thought.

When the chair of the department at UNC announced that a new search would begin for a permanent Jewish Studies position at UNC in the Department of Religious Studies, there was absolutely no note of recognition that Kal and I had been doing this for more than four years by now and that the success of those courses made a tenure-track appointment possible. No one knew about my private meeting with the governor except my closest friends and family. But there I have said it. The last straw came when Kal and I were ignored by the search committee, which chose David Halperin as its future appointment over two very distinguished finalists, either of whom Kal and I would have preferred. David turned out to be a brilliant and popular teacher who, after his retirement, became fascinated with UFOs and wrote several books about them. It was then that Kal coined the phrase "The Uncooperative Program." While we were truly insulted, it was not as if we didn't have our positions back at Duke and lots of wonderful students to teach.

The Joint Program survived in small ways, e.g., Duke subsequently paid for Modern Hebrew teaching at UNC for many years from the Joint Endowment until UNC made a permanent commitment to fund it. But to all intents and purposes, that was the end. Ironically, as I write this memoir, the two schools are growing closer together again in Jewish Studies as they should and have been running a joint seminar in Jewish history for many years along with other excellent joint programming.

15

Jerusalem Happenings, 1973–1975

THESE EARLY YEARS AT Duke and in Israel at the dig were great fun. Each of Uncle John's kids came on the dig, and Robbie later signed on as architect. John brought the whole family over for a tour in 1973 when we were encamped for three months in an apartment in Ramat Eshkol in Jerusalem, trying to finish the Khirbet Shemaʻ final report. Teenage cousin Janie Horwitz, granddaughter of Uncle Kurt and Aunt Eva, had come along as babysitter to help out. Carol and I and the girls became very close with Janie that summer and have remained very close all these years.

During the 1974 campaign at the Meiron site we were called and told that John was not doing very well and that Robbie should probably come home. And in another couple of weeks I got another call saying John was going fast and I should come home as well. Carol and Jim finished out the dig and packed up everything for the lab, and when I got back to Norwich it was near the end. Marshall had flown in from Buenos Aires, and we spent most days at John's bedside saying our goodbyes. And tragically at age fifty and in his prime he passed away. We were all absolutely devastated, especially his three kids. It was just awful.

I went back to Israel to arrange for work in the lab during the year, and the last days were spent in Jerusalem where our lab was. Norma Dever, wife of the Director of the AIAR at that time, Bill Dever, had been paying our bills in the off-season when inking and registration and special photography of objects were done. Norma's assistance in this regard was essential and the dig could not have operated in winter without such help. She was a co-signer of our MEP (Meiron Excavation Project) checkbook at Bank Leumi near the Institute, and while Bill in his memoir claims credit for much of this, Norma did it all. When she and Bill left we had to reorganize our laboratory work and were lucky enough to find Dina Kastel, an archaeologist with excellent people skills and an ability to store artifacts in a way one could find them easily. She took over this aspect of our work including supervising of pottery and artifact drawing until the MEP was completed. By that time we had rented space at the AIAR, and she was very comfortable working there.

Bill Dever and Eric at restaurant in Nogales,
Mexico, December 1983.

That summer there was also talk of Bill's leaving the AIAR for a variety of reasons. And when I got back to Duke, I got a call from the chair of a search committee from the University of Arizona, Albert Bilgray, who had met me earlier in Jerusalem The call was intended to get me interested in coming to Arizona to start a Jewish Studies Program with a dig component. Now they wanted me to interview on campus for a job there, and I was their first choice since they wanted an archaeologist who worked in Israel and who could help build a program in Jewish Studies along with Hebrew Bible and ancient Near Eastern Studies. In those days there were too few candidates to have a final list of three. Arizona had always been strong in scientific archaeology and in other areas but did not yet have anyone working in Israel. He said I was a perfect fit. As flattered as I was to hear this, I was just grooving into my job at Duke and starting to get graduate students. I had turned down several additional recent overtures to leave: Dropsie, the University of Florida again, and the University of Wisconsin with a prospect of a named chair this time. With lots of hard work and early tenure and Carol now on the verge of finishing up her PhD and still not yet in a position to get a regular appointment along with me at another institution, we decided to stay at Duke. I told Bilgray that Bill Dever was about ready to move back to the States and that he should call him in Jerusalem. Bill ultimately met with Bilgray and the Arizona search committee. Bill was offered the job, and he accepted it. It was a perfect match for a long while, and Bill built a fabulous program there. The Jewish Studies Program is still going strong there today under the able leadership of Edward (Ed) Wright. The Israel dig component ended with Bill's departure. For a variety of reasons Carol and I each have maintained very close relations with the program at Arizona through the years, not the least of which is our respect for and admiration of Ed Wright.

When Bill told Arizona that he would accept the job, things moved very quickly. Dr. G. E. Wright, who had more or less placed Bill in a job in Jerusalem at HUC years before, had succeeded in getting ASOR to move him to the AIAR as Director in 1971. Wright did not live long enough to learn of Bill's official appointment at Arizona or of mine to succeed Bill as Annual Director of the AIAR for my first sabbatical in 1975–1976. Wright's death in the fall of 1974 was not only a great blow to his family but to his many PhD students who loved him dearly. It was also a great loss for ASOR. Wright had been very fond of Carol after she had audited a class of his while she was at Wellesley. For his memorial service at Harvard I was not surprised to see so many of his former students reassemble from far and wide to pay homage to a man who had meant so much to every one of them.

After my mom's death, Carol and I decided to honor both Dr. Wright and my mother by establishing in ASOR a joint Shirlee Meyers/G. E. Wright Fellowship, first with the help of donations made in honor of Mom after her death. The intent was to subsidize young students' travel to participate in a dig. As of this writing, the endowment continues to grow, and there have been many worthy students who have received financial assistance to participate in a dig. My mom's support of my academic interests and career was essential to my becoming who I am, and pairing her with G. Ernest Wright, my mentor, in an endowed scholarship fund was just the right thing to do.

16

The Albright Institute, Jerusalem, 1975–1976

MOVING TO JERUSALEM WAS not too difficult since the AIAR was paying shipping and the director's house was huge and elegant, lots bigger than our house in Durham, with a large living room and dining room perfect for entertaining many guests. AIAR consisted of a hostel, several apartments, a common room, large dining room, a gorgeous garden, wonderful library, several labs, and great places to play for the girls. Omar Jibrin was the cook and since we liked to eat dinner at home as a family instead of in the institute dining room with the fellows, he often if not always prepared our favorite Arabic recipes and brought them to the director's house. We loved him, as did Julie and Dina. And part of the deal of being director was having lots of receptions; with Omar as caterer it was not a burden at all. There were always wonderful people coming and going.

Summer of 1975 was also a digging season for us at Meiron. While thinking of what to do at the AIAR that was new and different, well before summer, I had asked John Hanks, my voice teacher at Duke and tenor who specialized in the American art song, to perform in the AIAR Garden on July Fourth. John by this time was a seasoned archaeologist and a regular on our team. The Director's house had an upright piano and John brought over his regular accompanist for the occasion—her son and husband worked on our dig that summer and were already in Israel. We rented extra chairs and put up posters as did the East Jerusalem American Consulate. Omar was ready with his refreshments. Well the response was simply amazing. People had to go up to the veranda in the hostel and above the dining hall because there was not sufficient seating. Somehow we managed, and at the end we all sang patriotic American songs, the highlight

THE ALBRIGHT INSTITUTE, JERUSALEM, 1975–1976

for me being Irving Berlin's "God Bless America." A very good time was had by all, and for John Hanks, the angels heard him loud and clear. He was so inspired by the event that the next Christmas he brought the Duke Divinity School Choir to sing in Bethlehem in Manger Square.

Eric with Ephraim Katzir, president of Israel, and Avraham Biran, director of antiquities, November 1975, when Eric was director of the Albright Institute. At the president's house.

I was asked to teach a course at Brandeis Hyatt in Jerusalem in the spring of 1976, and when Ehud Netzer, then a PhD student and resident architect at the Hebrew University Institute of Archaeology, heard about it, he asked if I would like to bring my students to Jericho for a few weeks of digging as part of the course. I heartily agreed. We unearthed the Hasmonean winter palace those weeks. Just as during the first season at Gezer, we commuted to the site each day, leaving Jerusalem often in cold and rainy weather and arriving in Jericho in balmy temperature and with lots of sun. This was the beginning of a long and productive relationship with

Ehud, who nine years later would codirect the Joint Sepphoris Project with Carol and me. Having been students in Jerusalem just ten years before, it was enormous fun to come back in a positon of some importance and influence. Carol was also the Thayer Fellow that year at the AIAR, one of its most distinguished appointments.

We felt entirely safe in East Jerusalem. Both girls went to school in West Jerusalem, Dina at a Hebrew preschool run by WIZO (Women's International Zionist Organization), and Julie at the Anglican International School on Rehov HaNeviim (Street of the Prophets). Although one of us would walk or drive them to school, they would often go on Salah ed-Din Street, where the AIAR was located, alone, and the storekeepers knew who they were: Mr. Assad at Sindbad Travel across the street, the favorite confectioner from whom we bought peanuts and pistachios, the spice man, etc.

When the fall harvest festival of Sukkot came along that October, we decided to build a *sukkah* or booth in keeping with Jewish tradition. I was the first Jewish director since Nelson Glueck before the War of Independence, and Omar recalled that and said he and the Arab staff would like to help build it. And they did; and we all celebrated the holiday together by making *Kiddush* (blessing) the first night and having one heck of a memorable time together. We all thought we could make peace, thinking if we can do this in East Jerusalem why can't Israel and the Palestinians just do it. Fifty-some years later they still can't do it. Often that year, as a special treat after dinner, we would take the girls for special "American" ice cream in Ramallah at Rukab's.

1975 was also the year that Carol finished her PhD at Brandeis. Needless to say, it was difficult to collect on a promise from Tommy Langford from so far away, but purely by accident the very popular Bernard Boyd, James A. Gray Professor at UNC Chapel Hill, passed away that year and the search committee asked Carol to fill in for him in AY 1976–1977 while they conducted a search, which greatly eased our anxiety level about future employment.

I had a very memorable birthday party, June 5, 1976, at the AIAR. Unbeknownst to me Herbert (Herb) Paper, a good friend and colleague from the University of Michigan, on sabbatical for the year in Jerusalem, had worked with Carol and our good mutual friend Jonas Greenfield to play a joke on me. Herb's family had been in the bakery business, and he helped with the birthday cake. When it came time to cut the cake, which I was asked to do, I came upon some very hard stuff deep down in the middle. What was it?

Turns out that it was a big pottery sherd and everybody asked me what kind of sherd it was, and I said it was from Tel Beit Mirsim and identified the date correctly. Carol had picked up the sherd at a field trip to that site a few days earlier and had given it to Herb to bake into the cake! Well this along with a few vintage jokes from Jonas and Herb literally busted me up laughing. I also got a hernia that subsequently required surgery.

When it became necessary to have surgery weeks later, this meant going to Hadassah Hospital in Ein Kerem, supposedly the best hospital nearby. Well as you can imagine in planning the surgery, we had gotten good advice on who was the best person to do it; Menahem Haran had recommended someone who was tops. Well I had eaten that day and surgery was indicated sooner than expected and you are not supposed to eat before surgery. When the surgeon asked me after giving me a local if it hurt when he stuck a needle in my groin, I said loudly "yes" but still he continued. I tried to get up off the operating table. Indeed, I was not about to have hernia surgery fully awake and feeling everything. The doctor came out of the operating room to ask Carol if I had been taking drugs since he said I was a bit rambunctious. The surgeon returned to the operating room, and the last thing I remember was getting some anesthetic applied to my nose and mouth. The surgery was successful, and I'll never know whether lunch that day contributed to my difficulty with the anesthesia.

After surgery I awoke in a room with about six or eight patients, many of them miserable and very noisy—I called them "screamers." I vowed to get out of there as soon as possible. When I finally convinced the surgeon to release me, the orderly or nurse tried to find a wheelchair so I could get a refund on my bill (which included payment for several nights' stay, but I was leaving after only one night) and get to the car easily. It turns out there were no wheelchairs available: we were told that they were kept locked up so that they wouldn't become damaged from overuse. So I walked and walked to the office to settle the bill and then to the car, and it was not easy the day after abdominal surgery. When I arrived back at the AIAR the staff was a waiting for me, and they carried me, like a Hasmonean king, up to the second floor of the director's house on a throne—I mean chair. And what a relief it was to be back.

As our year in Jerusalem came to an end, we decided to have a vacation in Crete before returning to Durham. I should say that a vacation for the Meyers usually means a combination of museums and/or archaeological or historical sites and other more traditional fun things, like beach and swimming, etc. But this came only weeks after surgery, and I was not allowed to carry anything except a light briefcase if that. So in airports, boats, and at customs I would walk up carrying basically all four passports, and my wife and seven- and four-year old girls would be carrying all the luggage. In Greece the men cheered for me not the girls.

We made it back to Durham safe and sound to face a year in which my father's struggle with the angel of death ultimately failed. There were many false alarms and regular trips to Norwich and lastly to Yale New Haven Hospital. But Carol's year at Chapel Hill was a huge success, and UNC missed out by not appointing her to the chair, which went to John Van Seters. But somehow all the great feedback about her teaching and rapport with students got the ear of our chair at Duke, and she was appointed to a regular, half-time position. That's another story. As Carol rotated off the UNC faculty, so did Kalman and I.

17

Dad's Death (1977) and After

DAD'S CANCER PROVED TO be very aggressive, moving ultimately to his bones. We tried to keep him home as long as possible as he requested, but it took a huge effort, and as usual the pressure was on Mom and Connie who were less than an hour away. In those days if I was lucky I could get a connection to New Haven airport, but often it meant having to fly to LaGuardia and taking a Connecticut limo to Norwich. I think by the time Mom got sick I was flying to Hartford.

It was tough going back and forth, leaving the girls and all. But Karlchen, God love him, did not want to die, and his battle lasted much longer than any of us thought it would. On Erev Pesach 1977 he lost that battle and it was a Friday. This meant that the funeral had to be delayed till after Shabbat and after *yontif* for Passover, the longest delay Jewish law allows. This delay would have pleased him for sure, and it did allow for everyone to come to the funeral. Now I say *kaddish*, the mourners blessing, before first night Seder each year on his *Yahrzeit*, the anniversary of his death, and no matter it always feels like it was yesterday. Losing a parent is really hard and the feeling of loss never really dissipates. Uncle Kurt had died in the spring of 1976 and now my father. The German side of the family was quickly disappearing.

I had been very much involved with the Association of Jewish Studies (AJS) since its founding in 1968 but had become more involved with ASOR and SBL in recent years as my focus on archaeology and biblical studies became central. While my first paper at the AJS first Annual Meeting was on that very subject, how Jewish Studies related to material culture and archaeology, I saw that it did not have much resonance in the emerging field of Jewish Studies even though in Israel archaeology still was wildly popular at every level. But at Duke, the main framework for all my teaching was Jewish Studies with its centerpiece the archaeological summer program. Our field school at our summer dig remained extremely popular on campus, and we never had a problem filling our spaces to capacity. Julie and Dina came every year though when they got old enough to go to camp they returned early to go to Camp Judaea in the mountains of North Carolina.

My mom, now alone, regularly visited us in Durham a couple times a year and totally enjoyed being there and with the girls. She loved her room in the lower level of our house and was always one of my biggest boosters. Carol's parents were also regular visitors, especially for the Jewish holidays. Marshall of course was our biggest booster of all since he exaggerated more than anyone I have ever known. I was the greatest this or that, Carol was the greatest scholar Wellesley had ever produced, etc. You get the picture. If Marshall loved you, you were absolutely the best, no doubt about it. Marshall and his whole family visited once early on in the 1970s though he returned a number of times through the years as he traveled around lecturing. He once returned to preach at Duke Chapel in commemoration of Holocaust Remembrance Day. While it was memorable and unusual for the Chapel to have a Holocaust speaker in the 1970s, there was not a huge turnout that year.

18

Gush Ḥalav, 1977–1978

WE BEGAN OUR EXCAVATIONS at Gush Ḥalav, in the Arab village of el-Jish, in the summer of 1977. This would be our first dig in an all-Arab setting. It was about five km from Meiron and a healthy and somewhat difficult walk down the Wadi Jish to the site. One of the greatest challenges of working there was our negotiation with the Akel family that owned the land around the synagogue site. The synagogue ruin was situated right in the middle of a fig and olive grove with cows grazing nearby. While we could legally dig within the ancient site that jutted above ground and a few meters around it, if we were to excavate beyond that area, according to the law, the owners had to be compensated for every tree we had to remove, its produce and worth over its estimated lifetime. The cost projections were so great they were prohibitive, so I simply worked out a way to work within the above-ground limits of the site. We also had to agree on how to gain access via footpaths and Jeep. It was not easy to arrange but successful in the end, and several members of the Akel family worked for us.

We also hired two excellent workers from the village, Yakim and Suleiman. They were each large individuals and very lovable. Yakim in particular adored working with our group and became very close to Gary Termite, who regularly stayed at his house for weekends. Yakim also invited us and the family and a few students to his house for a *mansaf*, a special festive Arab meal. One dinner in particular was memorable since he slaughtered a lamb for the occasion. In addition to our family and some senior staff, three young teenage boys from Durham, who were on the dig that summer, joined: Mark Tetel, future stepson of John Hanks, David Lefkowitz, son of a future Nobel laureate, and Mark Lazarus, son of a prominent dermatologist at Duke. Well the feast was truly over the top but absolutely beyond delicious. With an abundant supply of arak at the table and wine and beer, one of our teenagers when we got back to camp did not recover easily, but he learned an important lesson.

Our other Arab worker who helped haul heavy architectural pieces with his Jeep was Hayal Khouri, a Druze, who assisted in a lot of technical preparations for conservation with winches, equipment, etc. He and Gary had to work very closely since we restored and raised up all the columns and consolidated the walls. Hayal invited us to his home also and to our great delight served *musht*, i.e., St. Peter's fish from the Sea of Galilee, grilled to perfection. Jim Strange loved them so much he won a world's record for eating fish in one sitting: seven and a half. No doubt the arak helped a lot. It was great fun. And when the dig ended Hayal gave Carol and me a bronze pedestal table that is in our living room still, but the Arabic inscriptions on it I cannot read.

19

Back at Duke, 1978–1979

1978 WAS A HUGE year for biblical studies, largely because the Ebla/Tel Mardikh discoveries had just been announced. The discovery of several cuneiform tablets were of special importance and became a popular topic in the news, so much so that David Noel Freedman embraced a reading of them that supported a revived high chronology for the patriarchal narratives in articles (see *Biblical Archaeologist* 41: "The Real Story of the Ebla Tablets: Ebla and the Cities of the Plain") and in lectures around the country. That meant for the public that the narratives had an historical kernel in them and that they were possibly written or conceived in the third millennium BCE. Several names that were in them also appeared in the Bible in their Hebrew equivalents (e.g., Abram, David, etc.).

One of those lectures brought Freedman to Durham. Carol had known him since her days at Ashdod before we met, and I had gotten to know him quite well during my synagogue site survey in 1969 and in the following years through ASOR. In fact he and I had already become rather close at the AIAR when he confided in me about being offered a job at the University of Michigan and wanted my reaction to accepting it after being involved so many years with theological education. I strongly urged him to accept the offer and he did. All this is to say that by 1978 Carol and I were pretty close to him and in regular contact, though as I said, Carol's relationship with him went back before she met me.

Though we strongly disagreed with him on the importance of Ebla for the Genesis narratives and his high chronology for the setting of the biblical text, i.e., moving them back to ca. 2000 BCE and giving them a strong historical basis, we remained very supportive of his work and valued his friendship greatly. Noel came over to the house the evening after his lecture at Duke presumably for a nightcap, but normally he drank regular Coke from morning till night.

Out of the blue he asked us if we would like to do an Anchor Bible commentary—a series for which he was the general editor—on Haggai, Zechariah, and Malachi. We were truly taken aback at the offer, and when we inquired why we should do it and not someone else who was more senior than us or whose research might be more focused on those prophetic books, he responded with sage advice: when you want something done and done well, ask someone you know who can deliver and do it well. He simply believed we would do a good job, and he informed us that he was a very involved editor. Little did we comprehend at that moment how involved an editor he would be. After due consideration we accepted and working with Noel was truly one of the highlights of our life in terms of working with a senior scholar of such renown.

When we sent him our first chapter to review, the comments he provided were longer than the text we had written! But his suggestions were usually wise, and we benefited enormously from his editing. I would not say that in the beginning it was easy going for me and Carol to work together, and we often fought over words, literary matters, and things that commentaries focus on. But knowing that Noel would ultimately respond to whatever we had decided would make us more certain about what we would want to publish. In retrospect, today we consider Noel one of our most important mentors in biblical studies.

In 1979 I began my first six-year stint as director of the Graduate Program in Religion at Duke. One of my greatest accomplishments in that position was hiring Gay Trotter, who served with distinction in her administrative positon for nearly three decades. She made working in that office a pleasure and it ran with precision. I also loved working with all the PhD students in their respective fields and learned a lot from them about subjects outside my specialties. And I was very good at helping them arrive at their ultimate goal of finishing with degree in hand. Many of them became good friends and have remained so long after they graduated. Meanwhile with New Testament scholars W. D. Davies and Moody Smith requiring their doctoral students to have a minor in Jewish Studies, in those days I was extremely busy with many New Testament students, which continued all the way through the years with E. P. Sanders and Joel Marcus.

BACK AT DUKE, 1978–1979

Eric in his office at Duke, early 1990s. Courtesy of the Duke Photo Department.

The Duke PhD in New Testament was distinguished from most others because of its strong Judaic Studies content, and Kal Bland and I took up the challenge with a strong commitment and gusto, if I might say so. In my forty-eight years of active teaching at Duke, I must have served on more than seventy New Testament dissertation committees and directed nearly fifty in Jewish Studies or Hebrew Bible, and several in New Testament. With Roland Murphy, O. Carm., and Carol in Hebrew Bible, and later James Crenshaw, we were pretty darn strong. And in New Testament, unique and special.

20

Venosa, Italy, 1980–1981

I HAD BEEN SERVING for several years, 1978–1982, on the World Jewish Congress committee on Jewish Heritage. Ronald Lauder had started it and was instrumental in encouraging work in this area when he became president much later. And in the course of numerous discussions with other members of the committee, we noted an interest and concern for Jewish antiquities in Italy, in Rome and Venosa in particular. It was about this time that the World Jewish Congress through its representative in Rome, Fritz Becker, also a highly regarded pipe maker, was negotiating with the Vatican a return of the Jewish catacombs in Italy for custodial rights. They had been assigned to the Vatican for custody in the days of Mussolini, in 1929. For reasons not entirely clear to me, the Jewish community had developed a deep distrust for the Vatican archaeological authority and was wanting a return of them to the government of Italy with custodial care to be assigned to the Jewish community. Doris Brickner and Estelle Brettman were at this time also involved in the discussions about future work in them, including restoration, and I was drafted by Doris to be in touch with Fritz Becker about such matters.

On one of my trips to Rome, Fritz put me in touch with Cesare Colafemmina, a priest who was an archaeologist specializing in Jewish antiquities in Puglia, in the south, and teaching at the University of Bari. We talked about a possible project in Rome and the south but it was quite clear he had one site in mind, Venosa, where recently a painted arcosolium tomb, a subterranean arched recess used as a place of burial, with Jewish symbols had been accidentally discovered and which he published. Doris Brickner actually visited the site with the chief rabbi of Rome in

1979 and had secured the support of the Italian Jewish community and its president, Tulia Zevi, to support an excavation there.

As a result of these discussions and actions we started a small dig there in 1980 before I left for Israel and the new site of Nabratein. It was possible to do a short dig of a month or so in Italy if we started in Italy at the beginning of May and then in Israel in June. The World Jewish Congress, the Institute of Christian Antiquity at Bari, and Duke were the main sponsors of the Venosa excavations. Doris did much of the fundraising with me appearing at a salon or private home to make the pitch. It was not difficult to raise money for a Jewish project in Italy, and when we discovered a hitherto unknown Jewish catacomb in Venosa, it made the front page of the *New York Times* on July 26, 1981.

Years later I learned that Cesare was quite upset with the interview, as was also the case in a film by Italian TV (RAI), but his English was not very good and English-speaking reporters were inclined to interview me. I always identified his pioneering work in Puglia regarding Jewish presence there and noted it was he who had discovered the painted tomb. Unfortunately, Estelle and Doris did not get along and fought over whose initiative it was that got the dig started. Worse still, there was the earthquake in 1981 that closed the dig for the foreseeable future and before we really completed all we wanted to do.

But my interest in Italian Jewish antiquity was kindled and a renewed effort to work in Italy began in the 1990s; more about that later. Today the Venosa catacomb we discovered has been beautifully restored so that visitors can enter safely and has been carefully explored again. For visitors to the region it is a successful archaeological park, its Jewish burial chambers being showcased in the very best light. A major publication about all the new work appeared in 2020.

Living in Venosa, ancient Venusia, those two summers in May and early June was so much fun. Of course we had to have two big meals a day as well, both with local red wine, Primitivo. The unionized workers took their midday breaks on schedule and often offered me their homemade wine on site. But the really great meals were at night at the Hotel Orazio (named for Horace the Latin poet who was born there), one better than the next and we had to drink wine again with our evening meal. The local wine was so heavy that our Duke crew (John Younger and Karen Dubilier) was taken aback by the color of their stools, which at first was a bit scary because they thought there was internal bleeding. Cesare thought this was pretty funny, because this apparently happened frequently to visitors to the region. He was not only a priest but one with a girlfriend whom he brought along to the dig. In the beginning he was a bit standoffish about it but in the end when he saw that none of us really cared, she participated freely with him.

In planning the dig I had visited several times in Bari and at his home parish where I often stayed with a huge cross over my bed. We also traveled around Puglia visiting places where he had discovered artifacts, often inscriptions, most of them pretty late by my standards, i.e., early medieval. But the remains at Venosa were surely from the fourth–sixth century when the Jewish community flourished there alongside a thriving Christian community.

To this day I treasure my time in the south of Italy and will never forget my work there. The rivalry between Doris and Estelle is long forgotten, and the new head of the International Catacomb Society in Boston, Jessica Dello Russo, and I are now email buddies. Despite the fact that some have thought that my relationship with Colafemmina might have been fraught, to the best of my recollections he was always collegial and very welcoming. We never let the rivalry between the two women interfere with our relationship.

21

Nabratein and the Ark, 1980–1981

HAVING TWO DIGS BACK to back like this for 1980 and 1981 in retrospect was a bit of a challenge, but by now our operation in Upper Galilee was running very smoothly. Our Gush Ḥalav excavation had run its course because we simply could not negotiate what I believed would be a fair price for the land around the synagogue. So we moved on to our fourth village site with a synagogue, en-Nabratein or Nevoraya. It was a bit of a *schlep* to get there each morning, and we were far away from anything so it seemed, but the site was in the middle of a magnificent JNF (Jewish National Fund) pine forest with a view to die for. The view to the north over towards Hazor and Dalton was breathtaking. We still maintained our dig headquarters in Meiron. For the rest of the staff it was a relief to focus on only one dig site at a time.

Nabratein was another site that had been surveyed by the German team of Kohl and Watzinger in the early twentieth century, so we knew quite a bit about it, so I thought. Tfilinski also had told me the story that he and Nahman Avigad, a distinguished archaeologist and biblical scholar, had visited the site years before at which time they discovered the famous Aramaic lintel inscription and arranged for it to be transported to Jerusalem. It is today at the Israel Museum in the outside exhibit area where many inscribed architectural fragments from ancient synagogues are displayed. The Nabratein inscription is unique in that has a date reckoned from the destruction of the Temple in 70 CE. That came to 565 CE, the date of the latest phase at the site. Tfilinski also said that their visit was memorable because when they were at the site they were threatened by a wild boar and of necessity climbed a tree where they were stuck for quite a while until the boar went away.

PART TWO: WITH CAROL

Eric at Nabratein, 1980.

The excavation proved to be far more exciting than we had anticipated. One of the reasons was that as we dug we discovered that the fill was deeper than we had thought and that the state of preservation of the synagogue and the areas around was better than we had imagined. Also, the sherds and stratigraphy revealed a longer and more complex occupational history. The soundings outside the synagogue to the north, for example, produced a clear layer of Early Roman material with an inkwell like those discovered at Qumran (first century BCE and CE). From an archaeological standpoint this was big news, and our expectations were sky high after that first season. While we had thought we were pretty isolated, since we were close to some venerated tombs of famous rabbis, there was a steady stream of mostly pious observers. Little did we know that they were not happy with us, our students, staff, and plans for the dig. This became apparent early on in that fateful campaign of 1981.

As the early phases of the synagogues were revealed in that second year, we began to restore the latest phase and put up a number of columns. We had also chained our tools at the site so we did not have to bring them back to camp each day after work and back again the next day. Early on that summer we began to note that balks were knocked down at night, several columns as well, and some tools stolen. We learned through Tfilinski that the *haredim* were upset that gentiles were working on a Jewish holy site, and that among them were women in immodest dress and that some wore crosses, and therefore we had to be stopped. So our protector who emerged to help us finish the season was Mordecai (Motti) Aviam who then worked for the Society for the Protection of Nature in Israel and headed a small group from the field school on Mt. Meiron. This group not only came to the site at the end of our workday, say around 1:00 PM, but camped there overnight as well with guns with live ammunition.

We did not fully realize how important this sort of protection was until we made a huge discovery on July 2, 1981. That discovery came in the form of a large stone that was removed from the *bema* in the southwest corner. Gary Termite arranged to lift it with a large winch, and when I leaned over I noted as soon as I put my hand on the underside of the fragment that it was well sculpted with some sort of relief figures. As we lifted the piece and successfully turned it over, we noted two beautifully crafted rampant felines or lions on top of a pointed pediment with a shell or half dome with a hole in the middle of it and a rosette in the apex. There was no doubt but that it was the top stone, or pediment of a Torah Shrine that many of us recognized from ancient mosaic art and even from modern synagogue depictions and structures. We knew it was a really important discovery but also realized that it would not be safe at the site or in Meiron if notice of its discovery was announced. So we did all we had to do in recording and photography as quickly as possible at the site and arranged for it to be transferred immediately to the Rockefeller Museum in Jerusalem where it was exhibited and remains there till this day.

Without the assistance and protection of Motti's young crew from the field school, we would never have been able to finish that season let alone deliver our finds and special ark pediment to the Antiquities Authority. We thought that this would be the end of the vandalism, but no sooner had the JNF made the site into a park than the ultra-Orthodox returned and destroyed the beautiful signage. They have done this numerous times and in recent years. Motti Aviam has called them the "Jewish Taliban" in the press, especially with their blind commitment to a form of aniconic Judaism with no images whatsoever, a very narrow view of—if not complete misunderstanding of—the Second Commandment.

PART TWO: WITH CAROL

Eric and Carol at Nabratein years later (2009), when it was a Jewish National Fund Park. The site has been vandalized numerous times by religious extremists who are aniconic and look at the relief sculpture with animals as heretical and in violation of Jewish law.

When Carol and I returned to Durham, we prepared a press release about our summer's work to be distributed by the Duke Communications Office. When we submitted our text we obviously noted that a special discovery of an ancient synagogue ark was the highlight of the season. We did not mention the fight with the *haredim*. We had handed in the press release in on Friday afternoon, and our plan was to fly to New York in a few days to join good friends on Shelter Island. On Saturday we got a call from the Duke person who was about to send the release out. He said to us: "I want you to go to the movies tonight before you leave and see *Raiders of the Lost Ark*." I said we were just packing and that we had no idea about the movie since we had been away for months overseas, etc. But Carol and I were so curious we rushed our packing and went to see the film. Upon leaving the cinema we kind of knew what he was thinking, namely that some people would assume that our synagogue ark pediment was the "lost ark" of the movie. We had no idea that in less than twenty-four hours that we would be inundated with calls from journalists all over the world and numerous invitations to appear on national TV. This happened as soon as we arrived at the home of our Shelter Island friends, Balfour Brickner, prominent Reform rabbi and social activist, and his wife Doris.

What our Duke colleague should have told us before we left was how to pack. We had only very casual wear, shorts and bathing suits and nothing appropriate for TV let alone for a serious interview. Several networks called and wanted an exclusive. We decided to accept *Good Morning America* since David Hartman was a Duke graduate, though we had never met him before. How else do you decide? We both had to go out shopping for some clothes; neither of the Brickners was close enough in size to borrow something. *People* magazine wanted to come right away to photograph the two of us, and they did, and it simply did not stop there. A photographer from *People* magazine also had to fly down to Durham, along with a reporter, for a few days to take more pictures of us and Jim Strange. And the radio and phone interviews continued for some time. All this was the same summer as the Venosa catacomb discovery. Carol was so worried about her future tenure and job security that she went to her dean to discuss whether all this publicity would hurt her. And Dean Ernestine Friedl, a pioneer in the quest for getting more women in academia, reassured her on that front and we simply enjoyed the ride. When the *People* magazine crew, photographer and writer, arrived in Durham they requested that we dress in *Raiders*-type apparel, and they photographed us in various places in the Duke Chapel, even in the underground crypt. It was actually lots of fun, and with the internet, all of that is now readily accessible for all to see and recall. And

PART TWO: WITH CAROL

often when one of us gives a visiting lecture somewhere the introducer or host will often begin with one of those pictures, all these years later.

Carol and Eric in Duke Chapel posing for *People* magazine in July 1981. This iconic photo has followed us around the world comparing us to Indiana Jones and Marion. Photo by Jack Vartoogian.

Eric and Carol with Jim Strange, July 1981, for *People* magazine. This photo shows the three of us at Duke in a seminar room working on an article, books spread all around us. Photo by Jack Vartoogian.

22

Oxford, 1982–1983

WITH THE SECOND SEASON of Nabratein behind us, our work in the Upper Galilee was coming to an end save for final publications. There was simply no way for us to continue in the face of such violent opposition. Also, the original goal of exploring village life and studying and dating the synagogues there had been met. In addition my work on regionalism had begun to take hold in other circles, and I wanted to move to the Lower Galilee and see how our material from the Upper Galilee compared. Indeed, this view was widely shared among our staff and a recent survey of sites clearly pointed to the urban site of Sepphoris as the focus of the next stage of our work. We also needed a hiatus for a number of reasons. We all needed a breather from the hectic pace of the last years.

Carol and I also needed to get cracking on our Anchor Bible commentary, and we had just gotten fellowships to go to Oxford University in the UK for AY 1982–1983. Our base was to be Noel Cottage on the grounds of Yarnton Manor, a seventeenth-century rural estate. The Manor was home to the Oxford Centre for Postgraduate Hebrew Studies (later renamed the Oxford Centre for Hebrew and Jewish Studies and relocated in downtown Oxford), We were appointed Visiting Fellows there. In addition, I was associated with Wolfson College, and Carol was a Visiting Research Fellow at Queen Elizabeth House. We were very excited for us and the kids to have another overseas adventure in a different culture. For me and Carol the big push was on for the Anchor Bible.

I had just taken over from David Noel Freedman the editorship of *Biblical Archaeologist* earlier in 1982 and also as first vice president of publications for ASOR. And I had to do all that long distance. The transition with Noel in Ann Arbor just before we left for England had not gone well since he had not wanted to step down from the position, which had a lot of power and responsibility to go with it. In visiting Ann Arbor with my new graphic artist Susan Leeb, we had to decide what to do with every single piece of equipment and also choose what we wanted take back to Duke. Fortunately, Jim Eisenbraun had been Noel's right-hand man for years as a graduate student at Michigan, and he was extremely helpful in accomplishing the task of closing down the ASOR office in Ann Arbor. A great outcome of this visit was the future of Eisenbrauns publications, which today is the standard in the field of Near Eastern Studies and Hebrew Bible (and recently becoming an imprint of Penn State University Press).

One day at Oxford I received a call from a former student and staff member from our digs in the Upper Galilee saying she had just been invited to join a new dig at Sepphoris in 1983 under the direction of Jim Strange. I was simply stunned to hear this. As far as I was concerned, we (Jim, Carol, and I) were on hiatus from digging but planned to excavate Sepphoris as the next phase of the Meiron Excavation Project. She added numerous details for the 1983 project, and I soon realized that Jim simply must have wanted his own project now and did not have the courtesy to tell me that. The fact is that Jim and I never had the opportunity or courage to talk about it, and it never surfaced before his death (in 2018). But I was darned if all that joint planning, digging, and surveys of the last thirteen years would not be realized in terms of my own research agenda and what our Galilee team had decided was the best strategy for the future.

We had as a group decided that Sepphoris was the next site to be excavated in our Galilee project. We had surveyed Sepphoris and noted that its early Roman materials and nearby Church of St. Anne hinted at a very strong relationship to Nazareth, just a few kilometers away, and would attract a lot of New Testament interest. As the capital in the time of Jesus and with an impeccable literary pedigree in Jewish sources and place where the Mishnah was edited, it was a most promising site. Thus I decided right away at the time that I was simply going ahead with my plans to excavate Sepphoris though keeping a hiatus of a couple of years. The dig would require a new staff, but there would also be plenty of holdovers from the MEP.

Though I was deeply hurt by Jim's inability to tell me about his plans and hearing about them from a third party, I did not allow this incident to stand in the way of my continuing close relationship with Jim and his family, even up until the time of his death. I even spoke with him by phone when he was hospitalized in his last days. This explains why Carol and I turned to Ehud to find a new partner to work with. Thinking about this all these years later it is quite possible Jim felt overshadowed by the two of us who are pretty high powered. But as old friends, we should have had it out over some arak or single malt. Fortunately, Sepphoris was big enough for all of us, though we have politely disagreed over a number of key components of the site, namely the dating of the theater and the time when the main expansion of the city occurred.

Eric and Carol with Governor and Mrs. James B. Hunt, Jr.
along with Rebecca Nagy, curator with me of the exhibit:
Sepphoris of Galilee: Crosscurrents of Culture,
the North Carolina Museum of Art, 1996.

The rest of our year at Oxford was a lot of fun marred only by the bullying Julie received at her school in Woodstock. That was remedied in the second term by having her transfer to the Cherwell School in Oxford. Dina loved the Yarnton village school, which had a wonderful music program that suited her aspirations. We loved looking out at the meadows across from Noel Cottage—the meadows often filled with sheep and later that spring with antique cars at a rally there. And we loved listening to the chimes of St. Bartholomew's Church near our cottage, which later became the vicarage for the old church. The academic program at the Centre was stimulating, and we met many scholars there, one of whom—Henry Near—became a fast friend. Henry was a British-born Israeli kibbutznik and Oxford graduate who wrote the definitive two-volume history of the kibbutz. He taught us punting, and we subsequently visited him at his kibbutz (Beit HaEmek) in Western Galilee virtually every summer that we were in Israel. And he came to Duke several times to lecture on Utopian communities.

We vowed not to let rain or inclement weather interfere with our weekend and holiday excursions, which included trips to Scotland and Wales as well as many English towns and cathedrals. That was important. Noel Freedman visited once that year and impressed upon us the need to ratchet up our commentary and to ignore the Doubleday people who wanted it to be more popular and accessible to the general public. The other important visitor that year was my mom around spring break.

The five of us drove in our new Peugeot diesel to the beaches of Normandy and over to Switzerland to visit Aunt Leni Heaton, my father's sister. That trip was truly memorable in every way: we all pretty much cried our way through Normandy, visiting cemeteries and World War II museums. I especially remember the girls in one huge cemetery running through the fields of row on row of crosses as burial markers and getting excited when finding Jewish stars. We really relished every minute of the trip and have plenty of pictures to prove it.

We spent winter vacation that year in Tunisia, and that was also memorable for many reasons, including a visit to Matmata, where an episode of the original *Star Wars* series was filmed and where all the buildings are underground, that is, cut into the soft tufa rock. The underground "hotel" where we stayed was unbelievable—UFB (unfucking believable) my mother would have said. Our room was a cave with a couple of beds, but no bathroom or electricity, on a ledge above a large space twenty feet or so below. While it was a unique experience we will never forget, it's good that our Arabic was weak since the owner of the hotel, such as it was, wanted to talk about Arafat, who was living in Tunis at the time. It was so cold that the one tiny blanket provided for each of us by the "hotel" proved inadequate and we all wound up together in two beds pushed together.

We also visited archaeological sites (e.g., Dougga, Thuburbo Majus, and el-Jem) in Tunisia, which was exciting and uplifting. The ruins are simply fabulous and well preserved. And the Bardo Museum in Tunis has more Roman mosaics than in Rome. Seeing the old Jewish community in Djerba was especially poignant. And our British fellow travelers were fun at our base hotel on the coast, singing and dancing every night. Julie got sick one day with a temp and we went to the hotel doctor's office. And when he tried to look at her throat with a used depressor we bolted and Julie recovered quite well on her own. And now our cousin Matt Bushell, married to Amanda Fuerstein, works in the embassy in Tunis—how cool is that!

Before returning home that summer I was invited to give a major lecture on our Nabratein ark at Chautauqua in New York State, the location of a fabulous summer festival with music, theater, seminars, and lectures, many of them outside. The honorarium was huge, and there was also to be a big joint appearance with the astronaut who had been to the moon on Apollo 15, James Irwin, and who now was trying to find the other lost ark, Noah's Ark in Turkey. It was an odd thing to do so soon before leaving England, but the money and fun of it was too good to pass up.

On my flight from London to New York, however, I had a little cold and developed an earache, which got worse and worse. Half way over the Atlantic blood started gushing out and the flight attendant tried to stop it and there was no physician on board to assist. It got so bad that the captain came out to see me and asked if I knew anyone who could meet me and take me to an ENT specialist when we landed since it was quite obvious I had a ruptured eardrum. Well, Henry Fuerstein's father, Sidney, was a very distinguished ENT specialist and surgeon in New York, and so the captain said he could call ahead to help make arrangements. Since Henry is married to Cousin Lisa Meyer I gave him Lisa and Henry's number and someone met me at the airport, I simply can't remember who, and within a short time I was in a chair in Sidney's office where he took care of me so I could continue to Chautauqua. What a relief to have had such great care so soon after landing. Thanks Sidney, *z"l!*

My lecture about the ark we had found at Nabratein was delivered without slides since the shed was too bright in the daylight to show slides, but my recent experience with the press allowed me to have a bit of fun and speak without notes to a very large and attentive audience. My appearance with astronaut Irwin a bit later was not as much fun, as he was quite a literalist and a creationist to boot when it came to the Bible. We duked it out fairly civilly, though after the conclusion of our exchanges we each went our separate ways and never interacted again. That's not too surprising. I was soon back on the plane, returning to England and to my family, this time with my ear healed.

23

ASOR and Yigal Yadin (June 27, 1984)

YIGAEL YADIN WAS SURELY one of Carol's and my favorite teachers; remember, we studied with him in 1964–1965 and excavated with him at Masada. As vice president for publications in ASOR in the 1980s, I was a member of the ASOR Executive Committee. Yadin had requested a meeting with the leadership of ASOR in late June of 1984 when he would be visiting the States. It just so happened that Leon Levy and his wife Shelby White agreed to host a dinner in New York City at their apartment, and all I knew in advance was that Yadin had something important to share with us. Invited to the meeting and dinner besides me were James Sauer, president of ASOR, Ernest Frerichs, dean of the Graduate School at Brown University and past president of the AIAR, Joy Ungerleider-Mayerson, chairperson of the AIAR board, and Richard (Dick) Scheuer, preeminent trustee of ASOR and the AIAR. After cocktails and a fabulous meal we sat down to listen to Yadin's proposal.

Yadin said he was concerned about the teaching of biblical archaeology in American universities and that, from where he sat, the future looked grim. What he also implied was that the study of the Land of Israel was declining as well and that if it could be shored up somehow it would be good for Israel and good for ASOR. So he proposed the following: he pledged that a new US lecture tour would be devoted to this aim with him as lecturer and that he would travel for expenses only and start a fund to promote biblical archaeology with whatever honoraria and gifts could be collected. But what he also offered was to speak to anyone and everybody we recommended who was potentially able to endow a program in biblical archaeology or Land of Israel Studies with archaeology at its core. The idea was to target the top eight to ten universities where such studies were available and strengthen them with an endowed position along with monies for excavations.

We all were enthused and pledged to do everything to support the effort. Joy Ungerleider-Mayerson had already been giving scholarships to work on digs in Israel through her Dorot Foundation to many key institutions and that program was to be the basis of the list of schools that would be assisted in raising such funds. With ASOR as the home for the effort, if the major schools could not assure such a home for the endowment, ASOR would find a suitable place to locate the monies. Our discussion only scratched the surface of what would happen if a person wanted to endow a position in Near Eastern archaeology embracing a larger area than Israel, but ASOR was well positioned to accommodate just that. All of us in attendance had no doubt that Yadin could pull this off. Among the schools to be considered at that time were in no particular order: NYU, Duke, Harvard, Penn, Cornell, Chicago, Brown, etc.

Yadin was flying back to Israel that evening, and when we all said goodbye well before midnight we were confident that this was a plan that would work. With such a charismatic and public figure as Yadin, we did not consider failure as a possibility. We all hugged and said *shalom*. Yadin left on the early El Al flight to Tel Aviv on the morning of the June 28 and after arrival went straight to his brother's Yossi's house on the coast to rest. There he died peacefully and suddenly that very day. When all of us heard the news about his death, we were of course shocked and deeply saddened.

What became of this effort, which to all intents and purposes was moot now? Joy Ungerleider-Mayerson did endow such a position at Harvard, the Dorot Professorships in the Archaeology of Israel, and Lawrence (Larry) Stager was subsequently lured away from Chicago to accept the position. The Levys also underwrote Larry's excavations at Ashkelon, and Joy had also endowed a chair in Jewish Studies at Brown but had not linked it to Land of Israel Studies or biblical archaeology.

Yigal Shiloh, the Israeli archaeologist most famous for his excavations of the City of David in Jerusalem, came to Duke as a visiting professor in 1986–1987, and I told him this story. As one of Yadin's best and most favored students, he said he would take up the task with me. Alas, by late spring and summer of 1987, Yigal, who had successfully battled cancer a few years earlier, had his cancer return and in November at age fifty he died. Yadin's fears about the decline in the field sadly have come true to a certain extent, and the area of study of biblical archaeology, or Land of Israel Studies, is

ASOR AND YIGAL YADIN (JUNE 27, 1984)

today, as I write this, still in need of considerable support at the Research One universities here in the United States. Israel Studies, i.e., the pursuit of the place of the political entity of modern Israel in contemporary history and politics of the Middle East, however, has become front and center and often dominates discussion of Jewish Studies in the university. Nonetheless, some Christian colleges such as Wheaton and seminaries have remained strong supporters of digs in Israel. While the practice of archaeology remains vigorous in Israel today, enrollments in university courses are falling, and it has all too frequently wound up in the middle of settler politics with its support coming from the extreme right—as in the case of Silwan, the City of David, Shiloh—or from conservative Christian supporters. Today there are so many digs in Jerusalem one can hardly keep up with them all, many subterranean. Archaeology, as part and parcel of politics, is alive and well in Israel. Between all the university programs in archaeology and the Israel Antiquities Authority, unsurprisingly, Israel has become a world leader in the field and will surely remain so for the foreseeable future.

Eric and Carol with the Mayor of Jerusalem, Teddy Kollek, and Joseph Aviram, director of the Israel Exploration Society, July 1985, garden of the Albright Institute, Annual Shwarma Fest.

PART TWO: WITH CAROL

Eric and Carol with Senator Patrick Moynihan and Leon Levy in the U.S. Senate Caucus Room, ASOR's 85th anniversary. Senator Moynihan's wife, Liz, was chair of the ASOR board, 1985.

24

Sepphoris, 1985–

BACK IN DURHAM, JULIE was poised to get her driver's license in 1985, and Carol and I couldn't wait so we could get off the carpool train. Julie took over carpooling Dina when she got her license that winter. Yeah!

Getting the plans together for Sepphoris was now a major challenge. We had broached the subject of a joint expedition with Ehud Netzer in person after learning about Jim Strange's plans, and it was now time to work out the details. One of the reasons for doing this was that I had thought Hebrew University would provide office and storage space in the off-season, and boy was I wrong. Ehud informed me that Institute of Archaeology on Mt. Scopus was overloaded and over stuffed, and we would have to find rental space somewhere else. I am not sure why or when I agreed to this, grudgingly, but we managed to find a small apartment in the Nahalot neighborhood of Jerusalem that Ehud knew about, and that became our storage area, but not workspace, until our split-up with Ehud six years later. The AIAR would not be available for a number of years.

There were signs even before our first season in 1985 that there would be some rocky days ahead. Hebrew University was not prepared to put in a single penny toward the dig in light of Ehud's other commitments, especially Jericho and Herodium. Also, Ehud informed us that we would have to reimburse him for his gas expenses, and he expected a rental fee for when he drove back and forth to the dig in his own vehicle. And the Israeli staff all had to be compensated while the Americans came essentially for free room and board. Almost an equivalent. Normally the consortium sponsor would pay the Americans' air travel and then a fee to the Joint Sepphoris Project, which is what we called the Sepphoris dig, and we would wave room and board. Lack of support from Hebrew University remained a bit of a sore spot, and it always seemed as if the Americans were picking up most of the tab, and we were.

Our first Israeli staff was fabulous though: Zeev Weiss, area supervisor along with Rivkah (Pukul) Berger and Rachel Bar-Natan, and Marva Balouka joined us in 1988. All of these individuals have gone on to distinguished careers with Marva and Rachel specializing in ceramics. I was doing all the pottery reading in those years, right on up to the end of the Sepphoris project actually. The idea of the joint project was great, but it only lasted for five years, and they were truly pivotal years for the study of the Galilee and for unraveling the history of Sepphoris.

Ehud and I had laid out the first squares and jointly decided on a strategic approach to the site: we would start on the western summit near the citadel, which we used for tool storage in those days, and move on down the hill westward. In addition, we would sink a large probe on the eastern end of the theater and do a series of probes in the pine forest to the south to see the extent of the ancient city. The probes in the forest were really a challenge since this was the heart of the Arab town of Saffuriyah, which had been bulldozed after the 1948 War and overplanted with pine trees by JNF. The result of the flattening of the modern town was that cement and rubble from 1948 was literally buried, making excavation in the area almost impossible. We did manage to find a few ancient ritual baths there, however.

Nonetheless, the strategy proved to be fortuitous and it was only after two seasons, in 1987, that we discovered the Dionysos mosaic on the peak of the summit and the wonderful villa in which it was housed. Needless to say this got everyone's attention, especially Hebrew University, which now was interested in helping more directly and not coincidentally in claiming full credit for its discovery. But it also got the attention of the National Park Authority and the mosaic portrait of a beautiful woman—dubbed the "Mona Lisa of Galilee"—soon won over everyone thanks to her smile and the "good stones" that made her a hot item in the middle of the first Intifada. Carol's interview on NBC television with Martin Fletcher was memorable and helped the process along hugely.

SEPPHORIS, 1985–

Biblical Archaeologist cover — *Mosaics of Ancient Sepphoris*

The discovery of the Mona Lisa mosaic at Sepphoris in 1987 made headlines around the world. The sobriquet was given by the press after seeing her and noting that her eyes would follow you in every direction. I was editor of *Biblical Archaeologist* at the time it appeared, in December 1987.

Carol's interview with Martin Fletcher of NBC News in 1988 helped to popularize the discovery a year later when the mosaic was removed for restoration at the Israel Museum in Jerusalem. The rollers in the picture have the mosaic attached and ready to be transported. Fletcher called them "the good stones" in a time when stones were being hurled during the first Intifada.

Between the excavation of the theater and the Dionysos Villa, Ehud became pretty much engaged; despite his ongoing work at Jericho and Herodium, and finishing his writing on Masada, he was fully committed to seeing the mosaic become the centerpiece of a national park that would take over the site. In addition, Ehud and I got the JNF to clear much of the theater that was not excavatable but added a great deal to the general attraction of the site for tourism. The three of us also had decided that we were trying to pass the baton to the next generation for leadership. Ehud had his eyes on Zeev, and Carol and I had our eyes on Jonathan (Jon) Reed, a New Testament scholar at University of La Verne. In the case of Zeev, he subsequently went on to lead the Lower City excavations at Sepphoris and to head the Institute of Archaeology at the Hebrew University. Jon's leadership did not work out for a variety of reasons, though he had one full season in 2000 and went on to become provost at La Verne. All this was happening when I was editor of *Biblical Archaeologist* (*BA*) and VP of

ASOR Publications. A number of our discoveries made the cover of *BA* and our cover story on the Dionysos Mansion and other articles on the dig had a huge impact on New Testament scholarship. Much of this came to a head in 1987 when during the dig an international conference on Galilee was convened at the nearby Kibbutz Hanaton.

Meanwhile, unbeknownst to Ehud, Carol, and me, *National Geographic Magazine* had been preparing a Christmas special issue on Jesus and Sepphoris with an argument that Sepphoris was a full-blown urban city in the time of Jesus with a pagan temple on the summit alongside the Dionysos Villa and theater. Jim Strange had been the main consultant on the project, and one day we saw a model of the city carried to the site by Jim alongside a professional photographer; it was a model of the reconstruction that was to be featured in the article. To our surprise and shock, the reconstructed model of the city covered our area of excavation and bore no resemblance whatsoever to what we had in fact uncovered. Rather, Sepphoris was depicted as a fully developed urban polis with Romans in total control of the Jewish population. We demanded to see the illustrations for the forthcoming article. After seeing them, we went ballistic and in fact threatened *National Geographic* with a lawsuit saying that they had used our data without our permission and grossly distorted it. The reconstruction drawings and illustrations by Robert Teringo, which we insisted on seeing in galleys and showing them to the scholars assembled at the conference, were anti-Semitic and condemned by all of the attendees. They depicted the Jews with pointy noses, beards, and swarthy complexions always wearing *tefillin* (phylacteries), and the pagan Romans as Aryans. And there were somehow pigs in the scenes as well. Jewish Studies scholar Lawrence (Larry) Schiffman, who was at the conference, and I wrote a blistering critique of the illustrations for *BA*. They later appeared in a book by Richard Batey, *Jesus and the Forgotten City*. Jim Strange's participation in this fiasco was another disappointment.

As I began this memoir, a new *National Geographic* Christmas issue was planned for December 2017. I had been consulted and visited Sepphoris with the author. Carol and I now have read the issue, and I can say that it truly reflects the dramatic changes in scholarship that have occurred since the incident. Indeed, the article, by Kristin Romey, and the illustrations got it right this time. Carol and I later (in the summer of 2019) spent time with her at Chautauqua in New York State where we all lectured; Kristin's interest in archaeology in Israel is still strong, accurate, and up-to-date. The large shed where I had once spoken years before was now larger and better prepared to handle illustrated presentations, though Carol and I presented outside in the small pavilion where attendees could see our slides on a big screen or on their own hand-held devices.

With the discovery of the Dionysos mosaic in 1987 at the end of the season we were faced with the question of how best to preserve it. We knew that we wanted it to be at the heart of the national park that would one day take over the site. The Antiquities people told the three dig directors that it was our responsibility to safeguard and preserve it and that we would have to come up with the requisite funds. So we reburied the mosaic in 1987 at the end of the dig. First, we posed as if in symposium formation, then covered the mosaic with sheets from a nearby hotel, and then piled gravel and dirt on top to keep it safe from robbers. We had the year to come up with the money. Nothing was forthcoming from Hebrew University, and when spring 1988 came along, there was no help in sight save for the regular dig budget. The plan was to have the staff of the Israel Museum, led by conservator Dodo Shenhav, do the work and they would have to be reimbursed. Dodo was also scheduled to consult with restorers from Cyprus who recommended a special procedure that would allow easy transport to Jerusalem after cutting it into seven sections, detaching each section from its plaster base, and rolling them up.

As the season neared I was off to Israel, still needing funds. Carol remembered that one of the Duke students who had been on the dig had mentioned that her parents wanted to "help." Carol spoke to the student's mother about needing some financial help and was told she would check with her husband. Meanwhile, Carol asked John Piva, then head of development at Duke, about how much money we might request from the parents of this student, Jane Gottesman. He soon called Carol back with the astonishing news that Jane's parents were owners of Edison Parking, about one-third of all parking lots in New York City. They made a generous gift that allowed us to preserve the mosaic in the most up-to-date fashion. The signage at the site acknowledges their gift in honor of Sadie Gottesman, Jane's grandmother. The restoration took a year in Jerusalem, and the mosaic went on display for three years at the Israel Museum. Ehud subsequently secured a gift to build a shelter for the mosaic at the site, and the national park became a reality as a result.

The idea of the national park consumed all of us for the next years, and Binny Shalev from Hoshaya, a settlement adjacent to Sepphoris, was the main person implementing the development of the site and seeing to it that everything in the antiquities areas was carefully guarded and preserved. Since the Crusader Church of St. Anne flanks the western summit and adjoins the orphanage there, I had the idea that the national park might include access to the beautifully preserved twelfth-century church, and Carol was totally on board. The Franciscans have had control of the holy places for centuries in the Levant, and St. Anne's, which marked the traditional home of Joachim and Anna, the parents of Mary, was one of them. We actually celebrated the 2000th anniversary of Mary's birth at the site one year. It would be so nice to enter the national park and exit after seeing the church. The Daughters of St. Anne manage an orphanage adjacent to the church.

But first we had to secure an agreement between the Israelis and the Franciscans. We were good friends with Michele Piccirillo, at that time dean of the Pontifical Biblical Institute in Jerusalem and best known for his writing on the mosaics of Jordan. When not in Jerusalem he lived on Mt. Nebo. He referred me to the person in charge of the holy places in Israel, the Custos Terra Sancta (guardian of the holy places), who resided in nearby Nazareth. The Custos was quite enthusiastic about the idea and agreed to pursue it if we could get the Israelis on board. There was the issue of the entrance fee, and the Israelis did not think many Israelis would want to see the church, which was mostly of Christian tourist interest. After much back and forth and no agreement how to divide the entrance fees, the idea was "cancelled" and never emerged again in any discussion. Today if one wants to visit the Church of St. Anne, one has to have a prearranged tour; and there is the additional impediment of having to drive through Moshav Zippori with all of its dozen or so speed bumps and no buses. Since the collapse of the plan, the *moshav* has closed their entrance to outside visitors except by special arrangement. I still think it was worth a try, and with the multicultural heritage of Sepphoris in antiquity, it was a natural goal to pursue.

Despite the increased visibility and prominence of the Sepphoris dig, Hebrew University did not help with ongoing dig expenses or maintenance of the Jerusalem office. Our relationship with Hebrew University and Ehud thus was even more strained. Now that Sepphoris was increasingly in the news and seemingly more important for studying early Judaism and Christianity, Ehud wanted to have more control of the dig, and this manifested itself in various ways. Access to our drawings and photos was complicated and difficult. Marva acted as if she owned them and took more and more pottery to the Hebrew University campus without telling me or Carol. She ultimately used them to teach her course in Roman-period pottery featuring Sepphoris, the topic of her MA thesis. Ehud leaned more and more on Zeev Weiss, and Marva kept leaving us out of the picture even though sending us bills for everything. Ehud also wanted us to dig faster and open up more areas as he preferred giving greater attention to the architecture. In light of our commitment to stratigraphic principles, we demurred and reached an impasse.

In 1989 at the end of the season we agreed to separate and allow the Hebrew University dig to move eastward to what turned out to be the Lower City. While the separation was amicable at first, allowing us to continue on the western summit with exclusive publication rights, Zeev and Ehud went ahead in secret and published in 1994, *Zippori* (Hebrew for Sepphoris), a small book featuring our joint work but adding information about more recent mosaic discoveries. This was a bombshell since the three of us, Ehud, Carol, and I had published a similar small book on Sepphoris in 1992, and much of the text of the new book and pictures were lifted from that. Clearly what had been a gentleman's understanding was now in need of legal definition. I consulted with the Duke office of legal affairs and Kate Hendricks, who specialized in intellectual property law. They considered this a clear case of violation of the law and of the antiquities law of Israel. Duke University filed a case against Hebrew University and Ehud and Zeev. A series of meetings was arranged in Israel, and Kate and I had to fly over to Jerusalem for a week to resolve the case.

After several meetings with all parties and the Israeli lawyer representing Ehud and perhaps the Hebrew University, an agreement was hammered out between the parties that governed our work until the year when we completed our final report of the Duke excavations at Sepphoris (published in 2018 by Eisenbrauns/Penn State University Press). The essence of that agreement was as follows: Duke would cede publication rights to the Hebrew University on the eastern end of the theater where the JSP had undertaken important soundings during several seasons in exchange for exclusive rights to all the domestic architecture and finds associated with it on the western summit. As for the Dionysos Villa, no publication could be approved without noting who the licensed archaeologists were at the time of excavation (Eric, Carol, and Ehud) and that they each would be given full credit—as in the case of *Qedem* volume 44, the volume on the Dionysos Mansion—on a title page. This painful procedure would leave a bad feeling for years to come. Our agreement also lacked specificity in regard to duplicate copies of photos and drawings, which until this day remains problematic. Ironically, the controversy over the dating of the theater and what was standing in the reign of Herod Antipas has united Hebrew University and Duke against the South Florida team of Jim Strange. Carol and I regained a sense of closeness to Ehud in his later years and were deeply saddened by his tragic death in 2010. We remain in cordial relations with Zeev to this day and do not blame him in any way for what happened.

By this time we had rented new laboratory space at the AIAR, all the space under the kitchen and dining room. The MEP had been renting the old G. E. Wright Lab for many years when Dina Kastel was running things and kept that additional lab space until MEP finished all its publication in 1978. Everything was meticulously stored, labeled, and Carol even made a diagram of all of this so when we communicated with Dina or someone else when we were in the States she could find the right box of sherds or a particular artifact.

Unfortunately, the director of the AIAR, Seymour (Sy) Gitin, began to encroach on the space we were renting in the Wright lab with his Tel Miqne materials, and when it came time for us to return the MEP materials to the Israel Antiquities Authority a good many of the Nabratein boxes were missing and were never found. We wonder if they possibly are stored mistakenly somewhere with Miqne materials. Carol and I feel awful about this, but Sy was just doing what he always did, taking care of his material first and foremost. The same thing happened with the Sepphoris lab under the dining area and kitchen, only we were paying lots more for it. Each time we came back to the AIAR there were piles of Miqne stuff or AIAR supplies being stored in our space, displacing our carefully organized materials. When we had just about completed the Sepphoris pottery volume and were preparing other plates for final publication, we found boxes of missing pieces of pottery that had been misplaced and not even been drawn or photographed, and we were forced to redo a number of the plates and add a few new ones. This delayed the publication of our Sepphoris pottery volume as you could imagine. We never got an apology from Sy or reduction in the rent. I fully realize that such mix-ups can happen and that the director might well have been ignorant of this when it happened. But with archaeology, the devil is in the details. The problem is especially acute when the leaders of the excavation have to return to the States to teach.

25

ASOR Presidency, 1990–1996

THE FIRST YEAR OF my ASOR presidency coincided with a year at the Center for Theological Inquiry in Princeton near Princeton Theological Seminary, and Carol and I also were named visiting fellows in the Religion Department at Princeton University. Our major task that year was getting our second Anchor Bible commentary, on Second Zechariah, in shape for publication. Having the chair of the ASOR board Gough Thompson (till 1992) there was a big help to me, and we often drove together to Baltimore where ASOR headquarters were then located. Dina was a first-year student at Duke, and Julie was an upper-classman at Hamilton. Our relationship with the university was a bit limited, though renewing our friendship with John Gager was a real plus. We actually worked hard that year and more or less did what we had planned to do and never quite got involved with the Seminary either. Jim Charlesworth, my Duke officemate in 1969–1970, lived down the street from us, and he pretty much dominated the biblical scene, despite Princeton Seminary having a very large and well-respected faculty. Carol and I loved walking on the trails and in the woods, and we even got to see an albino deer a couple of times—I thought I had imagined it the first time, but others had spotted it as well.

Eric in Sepphoris lab at the Albright Institute, Jerusalem, 1993.

As I noted earlier, I had been ASOR vice president for publications for some time before becoming ASOR president and had been traveling with my two predecessors Jim Sauer and Kyle McCarter to visit our affiliated archaeological institutes in Cyprus, Jordan, and Israel and their associated digs. As a long-standing member of ASOR's Committee on Archaeological Policy, Carol often was able to join these trips. They were a great way to recruit articles for *BA* and *BASOR* (*Bulletin of the American Schools of Oriental Research*) and line up manuscripts for monographs.

In 1989 a small scandal having to do with accounting practices was brewing in ASOR, which, along with some health concerns, forced McCarter to resign from the ASOR presidency. I was asked if I would be willing to succeed him and subsequently was elected to take over in 1990. ASOR's main office was located on The Johns Hopkins University campus then, and I would have to be there about once every six weeks or so. I truly got to love Baltimore, where my favorite restaurant featured food from Afghanistan. The Colonnade Hotel near campus became our gathering spot, and that's where I was introduced to Ketel One vodka, my favorite, by none other than ASOR trustee P. E. Macalister. But it was the Holy Trinity of the Board as I lovingly referred to them that made my terms as president so meaningful. It consisted of: Charles Harris of CAARI and Cyprus, former president of Seabury-Western Theological Seminary and Episcopal clergyman (Charles became ASOR chair in 1992–1994); Dick Scheuer, Reform Jew and chair of the board of governors of HUC; and P. E. MacAllister, Presbyterian layman and Caterpillar magnate. These three men would be my saviors for the next six years, in terms of support both financial and moral, as well as leadership. They were truly pillars of ASOR, and ASOR could not have survived this critical period without them.

After dealing with the scandal and office situation of ASOR in Baltimore and securing great on-campus office space next to Alumni Relations and the Eisenhower Library, a new challenge emerged. In addition to meeting the budget each year through the Annual Fund, in those years ASOR supported with direct funding the three overseas institutes with cash transfers. The largest recipient of funding was the AIAR in Jerusalem followed by CAARI (Cyprus American Archaeological Research Institute) in Nicosia and then ACOR (American Center of Oriental Research; now American Center of Research) in Amman. The reason for the AIAR subvention being so large was because ASOR was the legal owner of the physical facility. Aside from ASOR's modest endowments at that time, its main asset was the institute in Jerusalem. Since the 1967 War, the Arab nations surrounding Israel had boycotted archaeologists who had anything to do with Israel let alone dig there. The idea of Ernest Wright was that the overseas institutes could avoid the boycott by becoming independent with its own trustees and budgets. The idea also was that ASOR was to be apolitical and hence free to do work all over the region. But in 1990, as I said already, ASOR was still providing annual subsidies. The president of the AIAR at this time was Joe Seger, and the chair of the board (1988–1994) was Joy Ungerleider-Mayerson, a real powerhouse and strong-willed woman, museum director, and philanthropist par excellence. Somehow, she and a few other board members, probably including Dick Scheuer, wanted the AIAR building, once called the American School of Oriental Research, to be turned over to the AIAR board so that their trustees could take full ownership. ASOR was still paying the pension of Omar Jibrin, legendary cook, and paying a large annual subvention; but this became the cause célèbre of my first years as president. It was a doozy! P.E. Macallister, Gough Thompson, and Charles Harris thought it would be crazy for ASOR to give up its greatest asset for nothing. In those days it was worth well over seven figures though not yet declared an historic space and building. On the other hand, I as a past AIAR director and someone who was directing a project in Israel, was sympathetic to the request since the AIAR board was totally involved in the day-to-day management of the facility and was prepared to be weaned of the ASOR annual subvention in due time. The debate went on for several years and at times was quite tense and unpleasant; but in the end, reason won out and the transfer was completed. Gough Thompson had already stepped down as chair of the board to be replaced for two years by Charles Harris, and I convinced P. E. MacAllister to take over in 1994 and he agreed. P. E. remained chair of the Board until 2013. Reducing the large payment to AIAR and ultimately eliminating it made it far easier for ASOR to carry on its mission of running the annual meeting and publications.

At this time I had not known that in earlier years and quite recently ASOR had been directly involved in buying Dead Sea Scrolls back from Kando, the famous antiquities dealer from Bethlehem, and other dealers and intermediaries. ASOR had provided the tax write-off home for many donations, especially from Betty Bechtel, heiress and married to the co-founder of the Bechtel Corporation. She and committee members had used its Ancient Manuscripts Committee as the vehicle for doing this. Much of this became known to me in my third term as president as we undertook the task of organizing our archives. Looking back at how ASOR and this committee went about "rescuing" ancient scrolls and keeping them out of the wrong hands suggests that some of those funds might have been directed to other units within ASOR. I am not convinced that this was the best way to proceed, and the recent surge of Dead Sea Scroll forgeries in the market would seem to prove it.

Keeping politics of the Middle East off the table, so to speak, was a real challenge. *The Biblical Archaeologist* was thought by many to be an inappropriate name for a publication of an organization such as ASOR, which sought to be inclusive of the whole Middle East. The Bible after all was associated with Israel and the Holy Land and therefore was seen as being out of bounds for people working in Jordan or Syria or Iraq. So as my extended term as editor was coming to an end the Board conducted a membership survey about a possible renaming; and while the survey showed a clear majority wanting to retain the name of *Biblical Archaeologist*, the Publications Committee voted to rename it *Near Eastern Archaeology*. The journal has never quite recovered from this name change. When I was editor, subscriptions were about 7,000—after the name change they declined into the several thousands and today do not number 1,000.

In wanting to help publications along with funding dig reports and other subjects, I had the idea of producing an encyclopedia that would bring all the countries of the region together at least on the pages of an encyclopedia. I had found a willing partner in Oxford University Press and they had wanted to keep "biblical" in the title for purposes of marketing. It was crystal clear to me, however, that by doing so no Arab archaeologist was going to participate. Even with its name *The Oxford Encyclopedia of Archaeology in the Near East* it took a great deal of coaxing to get Arab scholars to write in a project that included Israelis. At the Annual Meeting on several occasions I quietly brought together scholars from both sides to meet, and soon we had commitments from most of the key people to participate. The five volumes came out in 1997, and I as editor in chief and each of the other editors had agreed to forgo royalties and honoraria in order to provide an income stream for future ASOR publications, today called the Opportunity Fund in ASOR. I must say I am very proud of this, and with the wisdom of hindsight I may note that this was an important beginning point for at least an intellectual rapprochement between Israeli and Arab archaeologists. Today the Annual Meeting regularly brings them together and serves as a model for the exchange of ideas in academic circles. And with virtual meeting becoming so popular in 2020, the coming together of scholars from so many different countries has become the norm.

Another major challenge came in my second term as ASOR president when Johns Hopkins University advised the ASOR board that we had better begin to look for new space since they would be taking over the space allotted to ASOR. This had been a perennial problem for ASOR, which had wandered from Yale to Harvard to Hopkins and had been other places as well. Fortunately for ASOR, Artemis (Artie) Joukowsky at Brown and who, with his wife Martha, had been involved with ASOR for years knew the higher-ups at Boston University and began to inquire about space there in Kenmore Square that would be free. Boston University was also interested in bringing the Archaeological Institute of America (AIA), and putting the two societies together in one building. This was accomplished the last year of my second term. When I first began to write this memoir Boston University had told ASOR that they must leave within several months.

ASOR subsequently found a new home in Alexandria, Virginia, and named it in honor of the late James F. Strange, whose widow Carolyn donated a substantial sum toward the purchase of the building. Who could have thought that academic life would involve so much real estate and complex business dealings? My father could not understand why an institution like Duke would pay me a regular salary with benefits to teach six–eight hours a week, at least so he thought that was all there was to it. Boy, could he identify with this. Real estate actually was real bucks and Artie's miracle was to get the two societies into this huge building at BU free of rent for nearly twenty-five years.

26

Mom's Death (1994) and Philadelphia

My mom died in 1994, less than a year after Uncle Marshall, and I was deeply gratified that several trustees, namely the Holy Trinity, Charles, Dick, and P. E, made contributions to ASOR in her memory. They asked me what I would like to do with the money, and I said I would like to establish a scholarship fund to allow students to participate in a dig. Carol and I have supported the endowment fund since that time. My mom, Shirlee, was always a big booster of mine and loved to say that her son was an ark-a-ologist—that's the way she pronounced it. When my father doubted my choice of careers, Mom was always supportive and proud. Honoring her together with Ernest seemed the right thing to do. Sorry I didn't think about this sooner so she could have known about it. She would have gotten a big kick out of it, for sure.

Losing a second parent was tough on me and of course on Carol and Connie and Shirl's girls: her granddaughters Julie and Dina, and Amy and Jennifer. Establishing this fund helped a lot to alleviate the pain of losing her. Coming so soon on the heels of Marshall's death made it even tougher. I had accepted an invitation to teach at Williams College in the fall of 1992 with the idea of spending every other weekend with her and commuting to Durham the other times. So we had had some quality time two years before, and I was grateful for that.

MOM'S DEATH (1994) AND PHILADELPHIA

Mom and Eric in Durham, early 1990s.

I had known how sick she was after a very bad fall at home in that spring and had visited her in the hospital, first in Norwich and then later in New Haven. But we had already planned a major excavation season at Sepphoris amid growing tension in Israel and an alarming escalation in terrorism and suicide missions. While I had considered canceling the season, in talking to university officials it was too late to do so since we had so many students enrolled for course credits, some planning to graduate early. There had already been two major suicide missions and there would be three more in 1994. This season we would have to be extra vigilant and not permit students to travel internally on buses, hitch hike, or travel in the West Bank. There was no way to cancel. Carol and I had to be there. I called home virtually every day to Mom or Connie as her condition deteriorated and fortunately arrived home in time for an emotional goodbye.

PART TWO: WITH CAROL

My sister Connie and I at her mother-in-law's 100th birthday party (Nana Perleson) in 2002. Nana stood in as "grandma" at Dina's graduation from Duke in 1994 when my mom was too ill to attend.

I should say a word about my year at the Annenberg Research Institute in Philadelphia in 1991–1992, since this occurred during my second term as ASOR president. I was supposed to have stayed at the Annenberg for at least three years with the possibility of renewal. This was the first year with the new name: the institute was previously known as Dropsie College and had a distinguished record of accomplishment in Near Eastern and Jewish Studies. Also, this was the last year that Dropsie could award degrees, and I signed the last of many MA and PhD diplomas that year as the last "president" of the college. I had a lovely apartment on the wharf not far from Independence Square where the gorgeous facility was located. I was on partial leave from Duke, kept all my benefits there, and spent a maximum of four nights a week in Philadelphia, commuting back to Durham for a long weekend.

Businessman and philanthropist Walter Annenberg was funding the operations more than 95 percent at that time and had paid for the new facility. We became quite good friends, and he invited me to his house and lunch numerous times. What I did not know at the time I accepted the job—nor did any of the trustees—was that Walter really wanted to merge the Annenberg Institute with the University of Pennsylvania on the model of the Annenberg School of Communications there. The board of trustees had no notion of this whatsoever when I was hired and was strongly devoted to maintaining the tradition of the old Dropsie College and wanted to stay independent. Mary Ann Meyers, head of the Annenberg Foundation at the time, and I met regularly and we got along well also. She had been secretary of Penn before moving over to the Foundation. She did not know of Walter's plans either until the day he sprang it on both of us at one of his lunches. When he did, we were both sympathetic and supportive and believed it was the right thing to do. Neither of us could have anticipated the harsh reaction of the leadership of the board of the Institute to the idea of merger with Penn.

Since the Annenberg Foundation through Walter's generosity was paying virtually all the bills, who would have thought that the chair, Seymour Kaplan and vice chair, Albert Wood, would have vehemently opposed it? In the case of merger they of course would lose much of their freedom to direct things at the Institute and would have to convert the current board to a board of advisors or something like that. In any case, I still thought it was a good idea, and I dutifully supported it in our conversations with the administration at Penn. Kaplan and Wood were furious, and while I was assured by the Penn Provost should the merger go forward that they would honor my contract if I decided to stay on at Penn for the next two years; but if I wanted to be tenured there, a search would have to take place in two years before I was renewed. It was clear to me that going back to Duke full time was the best plan—I had never intended for this to be a permanent or long-term move. Quite by accident, the Williams College visiting chair was offered to me on the occasion of their Bicentennial, and I accepted it and went back full time to Duke in the spring of 1993. By accepting the Williams offer and going back to Duke in the spring I was able to catch up on a lot of ASOR work and publications. The merger with Penn went through, of course, with Wood and Kaplan opposing it and then having to accept it. The Institute changed its name yet again to The Center for Jewish Studies at the University of Pennsylvania.

My year in Philadelphia was wonderful, apart from being away from Carol part of the week, and all told the best thing was being near Julie who was at Penn doing her MSW. I loved cooking for her once a week when she often brought friends and my niece Amy, always women. Once when I prepared Rock Cornish game hen for them I forgot to take out the frozen inner pieces that were inside. Julie discovered my mistake when I saw that the hens were not cooking as fast as I thought they should, so we had to drink another bottle of wine waiting for the hens to be cooked through. The worst thing that year was being away from Durham when Duke won another national championship in basketball. Oh well, there were a few more to come.

27

Frankfurt, Martin Buber Guest Professor, 1995

THE READER MAY WONDER by now why I seem to have had such a desire for overseas travel and study away from Duke as I am about to write about my 1995 Spring Term in Frankfurt as Martin Buber Visiting Professor at Johann Wolfgang Goethe University. A successful academic is always looking for a way to catch up on writing obligations, and Oxford and Princeton were the perfect places for that. Going to Germany for me was more of a "roots" sort of thing, a desire to see for an extended period what it was like to live in a major city where the Nazis had once ruled. My family connection is obvious and was a main factor in my deciding to accept the invitation.

My good friend Volkmar Fritz from Ulpan days in Jerusalem was now at the University of Mainz and arranged for me to lecture at different universities virtually every weekend (Freiburg, Giessen, Göttingen, Tübingen, Erlangen, Mainz, Marburg, etc.), and Carol had agreed to come over for about a month after Duke's semester ended. The university apartment assigned to me was near the botanical gardens and had been the headquarters for General Eisenhower during World War II and was now fully renovated. I had bought a new Saab that I picked up in Frankfurt and was quite mobile.

I was to teach two courses, one a lecture course on Second Temple Judaism and the other a seminar on Haggai and Zechariah, both in German. I had hired a German tutor in Durham for the previous six months and felt good about my language ability. Still, keeping up with the weekly *Vorlesung* (lecture) and seminar was a challenge. I had two assistants, however, who helped enormously and made it possible. I had most of my lectures prepared in advance and had translated a few of them. I also wrote a three–four page summary, *Zusammenfassung*, for my lecture each week. My assistant for that course corrected my German for the lectures and towards the end of the course said why not finish in English, which I gladly did.

In my biblical studies seminar, since I was "Martin Buber" Professor, I decided to use the Buber translation as a guide to the text. I did not need to prepare lectures for the seminar since the class was based on translation and exegesis of key sections of the biblical text. Consequently I asked my assistant for this class to help me prepare a list of words that would be central to a particular text and class and she would rehearse me for a couple of hours a week before the seminar. To my great surprise, after a couple of weeks, a member of the class came to my office with a request on behalf of the entire class: Could they please use the Luther translation because the Buber translation was too difficult and foreign to them. Of course I agreed, and the class continued without any further problems.

The dean of the Protestant faculty that year was Dieter Giorgi, who had taught New Testament at Harvard when I was a student there. He was a junior faculty member at Harvard at that time, and we had gotten to know one another somewhat. To my delight, he warmly greeted me and was eager to carry on regular conversations with me about two topics: Judaism, and the New Testament and the Holocaust. But in truth he wanted to talk about what he had done during the war, having served in the armed forces of the Third Reich, no less than as a gunner on a plane. Needless to say this was pretty heavy conversation, but his sincerity and wisdom were so convincing that when I think of these conversations I realize that they were cathartic for both of us. He had no choice but to serve; I had no choice but to forgive. When Carol came to visit, he and his wife took us to places of Jewish interest, insisting we see this place and that site. He made the semester very special.

Having Carol there was a highlight and her several lectures, especially at Frankfurt and at Marburg, where she was a huge draw and success. Julie visited for a week too, and Dina was just beginning her work for the Three Tenors and Hoffman Konzerte at that time and met us for several of her concerts that year. Leonard Rutgers, a former PhD student of mine, came from Utrecht for a long visit, and I drove him back to Utrecht where I lectured. He figures prominently in the Rome story that follows. Dale Martin from Duke, before he moved to Yale, was in Germany that year and spent a week with me as well, and so I was not lonely. In Heidelberg, Jürgen Zangenberg, who had worked with us in Sepphoris, was a gracious host, and today he teaches at Leiden and is still is a very close friend and colleague. He met me at the airport the day I arrived and delivered me to the apartment. He also took it upon himself to take me to old synagogues and Jewish cemeteries and demonstrated beyond any shadow of a doubt how so much of Germany had shown remorse for the Holocaust and had developed a sincere and profound appreciation for Judaism and the Jewish experience.

I subsequently went back to Germany twice to teach: once to do a mini-course for faculty and graduate students at the Free University in Berlin when Peter Schäfer was head of the Jewish Studies Program there; and later to give a course in German Jewish history for the Duke in Berlin Program. These cumulative experiences brought me much closer to my rich cultural heritage on my father's side of the family and a renewed appreciation for all that Germany accomplished after World War II. Despite all the reports of anti-Semitic violence increasing in recent years, there can be no doubt about the profound change in German culture vis-à-vis Jews in post-war Germany.

28

Rome and the Catacombs, Summer 1995

YOU MAY REMEMBER THAT my project in Venosa was actually a second choice to Rome. The accidental discovery there at Venosa of a painted catacomb tomb had pushed our group from the World Jewish Congress south with the blessing of the local Jewish community. Now fourteen years later Leonard Rutgers, one of my most distinguished PhD students, who by this time had written extensively on the Roman Jewish catacombs and had worked with us for a short time at Sepphoris, had convinced me that the time was ripe to do some serious work in the catacombs. He would bring the resources of the Royal Dutch Academy of Sciences, the University of Utrecht, and the Royal Netherlands Institute in Rome and I would bring Duke, ASOR, and the American Academy in Rome where our friend and Duke colleague Caroline Bruzelius was director at the time. I also had two donors who were prepared to underwrite most of the dig costs. Leonard was the director of the project and I was to be a kind of senior advisor and the licensed archaeologist. Another core member of our team was Nicolas Bucaria, a Sicilian by birth and former fellow at the AIAR, a specialist in Italian Jewry in antiquity, and at that time a translator for the EU parliament. Brigham Young University would be coordinating DNA studies and feeding that information into their vast databank and we were bringing Joe Zias of the Israel Antiquities Authority as the physical anthropologist.

We met in 1995 to plan our project and view the catacombs while staying at the American Academy. We set our eyes on the Via Torlonia catacomb on the Via Nomentana and the Randanini Vinyard catacomb. The Jewish catacombs had first been assigned to the Holy See and Vatican archaeological authority for oversight in 1929 by virtue of the Lateran Treaty signed by

Mussolini but now were under the authority of the Italian governmental archaeological authority. We brought Joe Zias in from Israel for the walk-through in the two catacombs, and he was blown away by the number of bones and their good condition. Even without touching them he could identify various diseases that were important in evaluating the health of the Jewish community at that time in antiquity. From afar he even noted that one skeleton had a deformity that was associated only with divers.

We knew full well that somehow the Rome Jewish community would have to be involved since by this time custodial rights had been reassigned to them after a big effort by the World Jewish Congress. As I noted earlier, I had supported their return to the Jewish community years before, having been overly influenced by some of the Jewish conspiracy theories that asserted the Vatican was hiding evidence from the Jewish community. In any case, Tulia Zevi was still head of the Jewish community in Rome and supported our efforts at first. Our team thought a major first step was to do a systematic DNA study of samples taken from long bones and teeth. Our plan was to turn over the bones to the Jewish burial society for reinternment after extracting DNA samples. We were prepared to have an Orthodox rabbi present to ensure the process was respectful. We also wanted to restore and re-measure and take new photographs of the tombs, frescoes, decorations and inscriptions before any further deterioration of them might occur. Some excellent work had been done on Christian catacombs, but the DNA study would help us better understand a number of ancient diseases and tell us something new about the ethnic background of those who were buried there.

In getting ready for our first season, we took up residence at the American Academy in the luxurious Villa Aurelia. Our Italian *permisso* (excavation permit) was in hand and we reestablished contact with Tulia Zevi. No sooner did we do this than she calls us all for an urgent meeting with the local rabbinic authorities. We assumed that all we had to do was finalize the protocols for turning over the bones as we had agreed the previous year. Caroline came along with Leonard and me, and Caroline asked the professor-in-charge of archaeology at the Academy, Elizabeth Fentress, to join us as well. Little did we know or could have anticipated what would happen: a small group of rabbis was waiting for us dressed in their traditional black suits and big, black Borsalino hats. Tulia greeted us and we told them in the most respectful manner what our plans were and that we would return the bones to them for reinternment after DNA removal from teeth and long bones. I carefully explained that this procedure would be most helpful in understanding diseases such as Tay-Sachs, which had so negatively impacted the Ashkenazic community. I also invoked the ethical principle that such examination of the bones would ultimately save lives. I tried to continue, but very soon the harangue and attack against us began.

We were accused of violating Jewish law, of desecrating holy graves though they had been left uncared for more than a millennium, etc. They screamed at us and said if we dare go near any of the catacombs they would bring the Eternal City to a standstill in traffic with demonstrators. There was no reasonable way to talk to them, and Tulia said that while we had a government permit she could no longer approve of the project in light of strong Orthodox opposition. To put it mildly, we were all in shock. We simply could not believe that after all we had done to avoid such a scenario, it now came down to either going ahead in light of such vehement Jewish opposition or not. In view of the fact that the Jewish community had custodial rights, we simply had to cancel the project and go home but not before having a couple of good meals and some great wine.

Leonard was inconsolable, and rightly so. It was simply one of the biggest disappointments of my professional life. Nearly thirty years later as I write this, and after returning from a wonderful semester in Rome, spring 2017, nothing has been done to preserve and care for these treasures of the ancient Roman Jewish community, though ambitious plans for Venosa have been implemented and exist also in a wonderful virtual reality form.

ROME AND THE CATACOMBS, SUMMER 1995

Eric, Carol, and Hershel Shanks in his office at *Biblical Archaeology Review* (*BAR*) after being named "biblical archaeology legends" in the magazine, December 22, 2014.

Eric and Carol in the Roman Forum when they were visiting faculty at the Pontifical Biblical Institute in Rome, Spring, 2017.

157

29

Leiden and Rome, 2016 and 2017

IN THE SPRING OF 2016 Carol and I set out to Leiden for a month at the university with Jürgen Zangenberg as our host. He arranged for a gorgeous seventeenth-century house on the river close to the university, just a ten-minute walk from the museum and department. We led a few seminars and gave lectures including a public one at the National Museum of Antiquities. Jürgen's publication team for Horvat Kur came for part of the time to consult with us, and it was truly a memorable sort of collaboration between staffs that I would heartily recommend. We also visited Keukenhof for the annual tulip festival and had a very special Passover in Amsterdam at a colleague of Jürgen's. Leiden is one of the most beautiful cities we have ever visited, and our time spent there is deeply embedded in our minds and hearts.

When Carol was invited to teach a spring-semester course in Rome at the venerable Jesuit institution, the Pontifical Biblical Institute (PBI), she decided that the only way she would go would be if I came with her and teach the course together. In consultation with the dean, we designed a course on the general state of biblical archaeology, a roundup of consensus views from the Late Bronze Age to the rise of Christianity after Constantine. This meant a lot of work on PowerPoint since it is nearly impossible to talk about these things without lots of images. We arranged our seminar to meet once a week rather than twice to allow ourselves maximum freedom to travel. The most delightful aspect of the class was our students, all male, all pretty much intending to teach within the Church system, all had multiple languages in their background including Greek, Hebrew Latin, French, Italian, and German plus their own native languages in Africa, Asia, and Europe. What a joy to present to such a diverse and dedicated group who were so appreciative of our presence. Carol gave one of her blockbuster lectures to the PBI community, and I gave one at a conference that closed out the semester and was subsequently published in a collection of the conference papers.

We were very close to the dean, Peter Dubovsky S.J., an Old Testament professor trained at Harvard. He took us on several excursions in one of the Institute's cars, including to a small Tuscan town known as "Little Jerusalem," Pitigliano. In visiting the small Jewish museums there we discovered that Peter's knowledge of Jewish customs and belief was quite limited and much of our talk on returning was on such odd topics as ritual purity, death and burial, etc. Talk about loving the land: we absolutely fell in love with Italy and remain enamored until today. We keep saying to one another "after the pandemic" we'll go back. Other members of the faculty also embraced us as friends, and we recall with special warmth our relationship with Craig Morrison O.Carm, and onetime student of our former Duke colleague Roland Murphy. We went several times to his parish for drinks and dinner. We were also frequent guests in the PBI refectory, and for the conference at the end of term we ate out at some fabulous restaurants.

It's hard to single out highlights of that spring, but the visit of Peter and Marilyn Ornstein was certainly one of them. And I think we wore out our sneakers walking all over Rome, sometimes seven–ten miles a day and once over ten miles in one day. Dina visited as well for a long weekend (four days) and wanted to visit the places she had stayed at when she studied in Rome as a Duke undergrad on a Trinity College program. She had stayed in a convent run by nuns. The night before she left we ate out with the head of her program with whom she was still in contact. Julie and her son Jacob also came for a week in May at our second and more spacious apartment on Via Annia near the Colosseum. (Our first apartment was beyond the Baths of Caracalla, with a view of the Aurelian wall.) What a joy to have them with us, and Jacob loved the pizza and the ice cream/gelato place nearest us that had almost one hundred flavors and needless to say we ended everyday there fussing over what to select.

Aside from incessant explanations from two archaeologist grandparents, Jacob and I managed to graduate from Gladiator School near the Appian Way and not too far from some of the catacombs, which he thought were pretty cool too. On another outing on the Via Veneto he visited a crypt where the bones of Capuchin monks were collected for hundreds of years and decorated the walls and altars below. Hopefully Jacob was infatuated with the city in a way that brings him back again and again and has instilled in him a love of the past in all its grandeur.

Another highlight was a visit to Florence to visit a former student, Giovanna Grassi, an art dealer in London, whose family estate in the heart of the city was truly something glorious. Her family not only welcomed us with open arms but gave us a separate, spacious house with all of her father's art books in it across the courtyard. Giovanna's dad had been an art dealer and specialist in the Italian masters, and we could sense his brilliance in this area when he took us around the Uffizi gallery one day and offered detailed explanations about some of the pieces in the museum. The red wine we consumed at their home was made on their own farm and was sealed in the old Tuscan way: by adding olive oil to the top of the bottle. When a new bottle was opened Giovanna's dad would suck out the olive oil and spit it into the sink. The wine was heavenly! We did not want to leave Florence.

For spring break we traveled to Israel and celebrated Passover at cousin Gaby's in the north with Aunt Naomi and her daughter, Anita. We also toured Sepphoris with Kristin Romey from *National Geographic* before her Jesus article appeared. And then back to Jerusalem to the Albright to see friends and talk more shop, i.e., archaeology.

Eric and Carol at Masada, December, 2009.

Eric working on an olive press at Qatzrein,
Golan Heights, October 2017.

30

The Meyer and Heschel Archives at Duke

ONE OF MY PROUDEST accomplishments at Duke was the acquisition of Uncle Marshall's papers and subsequently the Abraham Joshua Heschel archive, adding them to a growing human rights focus in the David M. Rubenstein Rare Book & Manuscript Library. If you have read about my early years, you know that each of these individuals played a significant role in my development. Of course, Uncle Marshall's role was more direct as part of the immediate family, only a block away.

Aunt Naomi and I had thought the right place for all his material would be Dartmouth, and after his premature demise Naomi began to explore how that might occur. Marshall was an inveterate saver, and there were probably a hundred boxes of material to be catalogued and accessed. The Baker Library people at Dartmouth were indeed interested but were not willing to offer much in the way of help or money. A close observer of all this was Susannah Heschel, a faculty member at Dartmouth who possessed her father's archives and was considering what to do with them.

Naomi expressed her growing disappointment with Dartmouth and asked me what I thought she should do. So I said I would explore with the librarians at Duke and see if it might be possible to do something in Durham. A new building facility had just been completed and was state of the art, and I used all my connections to see if we could bring Marshall's legacy to Duke. Marshall did not really publish a lot but had saved every sermon and letter he had ever written or received.

After much back and forth at Duke, I got a green light but with the condition that the library would only pay for shipping, the value of the collection would have to be written off as a tax benefit to Naomi. To my delight, Naomi agreed and Dina who was living in New York at the time and Marshall's daughter Anita agreed to pack things up with Naomi, which was a huge effort. FedEx delivered the boxes successfully and then the archivists took over.

Together, Jewish Studies and the library team began to plan a series of events that would promote the Meyer materials and the human rights component of them that centered on his fight against the government during the Dirty War in Argentina. Patrick Stawski's assistance in bringing all this to fruition was incalculable. Patrick is a special collections librarian and specialist in human rights materials. Since I was Director of Jewish Studies at Duke I still had a bit of administrative leverage and funds from my endowed chair. I retired only in 2015. My remarks at the dedication may be found in Appendix D.

In addition to me, Naomi spoke and a special invited guest was Susannah Heschel who also shared remarks. Patrick and I had already been thinking of bringing the Heschel archive to Duke and reuniting student and mentor together. The idea was seeded that evening at a lovely dinner that followed, but the real challenge was coming up with the price tag that was attached. The Meyer archive attracted numerous scholars pretty quickly, and Patrick was kind enough to suggest to them that they come to my office to meet me. That was really nice and the archive attracted a wide variety of scholars: some were interested simply in Jewish life in Argentina and the new liturgical approach of Marshall or details about the Timmerman family and how Marshall succeeded in helping earn Jacobo Timmerman's release. But Marshall's activities during the Dirty War and prison visits and efforts for human rights became the most popular and important components of the archive.

Years later, Pablo Stahlman, who often accompanied Marshall to prison as his driver, where Marshall had hopes of saving their lives and getting them out of prison, endowed a human rights research fellowship in Marshall's honor at Duke. Pablo was married to Anita for many years, and Anita and Pablo had stayed with us at the AIAR as teenagers in the spring of 1976. The Triangle Jewish Chorale, a few years later in 2012, sang a concert in Marshall's honor, bringing his son Gaby down along with Naomi. Gaby sang a few songs in Spanish, all in the Divinity School Goodson Chapel, outside of which the full audience of ca. 450 could see the traveling exhibit of banners featuring highlights from the Marshall T. Meyer Collection, which Patrick had prepared.

Seeing the keen interest of the Rubenstein Library in housing Jewish archives, I pushed the idea of bringing the Heschel archival materials with the Jewish Studies Executive Committee. When seeing an inventory of what it included they got very excited and it was not too difficult to find all the monies with their enthusiastic endorsement. Soon enough we entered into negotiations with Susannah—I recused myself for personal reasons—and as told to me by Patrick and others it was not easy going. But in the end it all worked out and the boxes began to arrive again and new plans were made for another dedication. My remarks at that occasion and questions I addressed to Susannah may be found in Appendix E. Susannah did not want to give a formal talk nor have her remarks recorded.

Part Three
Other Matters

31

Music and Singing

THE READER KNOWS QUITE well from the beginning of this memoir that music was an important part of my life from a very early age. As I have written, it also included being a part-time cantor these many years, mostly at Beth El after moving to Durham in 1969. This has also included doing many weddings here in North Carolina, especially since for many years there was no one else who would do mixed marriages. My simple criterion for doing them was this: that the family commit to having a Jewish household and raising the kids Jewish as best they could. North Carolina only insisted for legal reasons that the officiant be a recognized leader in his or her religious group. You'd be surprised as I have been at how many couples came to me and had never really worked out how they would manage this. Some even had never even discussed it. In those cases, I chose not to do the ceremony. Through the years I have had numerous couples or their parents tell me that helping them through this special event and time period was so important to their families. And I have been overjoyed that any number of families have adopted a Jewish lifestyle with enthusiasm and joy. My delight at seeing so many of them thrive within the Jewish community is one of the most satisfying aspects of my life in retirement.

But singing for the holidays has been a great honor for me these past decades, five now, and I have told Carol and Dina mainly, that when the voice begins to fail me let me know and I will retire. So far at age 82 the voice is still strong as ever and seems quite OK. But it takes longer to get in voice every year, and my training program has really helped. We'll see, you never know. Being honored in 2019 by having the High Holiday ark at Beth El named in my honor for my *davening* (chanting) all those many years was a huge surprise and special occasion. And preparing a virtual service with Rabbi Greyber during the pandemic in 2020 and 2021 was challenging but hugely rewarding, and I believe a real success. Given the phenomenon of Zoom fatigue, shortening the length of services was key, as was making other accommodations.

One High Holiday in particular stands out in my memory and should be noted, 1973. This was the year of the Yom Kippur War. Beth El's rabbi at the time was Rabbi Herbert Berger, who was more Orthodox than Conservative, though he had a degree from the Conservative seminary. Rosh Hashanah had been quite normal and went without incident. But Yom Kippur was something else. It was on the morning of Yom Kippur that we learned that the surrounding Arab nations had invaded Israel and that Syria was poised to make deep inroads into the north of Israel. Since Rabbi Berger was very traditional he had not turned on his radio or TV that morning and had no idea what was happening. I had to drive into town to Beth El and heard on my car radio what was happening. When I arrived at synagogue I told Rabbi Berger what had happened in Israel and asked him if I could run out to listen to the radio regularly to brief him and the congregation on the state of affairs. Fortunately, he agreed and when not chanting or leading I went to the parking lot to hear the latest and then report from the pulpit. It was a very emotional day to say the least, but we got through the day and the pretty much negative news and into the next week, when things turned around for the better. The mood in synagogue that day remained grim, and I shall never forget it.

I had always done annual recitals while studying with John Hanks, and they consisted mainly of German *Lieder*, Schubert and Schumann, etc. and arias from Italian, French, and German opera. In the early years of doing this when the girls, Julie and Dina, would come to the recital, I would end the performance with Kermit's song: "Being Green" from *Sesame Street* in my own fashion. John also had me learn many of his American art songs for which he was famous, especially performing the songs of his former colleague at Smith College, John Duke.

John also organized an annual Jewish Music week concert, already in the 1970s, well before the birth of the Triangle Jewish Chorale (TJC), which was around 1997. John and I were the main performers and Isabel Samfield was also involved—she later became director of the TJC—but we got all sorts of others involved as well. In 2000, I organized a tour of Israel for the TJC and other singers from the area with David (Dave) Stuntz as director—Dave was long-time director of music at Blacknall Presbyterian

Church and part-time instructor in choral music at the North Carolina School of Math and Science, and retired at the end of 2020. We had a full bus, forty-nine people with about seven non-singers. 2000 was the year of an almost successful peace effort in Israel and the trip was a huge success. A number of us have also participated in overseas trips with the former Duke Chapel Choir director, Rodney Wynkoop. These tours have included South Africa and Namibia, Brazil, Cuba, and Spain. Nancy Clapp-Channing was the principal organizer of those, and Carol has gone on all these wonderful trips and became an official alto singer on the second one. Our TJC traveled to Argentina in 2016 and Dave Stuntz joined Lorena Guillen our director as co-director for the tour. Pablo Stahlman our Argentinian cousin was hugely helpful in making the trip a success.

A highpoint in my Duke musical career was in 1988 when Rodney's predecessor as director of the Duke Chapel Choir, Benjamin (Ben) Smith, invited me to be the cantor soloist in a performance of Ernest Bloch's *Sacred Service*. John Hanks was thrilled and was ready to rehearse me and get me ready to sing with a chorus of around eighty souls and an orchestra of around thirty to forty, mainly musicians from the North Carolina Symphony. By way of practice and extra rehearsal, Ben asked me to sing small snippets in Sunday worship, which I gladly did, and it took some effort getting used to the three-second delay in the Duke Chapel. We only had two rehearsals with the orchestra, but that actually was enough since the choir and I had been rehearsing for months. Ben was the sweetest guy in the world and was very emotional. John had warned me that he often lost himself in the music so I would always have to be ready to do the music as written and as we had practiced just in case. My mom and sister came down for the performance and it was a Sunday afternoon. Ben was doing this to honor the Jewish community, which at that time thought it was celebrating the centennial of its first settlement. It turns out it was a bit older than a hundred that year.

The big Duke Chapel filled to overflowing—official seating capacity is 1800. Before the performance Ben pulled me aside with an arm around my shoulder, walked me out in the front of the Duke Chapel to the main entrance, and said to me with tears in his eyes: Duke Chapel and Duke University have not always been the most welcoming places for Jews and others, meaning blacks. This performance in Hebrew is a sign to all that this Chapel and this place is now a place for everyone to feel at home. He hugged me and we cried a bit, and he wished me good luck, and said "Break a leg." Little did I know that in a few short months Ben would be diagnosed with AIDS and not survive another year. Before he died, when I visited him at home and in the hospital, surrounded by his gay friends, he asked me to be an usher at his funeral. He said they would play our recording of the mourner's blessing from the end of Bloch's *Sacred Service*. So I literally sang at Ben's funeral. Miss you Ben after all these years. I performed the *Sacred Service* a few years later in Wilmington, North Carolina, with the Wilmington Chorale with organ accompaniment.

Carol and I have always been avid concertgoers, and Duke has had an illustrious history of bringing famous musicians to campus. One year Isaac Stern, the eminent violinist was on campus, and not surprisingly was a good friend of Uncle Marshall. We arranged a meeting in the lounge of our department and, as a result, Isaac put me in touch with his then wife, Vera, who was very involved with music in Israel. John Hanks had done a very successful concert and recording of Canadian art songs and wanted to do that for Israeli art songs, and so Vera Stern arranged for John to meet key composers in Israel and John collected all sorts of music of art songs and performed a selection of them on campus. Unfortunately, when John died, the corpus of music he had acquired seems to have been lost by Duke's music library or those who cleaned the house when his wife, Joan Tetel, sold it.

One more music story that I think is important has to do with my good friend George Gopen whom I had met at Brandeis years before when Carol and I were dorm and Quad counselors. Somewhere around the time of John Hanks' retirement from active teaching at Duke, 1988 or a bit earlier, George and I started doing music together, with George a very accomplished pianist and genuine connoisseur of classical music too. Together we commissioned several songs by an upcoming PhD student of Stephen Jaffe in music composition, Penka Kouneva, today a very well-known composer of Hollywood and TV music scores. Having just finished the first of two large volumes with Carol on Haggai and Zechariah, I thought having music that featured the story of the Exile and Return of the Jewish people to Israel would be a very positive thing to do and excellent story line. Penka started us off with some Psalms and the commissioning fee we paid her helped a lot with her expenses as a graduate student. Soon she expanded what she had done to include texts from Haggai and Zechariah. George and I performed the Psalms at the opening of the Sepphoris Exhibition at the North Carolina Museum of Art in Raleigh in 1997, and I subsequently performed them at an ecumenical service of worship at Illinois Wesleyan University where Dennis Groh was chaplain. Dennis had been a member of the Upper Galilee excavation team and later joined Jim Strange's staff at Sepphoris.

On a lecture visit to Stanford soon afterward I met Patrick Hunt, a faculty member and archaeologist who worked on Roman remains in Italy, France, and Switzerland of all places. It turns out Patrick is also a very distinguished composer. He invited me to his home, and he played me some music he had written and told me about his involvement with music at many levels, especially opera. I told him about Penka, and he volunteered to write a few songs to complete our new song cycle; and since he knew ancient Greek and Hebrew, he vowed to have the music reflect ancient modes of music. The result was just fabulous, and George and I somehow received an invitation to premier the entire cycle at the Israel Embassy in Washington, DC. We later performed it at the North Carolina Museum of Art and at various venues in Durham, e.g., Judea Reform Congregation on the occasion of the retirement of Rabbi John Friedman, but especially in soirees at George's house. We even have recorded it, and Patrick Hunt has featured parts of our performances on his web site (http://www.patrick-hunt.net/images/music/duke.jpg).

32

The Havurah

I WOULD BE REMISS if I did not mention our Shabbat *havurah*. *Havurah* means "fellowship" and our small group of couples—Marilyn and Peter Ornstein, Susan and Joel Leeb, and Elaine and Lee Marcus—have been having Shabbat together once a month for about twenty-five years as I write this except for during the pandemic. We have also celebrated many joyous occasions together. Actually, we could call our *havurah* our local family since we stand in for each other as a family member might. The toughest part about coming to North Carolina in 1969 was leaving our families back in Connecticut, Pennsylvania, and New York. By aligning ourselves together we in effect established a broader family network to simply be there for one another at a moment's notice. As we have gotten older, in years only I should say, this has become even more important. One of the reasons is that all of us have lost our parents and some of us, especially the Marcuses and Meyers have all of our loved ones up north (the Leebs and Ornsteins have one or both of their children nearby). It is tough to be so far away, but this is part of modern life that most of us have come to accept for better or worse. In thinking about my youth and growing up in a small town where all the family lived, most of my memories are associated with my extended family on both sides that had so great an influence on me. It was a defining part of my life.

The fact is that Carol and I miss our family, our girls, and our grandkids terribly and it is tough to accept FaceTime, Zoom and phone calls, text and emails, instead of having them close by—they help but it's not the same. But we have our local family and more than fifty years of connections here with many friends to make it easier to stay than to leave. The pandemic, however, has of necessity worsened everything, and Carol and I feel as if we have lost a year or more. On the other hand, because of our deep love and respect for one another being stranded at home has not been as bad as feared. And not having to worry about job security or money has taken away any sort of mental strain. Durham is our home, and we are happy to be here despite these reservations.

I should also note that there have been many friends besides the *Havurah* that have meant so much to us and continue to be important in our lives and not to mention family members in many different places but mostly in the northeast. The *Havurah* gave us continuity when we needed it and continues to do so, and we have often combined several of these groups to celebrate events such as secular New Year.

33

Health Concerns

It's so nice to be writing this years after having been properly diagnosed with Lev's disease or Lenègre syndrome, i.e., a complete loss of the electrical system that keeps the heart pumping, or in simple terms, complete heart block. Until June 2010 I had been misdiagnosed with a neurological disorder that caused syncope from time to time, the first episode occurring at Dina's when she lived in New York in the late 1990s. I passed out at her breakfast table one day and wound up at Columbia Presbyterian Hospital diagnosed with a TIA without deficit by the head of neurology there. Before allowing me to be dismissed from the hospital, the chair of neurology, an ancient history buff and not Jewish, prepared a pop quiz for me to see if my mind was OK. Most of the questions were about Masada and the Great Revolt, and I passed with flying colors. I was so relieved to leave and get back home to Carol. Several other episodes put me in Emory hospital once and at Duke, but I was still treated for anything but a heart disorder. The last diagnosis in Duke Neurology was that it was my old head injury from falling off the photo tower at Sepphoris that caused the syncope.

But on the first hole at Duke Golf Course in June 2010 playing with George Gopen, I keeled over out cold on the first tee only to "wake" up with an EMS attendant telling me I had to go to the hospital because of a severe bundle branch complication. I told him that this had occurred before and that I was certain it was my old head injury that had caused the syncope. But this was different: I fell from a standing position, injured my head and bruised my eyes, so I called my primary care physician (PCP). He said to read him a certain number on my EKG that had been taken, which I did; and when he heard what it was, he said get yourself over to Duke's emergency room—this is very serious.

HEALTH CONCERNS

By this time Carol was with me and drove me to the ER. In the intake examining room my heart literally stopped again, for I don't know how long, and the next thing I knew I was waking up with paddles on my chest and lying on a gurney and being rushed to surgery. That was when the diagnosis was finally made, and of course it was Friday afternoon and the right people were not around to put in a pacemaker and new leads to the heart. As a result, the ER team did a temporary job, which meant I was immobilized till late the following Monday morning when my surgeon, Dr. Sana al-Katib, put me on a device with two new leads to literally keep me alive. At first, I was completely dependent only on one side of the heart to provide the necessary electrical output to stimulate the heart, but ultimately, within a few years, I was completely dependent on both sides.

By 2016 I was not feeling well or very strong and when I complained to someone at Duke's Picket Road clinic and the resident there, an aspiring electrophysiologist, sent me to Dr. Thomas Gehrig for an appointment via my new PCP, Dr. Jeff Clough. At Dr. Gehrig's office I did a number of tests including a stress test, and he asked me not to leave the premises except for lunch. After more tests that afternoon, he said he had scheduled me in a few days for a surgical procedure to examine all of my arteries. My pacemaker, he said, was not doing a good enough job any more, but it could be that one or more arteries were blocked. After the procedure several days later he came to my bedside at Duke Hospital with Dr. Jason Koontz and said the good news is that my arteries are clear; the bad news is that I need a new pacemaker right away and an extra lead wire on one side. This would take place in less than a week.

Well it was certainly scary enough, but the outcome has been nothing less than amazing and life-changing. My new bi-ventricular device with three lead wires was helpful from day one out of the hospital, and years later I feel the best I have felt in decades. I am today simply a miracle of modern medicine and ever so grateful that my episodes in 2010 and 2016 were so close to Duke and that the first one did not occur a few minutes earlier when I was driving on the highway to the golf course and could have killed a bunch of people.

The new device, made by Boston Scientific, as you can imagine is quite sophisticated. After implantation, the one at my bedside was not a nurse but the computer technician from Boston Scientific in Minnesota. He was programming this and that and explaining to me about the scanner that I was to take home, which needed to be programmed as well. It was to be placed in a spot that could read my device at a given moment and report any abnormalities to the Duke Heart Center. It could also record an EKG easily, chart my breathing, as well as keep tabs on me. Can you believe it? That scanner is at my desk at home now watching over my artificial electrical system and doing a pretty good job.

All this came to a head on December 1, 2019, at Dina's when my implant device recorded a heartbeat of around 300 per minute as opposed to 62, to which the device was set. I had told Dina I was not feeling great but did not really make much of it. When we got back to Durham a few days later Dr. Koontz called and put me on the blood thinner Zarelto right away. Tests done at Duke revealed I now had A-fib and was in danger of having a stroke without blood thinners. A cardioversion (shock therapy to the heart) set my heartbeat back to 62 after a team of specialists did another miracle. Time will tell. Meanwhile my two knee replacement and one hip replacement are doing just fine, and I am still walking eighteen holes at the golf course.

34

Israel, Zionism, and the Jewish People

WHOEVER READS THIS MEMOIR one day might be asking at this point: after spending so much time in Israel over the course of some sixty years as of 2021 with my obvious liberal leanings, how have I managed to stay so attached to the Land and its people given the circumstances of the Occupation, the domination of the Orthodox right, and the blatant use of archaeology for political purposes? It has been a struggle for sure, especially when I observe the corrosive effect of some aspects of these factors on the moral compass of many fellow Jews as they continue to denigrate Arabs and accept their second-class status in the Land. While many Jews have not agreed with the direction of the Israel government these past decades as women have been banned from praying at the Western Wall, the Reform and Conservative movements labeled heretical and non-Jewish, and settlements kept and keep on getting more plentiful on private Arab lands, there have not been many opportunities for individuals like me to do anything that has had an impact. I pretty much always have spoken my mind on these matters, joining Peace Now in the 1970s and more recently being associated with J Street. I am also a big supporter of Emek Shaveh, which is laboring to save Jerusalem from fundamentalist bias and settler overreach in the City of David with its planned new museum at Dung Gate and cable-car plan. While the cable-car plan was overturned by the Supreme Court in March 2021, attempts to revive it are in the works.

The Jerusalem digs are all very well done, and with all outside monies flowing in they get the best staff archaeologists and do amazing things. But the Jerusalem excavations are not an inclusive project, and have not had a positive impact on or recognition of the people of Silwan. In fact, more and more houses there have been taken or demolished in the name of archaeology and tourism. Also, the true impact of Islam on the holy city, despite the Temple Mount with its two hallowed mosques, has not been allowed to be fully appreciated and observed. While the Temple Mount has been under the supervision of the Muslim Waqf for centuries and reporting to the Hashemite King, it has been reported that the Trump administration tried to get the reporting mechanism diverted to Saudi Arabia, hence tensions in early 2021 between Jordan and Israel. For the time being, however, Jordan remains in control of the holy places.

To be sure, the Palestinian Authority and its archaeological staff through the years have attempted to deny Israel's historical claims and most egregiously in clearing the underground space for the expansion of Al Aqsa Mosque on the Temple Mount threw out the excavated debris. The Israelis collected the debris and continue to sift it to this day and find ample evidence for Israel's presence on the Temple Mount in the first millennium BCE. But this is part of the political circus that surrounds Israel–Palestine talks today, and until each community recognizes the other's history and its uniqueness there can be no progress. The fact of the matter is that the ancient Israelites and Canaanites were both displaced peoples of common ethnic background who came together in the Holy Land to begin a new life apart from Egypt where some were slaves and apart from the city-states who oppressed others including the Canaanites, ancestors of the Palestinians. Recognizing this common beginning should help bring us together one day, with God's help, *inshallah*.

In recent years (2016–2019) Carol and I have led tours to Israel and Jordan either with the sponsorship of the local Jewish Community Center (JCC) or Duke Alumni Office that have focused on the historical heritage of the three religions of the book and the great empires of antiquity such as Greece and Rome, the purpose being to show how multiculturalism thrived under diverse auspices. A major case in point has been our work at Sepphoris whose residents did not participate in the Great War with Rome in 66–70 CE. Its decision managed to save the city and enable it to grow and prosper with a diverse population. By also going to Jordan we hoped to show how an Islamic nation, along with Israel a close neighbor and ally, deals with its population and modernity, and how it deals with the multicultural heritage of major historical epochs that are reflected in the material culture within its borders. We also intended to show that Israel's Arab neighbors are regular people with the same cares and concerns as their Israeli brothers and sisters over the Jordan River. While Israelis can travel to Jordan, in view of ongoing tensions in the region Israeli tourism to Jordan is down to a trickle in the 2000s. But at least Americans can develop a broader outlook on the state of affairs and can see a glimmer of hope for peace one day.

I was more hopeful before the two intifadas, but the explosion of horrendous acts of terrorism and suicide bombings in the late 1980s and early 1990s and then again later crippled if not killed any rapprochement between the children of Abraham. Carol and I were only a block or so away from one of the worst suicide bombings in Mahaneh Yehudah on July 30, 1997. When we heard the noise and felt the ground shake and saw smoke rise, we ran immediately back to our hotel. We turned on TV and wept, and cried, and hurt deeply. Those events set the peace movement back and it has never recovered.

In the Durham community in recent years Israel has become a subject so fraught that congregations and even our Jewish Federation have had to hire facilitators to have a civil discussion on aspects of the *matzav*, i.e., the Situation, and lack of progress in peace negotiation on any sort of level since at least 2000. The continuing conflict has also made it easier for anti-Semites to link the Israel conflict with their racial hatred of the Jewish people.

At Duke I have been working even in retirement with various colleagues to offer a greater variety of courses, internships, lectures for students of a more liberal inclination in respect to Israel affairs vis à vis Arabs. And in the fall of 2019, a former student from the 1980s, Bobby Green, today a physician and medical entrepreneur, established an undergraduate scholarship fund for students in Carol's and my honor to work in the areas of social justice and human rights in the US and/or Israel. Pretty proud of that, I must say. In all, despite what has happened, I have remained critically attached to Israel, emotionally involved in its history past and present, and committed to its future as an inclusive nation that is a beacon to its neighbors in the Middle East and beyond.

35

The Jewish Heritage (Foundation) North Carolina (JHNC)

HENRY GREENE, LEONARD (LEN) ROGOFF, and I have been leading this organization for around thirty years now and just in 2019 changed its name and took out the word "foundation" from its title since many individuals mistakenly thought we were in the business of making grants. The real purpose of the organization is to encourage the Jewish population of the state to learn about the history of Jews in North Carolina and to embrace and take pride in the unique story of North Carolina Jewry.

Before this not-for-profit was started, a small group of bibliophiles led by three Duke professors—Albert Heyman, Sydney Nathans, and me—had the idea of commissioning a history of Jews in Durham, and we turned to Len Rogoff to write it. About that time Duke Chapel had announced it was performing Bloch's *Sacred Service* (see above "Music and Singing") in honor of the local Jewish community and its long and distinguished history of one hundred years. Our bibliophiles group soon morphed into The Centennial Publications Committee because we thought that the Jewish community was around a hundred years old at the time but soon learned from Leonard that it was considerably older. On our committee was the future mayor of Durham, Steve Schewel.

Leonard's first book, *Homelands: Southern Jewish Identity in Durham and Chapel Hill, North Carolina*, appeared in 2001 at the University of Alabama Press, and soon after he organized a small exhibit of Jewish life in small towns in eastern North Carolina. One of my students, Robin Gruber, wrote a senior thesis in 1986 titled "From Pine Street to Watts Street: An Oral History of the Jews of Durham, North Carolina." Her tapes were essential listening-material for Leonard, especially the ones of Beth El Synagogue's

THE JEWISH HERITAGE (FOUNDATION) NORTH CAROLINA (JHNC)

chief *gabbai*, Gilbert (Gibby) Katz, whose account of anti-Semitism in the 1920s and 1930s is an alternative reading of history than that of Eli Evans's much more positive assessment in his *The Provincials*. In my years as president of JHNC, I commissioned a cantata to tell the story of our North Carolina Jewish community and Katz's tapes comprise a whole movement, "Say you can and you will." Alexandro Rutty, Professor of Music Composition at UNC-Greensboro, was the composer and selected texts from our archives to which he set appropriate music (see below).

Henry Greene, a close friend, an optometrist, and world-class specialist in low vision care, was our pioneering first president, and he led us from doing small exhibitions at Judea Reform Congregation to undertake an ambitious program of a statewide exhibit to commence at the North Carolina Museum of History in Raleigh and then travel around the state to other venues. In planning, we also decided to have Len Rogoff expand his purview and write a much larger book on the history and legacy of all of North Carolina's Jewish communities. The title of the exhibit, book, and cantata was *Down Home: Jewish Life in North Carolina*. After doing new interviews on video, yet another iteration of *Down Home* was born: the film. Produced by Henry Greene and award-winning videographer Steve Channing, using the JHNC Executive Committee as an advisory committee, the film also emerged as a huge success and is seen regularly on UNC TV and in synagogues and churches. Henry was an awesome fundraiser, and the exhibit and book and film required almost two million dollars to see the light of day. The Charlotte and Greensboro communities led the way, and the exhibit was a smash hit; the book is required reading for all Jewish newcomers to our great state. Henry's success in this phase was nothing short of phenomenal and wanting a rest turned over the reins to me in the early 2000s, and he remains treasurer to this day.

As the second president of JHNC, I wanted to tell the *Down Home* story in a musical way and collaborated with Alexandro Rutty on the text of the cantata, with Len's inputs as well. Our first performances were a big success, and the music and choral singing got universal high marks in reviews; they can be accessed on the web site: https://jewishnc.org/about-jhnc/ or the web site of the TJC: https://trianglejewishchorale.org/. Only one movement in the cantata was not based on JHNC's archival holdings and tapes: it was based on an interview Alexandro and I did with Henry Landsberger, a survivor of the *Kindertransport*. It was a novel way of treating the Holocaust, which obviously plays a huge role in our state as it does everywhere. Henry Greene and I ultimately got the Levine JCC in Charlotte to take some of the items from the exhibit and put them on permanent display.

In taking down the exhibit I realized that many items had been gathering in the suite of offices I had arranged for JHNC on the Duke campus, many of which we had no intention of keeping. JHNC was not to become a permanent museum, though we had been accepting things that were not display worthy for years. In rethinking many of our priorities, it was clear that the tapes and videos of our oral history work were invaluable and needed to be properly preserved and stored. JHNC was not equipped to do so. We also had to decide what to do with a collection of rare books, manuscripts, synagogue records, and other objects including some rare maps of the Holy Land that had been donated and other original art works of Jewish content. Since they were already on the Duke campus in Trent Hall near Duke Hospital South, we invited people from the rare book and archives section to assess what we had and see if they were interested. After several meetings, the Duke Library team said they were interested in most things, but a significant group of artifacts were simply of no historical or aesthetic value and could in no way be transferred to the Duke collection. Then came the big issue of who was going to pay to catalog the collection and make it accessible digitally. Well as director of Jewish Studies I still had some influence and some funds. After a bit of haggling, Duke agreed to take possession of the collection and to weed out what was not worthy. This work took nine months and cost lots more than we had anticipated. In the end it is now part of Duke's holdings in the David M. Rubenstein Rare Book & Manuscript Library at Duke (https://archives.lib.duke.edu/catalog/jhfnchistorical). Many of the rejects are still in storage at Duke in Trent, and JHNC has a plan to divest of them by auction or giveaways. Several items are now on display at the museum of the Southern Jewish Experience in New Orleans, and several pieces went on display at the North Carolina Museum of History this spring, 2022.

36

The Professoriate

Teaching as a Calling (*Beruf*)

I HAD NEVER PLANNED to be a field archaeologist until after meeting Carol. Once I decided to stay in graduate school and pursue archaeology and biblical studies, however, I knew I wanted to be a teacher at the college and university level. Little did I know that in developing a field school program for the excavations I could have both: I could continue teaching and mentoring in summers while excavating. In fact the kind of teaching and interaction with students that one has on a dig cannot be replicated on campus, except perhaps in a scientific lab, which is probably more oriented toward graduate students. Our staff on the dig was always composed of PhD students and professors, and whether it was in the trenches during the digging hours or at pottery reading and washing or registry, or at after dinner lectures, learning was at the core of the field experience. Also, on most weekends we organized study tours to the most important sites in the country, and sometimes to Jordan and once to Egypt. But in such an intimate environment close friendships were made, not only among the students but also between the faculty and students. The relationships formed on the dig go back over fifty years and Carol and I are in touch with many of them even today. Of course relationships formed in the classroom at Duke are also memorable but somehow the experience of digging in the dirt together brings about a sense of discovery that is hard if not impossible to replicate on campus. What one often discovered on a dig aside from ancient coins and pottery and other artifacts was one's own self, and the implication of that is realizing that one's own individual importance has to be understood in the long view of things. Archaeology surely puts things in perspective. And when all that is combined with readings, tours, lectures, etc. history becomes real and alive, and meaningful. The fellowship of diggers is unique and I know it often changes lives. It changed mine.

That is not to say graduate teaching and mentoring cannot result in the same sort of lasting relationships between student and teacher. Another unexpected surprise in my career was how much I would enjoy graduate teaching and how much I would derive from it in return. In selecting Duke as my "first" choice, I was influenced by both Professors Wright and Cross who thought that my position on the graduate faculty at Duke was very important to carry on the Harvard tradition: in their mind, that was the Albright tradition. In my view that meant that archaeology and material culture must be essential tools in learning about the social world of the Hebrew Bible, the New Testament, and the world of the rabbis and early Christianity. While today I can say that all these fields have been enriched by such interdisciplinary work, many graduate programs in their retrenchment are inclined to cut archaeology first because it is so expensive to sponsor, and often archaeology PhDs are a bit too narrow in their scholarly outlook to warrant a position in a program in biblical or religious studies. And in recent years I have been saddened to see the humanities decline at many Research One universities, less so at the small colleges. I would like to think that the students who have worked with me or Carol at Duke or in the field will carry on the tradition of combining a detailed knowledge of material culture that is relevant to their special field of interest. Carol's total engagement and familiarity with the material culture of the Iron Age has enabled her to recreate the daily life and the personal, everyday religious lives of women and men as few others have been able to do. Without my first-hand knowledge of the facts on the ground in the late Second Temple and early Roman period there is no way I could have so fully understood the literary sources of the period and the world of Jesus and the sages. Conveying these realia without the benefit of seeing the material remains and stepping physically into that environment is a genuine shortcoming of teaching such subjects only on an American campus, but it can be done with much effort and lots of PowerPoints and augmented reality. The mute stones, however, speak with the greatest clarity.

37

Epilogue

LOOKING BACK OVER FIFTY-PLUS years in Durham and Duke, the world has changed and so have all of us. The great thing about teaching history and archaeology let alone the sacred texts of tradition, is that one must remain humble and insignificant in the shadow of centuries of human accomplishment and achievement. Having had the opportunity not only to bring students to experience the past through uncovering it, but to excite their imaginations on campus as well, has been a blessing for Carol and me. To learn authentically about the past is to learn about oneself and discover how one sees him/herself over against earlier generations.

When I hear today that fifty percent of all American students today have never heard of the Holocaust, I am astonished and fearful. Focus on the present is apparent everywhere and I believe it is not healthy. Looking backwards into the riches of the past allows us to understand the present with new and fresh eyes. The pragmatism of the residents of Sepphoris to sit out the Great Revolt against Rome allowed it not only to survive but to prosper as a multicultural city and center of Jewish learning. Observing the grand sweep of cultures and peoples that overran the Levant and greater Middle East in antiquity—the Persians, the Greeks, the Romans, the Christians, and Muslims—allows us to appreciate better how individual cultures and peoples responded to those changes. In so many instances the response has been positive and creative, though in some cases negative.

ASOR, the American Society of Overseas Research, has been the preeminent organization for facilitating archaeological work in the region of the Middle East since 1900, and even before if we count its predecessor organization, the American Palestine Exploration Society. Today it embodies the very best of America's love of archaeology and has rightly changed its name to signify the shedding of its colonial roots. In recent years its adoption of and expansion of its cultural heritage initiative demonstrates how the field has evolved and continues to change for the better.

Sensitivity to the cultural heritage of Others as ASOR has chosen to foster, lies at the heart of archaeology and the world could use a big dose of that today. Archaeology can bring to life again the hidden voices of the past that may not have survived the publication of books and sacred texts that often pass over some of those voices. The people they represent may not appear in the monumental remains such as a temple or theater but arise out of the everyday remains of a kitchen or a simple room in a house. Those voices can be recovered only with greater attention to the quotidian household items that allow a family to exist day to day, which is where the discipline of archaeology is rightfully headed today.

Looking backwards to the past is a healthy way of looking to the future and an essential tool for understanding the present.

APPENDIX A

The Meyerowitz Family from Königsberg

APPENDIX A ON THE MEYEROWITZ FAMILY is adapted from a presentation at Duke and published in abridged form in *Nexus: Essays in German Jewish Studies*, vol.2, edited by William Collins Donahue and Martha B. Helfer. Rochester: Boydell & Brewer, 2014, "The Meyerowitz Family from Königsberg: Contemporaries of Hans-Joachim Schoeps," pp. 29–32.

My father, Karl Otto David Meyerowitz, was born in East Prussia in 1909, in Königsberg, home of the Jewish Reform Movement. The intellectual and religious currents unleashed in the Jewish Enlightenment or *Haskalah* in the eighteenth century were still being played out in the lifetime of my father.

My father was born into an aristocratic Prussian Jewish family. His father Benno was a wealthy textile factory owner, with a summer house on the sea and a schooner with a captain and mate as well. Benno Meyerowitz married Käthe Supplee, a Protestant Huguenot whose ancestors were from St. Petersburg; she converted to Judaism when Hitler came to power as a sign of resistance and family unity. She was a concert pianist and accomplished soprano. Benno was a co-founder of the Society for Königsberg Opera (Die Königsberger Operngesellschaft mbH) together with Bruno du Voitel in 1921, and they succeeded in ensuring that for the next years operatic programming would continue in the several theaters of the city. As successful businessmen, Meyerowitz and du Voitel guaranteed the performances in those hard economic times. Among the operas performed at that time were ones by the Jewish composer, Erich Wolfgang Korngold, *Die Tote Stadt* (*The Dead City*), and Alban Berg's, *Wozzek* (see http://kultur-in-ostpreussen.de/index.php?option=com_conten . . .). Opa Benno worked

APPENDIX A: THE MEYEROWITZ FAMILY FROM KÖNIGSBERG

as a volunteer and unpaid impresario and continued to promote opera and music in the several city venues for years. Ultimately he became Dirigent of the Königsberg State Opera as an unpaid manager and the family spent several nights a week either in the front row of the opera house or backstage watching the action unfold. My father knew Puccini and Verdi in German and studied voice while preparing to take over the family business after attending university. There were two older sisters, Eva and Leni, and their fateful lives also illuminate the social and intellectual world of Prussian Jewry in the 1920s and 1930s.

In 1922 my father became a Bar Mitzvah in the Great Liberal Synagogue of Königsberg where men and women sat separately and the men on such occasions wore cutaways and high hats as they did on all holidays. On Rosh Hashanah all the women received roses upon entering the synagogue. The cantor there was Manfred Lewandowski, great grandnephew of Louis Lewandowski, who died in 1894. The religious garb he wore included a high yarmulke and in his liturgical robe and collar could have been mistaken for a Lutheran pastor. While the holidays were celebrated at home after a fashion, the Jewish calendar did not greatly influence the lives of the Meyerowitz family. Passover seders were mostly celebrated at friends' houses. The click/clack of the boots of the Nazi Movement did, however, and the hopes and dreams of each of them were forever changed on that fateful day in January 1933 when Hitler came to power and Oma Käthe decided to become a Jew-by-choice.

Opa Benno could hardly believe that the Nazi Movement could succeed after he had achieved so much and considered himself to be the epitome of the good German citizen. His closest friend in the musical world was Richard Strauss who often visited in the Meyerowitz home to smoke and play Skat, and my father remembered sitting on his lap as a little tot. All of the Meyerowitz family loved Richard Strauss and his music and whenever criticisms of his behavior during and after the war would emerge, they would defend him and say he was not an anti-Semite and whatever he did was only to allow him to forge ahead with his music. Be that as it may, the love of Strauss at any cost symbolized for the family the halcyon days of life in Königsberg when there was no hint of the dark days that were to come.

A few more details about the family and then a concluding story that I believe sums up Benno's love of the Fatherland. Leni was a free spirit and wanted to be a ballerina, but Opa did not think this was a good life for an upperclass Jewish aristocrat. But Leni left home and became a

APPENDIX A: THE MEYEROWITZ FAMILY FROM KÖNIGSBERG

ballet dancer with the Hamburg Stadt Oper, and during her time there met and married a dentist, Peter Starke, some of whose family members were Nazi officers. Soon after Leni got pregnant, she and her husband moved to Persia where Starke served as the Shah's personal dentist. The son born to them, Tom, subsequently married one of the Shah's daughters. Leni ultimately divorced Starke and met and married a BP oilman, Dan Heaton, and moved to Isfahan just before the war. During this period she became a Christian and a British citizen and during the war was a translator from German to Persian and to English of messages intercepted by the British Foreign Service. She worked out of the British Ambassador's office in Teheran. Her wartime services in behalf of the Allied cause were recently recognized by the British Foreign Office after her death at age 102. She taught at the Laban Dance School in London after the war and retired to Switzerland where she passed away.

Eva, the older sister, married a Heidelberg-trained physician, Kurt Oppenheimer from Frankfurt, and they had a wonderful life in Prussia till things began to fall apart. In 1938, shortly after Crystal Night and after a terrifying visit from the Gestapo when Uncle Kurt and Walther Lehman, a close friend of the family and lieutenant governor of East Prussia and Jewish, were both briefly jailed. They were eventually freed with the intervention and assistance of an SS officer who had known Walther Lehman and no doubt was indebted to him in some way. There had been an escape plan for some time, and Eva recovered the name of the officer who would help in an emergency from a secret hiding place at home. With Kurt's and Walther's removal from prison the SS officer somehow secured safe passage for two months, which ultimately allowed the Oppenheimer family with their two girls, Susie and Hanni along with Walther, to escape to Cuba. After several years in Cuba and with the assistance of my father and his wife's family as well as Leni and friends who collectively had to offer a guarantee of employment and proof of financial wellbeing, the Oppenheimer family immigrated to the United States and settled near my father and his new family in Norwich, Connecticut.

My father had left earlier to the States on November 2 1934, and his first job in the US was as a singing waiter at Sardi's in New York City, singing arias and light operetta songs. He was met at Ellis Island by Opa's brother Eddie who had changed his name to "Meyers" and told Karl to do the same. Eddie was a real estate agent who once had had the Empire State Building as a property but also had many wives and lost most of his earnings. Karl somehow found his way to Norwich, Connecticut, where he worked in the familiar textile business for one Harry Land, whose son Edwin invented the Land Polaroid camera and attended my high school, the Norwich Free Academy, and Harvard, briefly. Father also met my mother there, Shirlee "Meyer" without an *s*, the daughter of a recently arrived pants manufacturer, Isaac and his wife Anita Meyer, formerly of Brooklyn, New York.

With Leni in Persia, Eva in Germany still, the most astonishing thing happened: Oma Käthe decided to come visit her only son in 1935 for one week in September, which she somehow managed to do and subsequently returned to Königsberg. Opa Benno came to visit his beloved "Karlchen" in October 1936 and was thrilled to see his son doing so well in Connecticut. After a brief visit he returned by ship to Königsberg just as Käthe had done the year before. The enigmatic question to all surviving members of the Meyerowitz family is this: If the two of them could get passage to the US so late and even manage to go back, why did they not leave or at the least encourage the Oppenheimers to leave? The answer is complicated, but in a sense the Prussian in Benno still believed that the Nazis would not succeed and that this awful era would pass and he would see his family in better days, which were not to come. The story until about twenty years ago was that Benno and Käthe stayed in Königsberg until the Nazis withheld his insulin medicine from him till he died. However, Käthe escaped and went underground. A death notice filed by my father and Aunt Eva in the German-Jewish publication, *Die Aufbau*, lists his death as having occurred on June 5, 1942, exactly two years after I was born. More recently, Michael Wines reported on a front page story in the *New York Times* on January 31, 2000, that all remaining Jews in Königsberg were rounded up and the men shot in a death march to the sea in 1945. Some of us thought that Benno could have been among them. In a recent interview with me in October 2012, Hanni Curland née Oppenheimer recalled that Benno was taken by the Nazis when mixed marriages were first targeted and forced to assemble in public, presumably in 1942; Käthe escaped but Opa was shot. Hanni also recalled that Käthe walked all the way from Königsberg to Poland where ultimately she found her way to a convent where nuns took her in until the war ended and she was able to reunite with Benno's family in Freiburg where his brother Felix lived. Felix's family had been spared due to the fact that the Allies had bombed city hall where all trace of their Jewish ancestry was destroyed.

APPENDIX A: THE MEYEROWITZ FAMILY FROM KÖNIGSBERG

Hanni also informed me how Oma Käthe was reunited with the Meyers and Oppenheimers in Norwich in 1947. For several years she had tried to make contact with the family without success until one day in a DP camp after the war she met a military person in charge of reuniting families who just happened to be from Norwich, Connecticut, and knew the Oppenheimer family well and undertook immediate steps to bring them together. While it was a joyous reunion, Käthe was never able or refused to tell her children all the details of how she survived except for what Hanni now recalls. Within several years she lost her mind to the point that she had to be permanently institutionalized. Her last years were spent in the Norwich State Hospital where we all visited regularly and she recognized no one and knew not who she was or where she was. However, and this is the most important part of the story: She played the piano like a professional still and sang songs to the other patients and never missed a word. Oma Käthe could play and sing *Fledermaus* for us, but the dark days of the Nazi era somehow had to be blocked out. Music was her last and only way of calling up the past, which was simply too awful.

Except for the survival of all three of the Meyerowitz children and their successful lives and their children's lives, this Prussian family saga had a rather unhappy ending. In Benno's love of Germany and Prussia in particular he shared much with so many other German Jews. Like so many other survivor families, however, the details of the Holocaust or the facts relating to the deaths, escape, or survival of relatives were hardly ever discussed at our home though the Jewish community in America found other ways to deal with the tragedy: through HIAS, the Hebrew Immigrant Aid Society, and its resettlement activities and through Zionism. But that is not a part of this story. Benno Meyerowitz believed in the absolute "Germanness" of German Jews. In the end, his confidence, I believe, was misplaced.

*I would like to express my sincere thanks to my cousin Jane Frieman of Harrison, New York, who in her passion for family history has helped with portions of this essay. She is the daughter of Susie Oppenheimer. I would also like to thank Hanni Curland, Susie's sister, for being the person who after all these years remembered so much and could talk about the past with such honesty and directness. May Susie's and Hanni's memory be for a blessing.

APPENDIX B

Dartmouth Phi Beta Kappa Address

Dartmouth Phi Beta Kappa Address, Graduation 2012
Eric M. Meyers, class of 1962

YOU MIGHT WANT TO ask why a member of the class of 1962 is being inducted with you today and addressing you at these ceremonies today. You might want to ask me, I suppose, if it has to do with my Fiftieth Reunion, which I am celebrating this weekend, and indeed it does. And yes, I have gone on to publish many books and articles and to achieve success in the academic world at Duke, which may or may not be of interest to you, but quite apart from my field of specialization I have a feeling that I have a few things to say that might be of interest to you as you set out on your careers. It's a whole new world for sure out there, and all the technological advances have not made it any easier, even though it may seem so. I had no cell phone when I was a student here and called home only once a week from a dorm pay phone, collect, to brief my parents on what I did in the week before, and normally that was Sunday night. I also was expected to write letters, which I faithfully did at least once a week. And I looked forward to the letters I would receive from family and friends for all special occasions, and I still have them.

My first question to you all is this: have you saved your favorite emails? You know you can with Google. I was pleasantly surprised when I turned 70 that my younger daughter had saved some of my best emails to her, and quoted from them at my birthday party. So don't miss out on saving some of these communications now that we live in cyberspace. By the way, in high antiquity literate civilizations kept their records on baked clay tablets, which were pretty much indestructible. So think twice when you switch computers or hard drives. And by the way, nothing can replace the importance of the spoken word! We also had no Xerox and no computers either in those days; it took an "all-nighter" for me to type up my term papers on my portable Olivetti along with correct-o-tape.

Dartmouth was single sex when I attended, and many of us felt seriously shortchanged by not having women around on a regular basis in the classroom and as social partners. So how did we deal with this? We got in our cars virtually every weekend after Saturday AM classes and schlepped to Northampton or Boston for a Saturday date. I found my future spouse in Boston at Wellesley College in grad school, but it took some doing. I did not find her at Bennington, which was always a targeted destination because the women there were so ahead of the times in certain ways. And in the process of going to Grad School in Boston I soon learned the kind of mentor and teacher I wanted to be, like the ones I had at College—at Harvard I learned how I did not want to teach and mentor. But I did learn in grad school the kind of scholar I wanted to become.

When I was invited to give this talk by the College I was told that often the speaker would try to be funny and that this was not a bad strategy along with being brief. So let me tell you about my first visit to Dartmouth in the spring of 1949 when I was almost nine years old. My uncle Marshall was a member of the class of 1952, and later the recipient of an honorary doctorate from the College; he was also my childhood mentor and principal babysitter, and he invited me to visit, a practice I continued every year even when he went to graduate school in New York. I went alone by train and was met at White River Junction and was welcomed to Wheeler Hall with great warmth by roommates and classmates alike. I opened my luggage and my grandmother's home-made cookies were consumed in short measure. After visiting classes and hanging out for a few days I got quite sick with the mumps, and soon a good portion of the dorm came down with them. My dad had to come get me from Connecticut since I was running a fever. The surprising thing was that the same gang let me come back the next year, and the next. There was no doubt I was going to go to Dartmouth from that time forth.

As a member of the class of 1962 you might not believe this but we actually had food fights in Thayer, protesting what we believed was the poor food we had to consume, especially the mystery meat and the fish on Friday. I'd heard about hazing and drunkenness in the fraternities but never experienced it firsthand since I never joined. I am genuinely upset with the recently reported forms of extreme behavior I read about, but leave it up to you leaders of the class of 2012 to help remedy a situation long overdue for a full review and overhaul. A group of us from the Dartmouth Players also often came marching into Thayer, shoulder to shoulder, to make fun of what we had to eat on a particular day, but today this seems kind of mild in light of what I have read recently. Practical jokes were not limited to food fights, however. One of the best ones we did was to empty out the dorm room of a graduating senior and put in sod on all the floors and then filled up the room again on top of the freshly laid lawn. When we were discovered we had to pay back the College for the sod we snitched for the joke, but watching that senior enter his room and scream out is something I will always remember. And at the Harvard–Dartmouth football game my senior year in Cambridge we somehow managed to paint the toilets green in a couple of dorms, including where I was spending the night. The next day at the game, however, the Harvard Marching Band mooned all of us on the Dartmouth side. So, lighten up a bit, and keep a sense of humor. I did experience some bullying and prejudice while here and have written about it in my reunion book. All I can say is that it has no place whatever in college life or in life at all and one needs to fight it at every stage.

As honorees for academic excellence you have a special opportunity to shape the future in your respective disciplines and professions. You are the very best that the College has to offer, at least at this stage. But remember you have benefitted somewhat from grade inflation and other factors, so don't be too overconfident: the real tests lie before you. What are some them? You will certainly see soon enough how smart you are and how those skills you strived so hard to achieve may or may or may not work for you. One can only do so much with the knowledge learned and the skills you honed here in College. Hopefully, you have also learned from your parents and friends here that a caring eye, a helping hand, and a listening ear will stand you in good stead in the world you enter and are a part of. Pure knowledge without good deeds can hardly make a difference; together, however, they will help create a better world. And be sure to judge every person on the scale of merit. As for the world of liberal arts that has opened up to you here, hopefully it will allow you in your everyday affairs to appreciate the beauty and variety of the arts as a means of enriching your individual and collective lives.

Eleazer Wheelock, a Yale graduate and founder and first president of the College in 1769, conceived the College as "The School of the Prophets," after the example of Elisha the prophet in the Hebrew Bible (2 Kings

6:1–7). While in those early days in the aftermath of the Great Awakening "School of the Prophets" meant the preservation and dissemination of true religion for people of all colors and background, we may also take from Eleazer's platform the ongoing call for education to be infused with the moral imperative that we take from the Hebrew prophets of old. At Duke all undergrads are subsidized and encouraged to participate in programs and activities that have a moral imperative and that encourage good citizenship, and that program is called "Duke Engage." So to you the best of the class of 2012, go forth from these hills with the lone pine above it and circle the girdled earth and make a difference; I know you will.

APPENDIX C
ASOR Obituaries/Tributes

ADDING THESE FEW TRIBUTES is simply my way of honoring their legacies in ASOR. As I note above they were my Holy Trinity and together made it possible for ASOR to move into the twenty-first century.

Scheuer Obituary

When Richard (Dick) Scheuer died in 2008 I wrote this obituary for the *ASOR Newsletter*:

Dick Scheuer (b. July 14, 1907, November 9, 2008) was one of ASOR's holy trinity, along with our board chair, P. E. MacAllister, and the late Charles Harris, past ASOR treasurer and longtime CAARI President. Dick was also an indefatigable supporter of the Albright Institute in Jerusalem within the ASOR family. As the 2007 recipient of the Richard J. Scheuer ASOR Medal one of the first things I did after receiving the award was to call Dick at home and he was absolutely thrilled with my selection. We reminisced about our long association and friendship and we talked about the future: how the archaeology of the region of the Middle East would take shape over the next years and how it might affect the peace process to which we were deeply committed. Dick Scheuer was a man of great insight and foresight; he knew what we did in Jerusalem and in the region was of great moment and would influence the politics of the region for good or for bad for a very long time.

My wife Carol and I got to know Dick when we were fellows at the HUC in Jerusalem in 1964–65 when we were enrolled at the College and participated in the 1964 seminar on biblical archaeology. Our guide in the Negev was Nelson Glueck, and Frank Cross was outgoing director of the school and our teacher in the summer seminar at HUC, later to be known as the Nelson Glueck School of Biblical Archaeology. Frank Cross was succeeded in the fall of 1964 by G. Ernest Wright. It was in that fall that the excavations of ancient Gezer began and Carol and I were part of the original staff on the team till 1969. During these years we came to love the Hebrew Union College in Jerusalem and got to know Dick and Nelson as the College embarked on a unique expansion of its Israel program. One of the things I remember most vividly from this time is the vision and commitment of Dick and Nelson to making a Jerusalem experience and the Jerusalem school a requirement and major part of the Reform Jewish experience, a requirement that went into effect in 1970. The new campus on 13 King David St. is in great measure the result of Dick's efforts and he was responsible for the hiring of the famed Israeli architect, Moshe Safdie, to draw plans for the expansion of the campus that was completed in 1986 and was featured in the Venice Biennale of 1991. Dick's efforts in behalf of HUC and the city of Jerusalem were recognized in Israel when he was awarded the highest honor of the city: "Yakir of Jerusalem," Beloved and Honorary Fellow of Jerusalem, an honor bestowed on only a select few. Dick was chair of the HUC board of governors from 1983–1990 but served on its board from 1962.

Dick was also a lover of his *alma mater*, Harvard College, from which he graduated in 1939 in Classics. In recent years he was instrumental in the campaign to build a new Hillel house at Harvard. Thirty years after his graduation from the College he graduated from New York University with an MA in Near Eastern History and Archaeology, which led him to his profound love and commitment to the archaeology of the land of Israel and of the greater Middle East. His support of ASOR and ASOR publications and the Gezer publications led the director of the Albright Institute, Sy Gitin, to comment: "He believed that if it wasn't published, it was as if it was never excavated." Dick Scheuer knew what it meant to be involved in archaeology and he challenged all of us to respond to its demands with all due efforts.

Dick also loved Jewish art and served as chairman of the board of the Jewish Museum in New York City from 1971–79 during which time I taught several courses there commuting from North Carolina. Dick's involvement with Jewish museums led him to help support the creation of the Skirball Cultural Center in Los Angeles and to establish the Art Committee for HUC-JIR New York's campus, a committee on which he served until his death. In 1979 he helped launch the organization of American Jewish

Museums. Dick was also an avid sailor and with his wife Joan raced a 210 class sailboat on Long Island Sound.

These details are but a snippet of the long and productive life of one of ASOR's and AIAR's angels, and one of the giants of those who have supported and participated in the expansion, growth, and maturation of biblical archeology. Richard Jonas Scheuer was a man of rare talent and energy and saw in the day-to-day workings of ASOR and AIAR the workings of something very special that could translate into a new vision of the Middle East as we know it. Dick was up to the minute about every detail of the Middle East peace process and was as downcast as the next person when terrorism struck. But as a student of ancient Near Eastern history and culture, he knew full well that better times would come and that an all-inclusive organization such as ASOR was best poised to help us realize a Middle East in which all parties could participate. While he did not live to see this happen, he at least saw in his mind's eye the hope all of us in ASOR share: that one day not in the too distant future, all peoples of the region would search into their past to rediscover their present and their future, just as HUC had done when it set down its roots in Jerusalem.

We in ASOR will miss Dick Scheuer for his vision, for his generosity of spirit, for his undying support for the Albright, and for all the nitty gritty things that ASOR has to do in order to fulfill Dick's dream that each dig in order to be a successful one must be one that publishes its results in a readable and timely way.

Dick was truly an angel, and because of that status he is still watching over us today and encouraging us to get over the current crisis and move ahead by making the past a road-sign to a better future. Dick: we miss you sorely and will never forget you. May you rest in peace and watch over us as we seek to do what you have always urged us to do.

Pershing Edwin (P. E.) MacAllister Tribute, 10/21/2019

Chris MacAllister, the son of P. E. MacAllister, asked me to write a one-pager to be read at P. E.'s funeral, and here it is:

As an academic and Biblical scholar for whom history is always a "teachable" moment, knowing P. E. all these years, from the early 1980s, has been a sheer pleasure and joy. Our mutual love of history and the Bible made us friends in the best and deepest sense. We often turned to the past to learn about ourselves and the present. And often the Bible spoke with a clarity and wisdom that reminded us of our common roots in the ancient Middle East. But we were united also in other voices of the past that we deeply respected and admired from the Classical World. Why do persons like P. E. and me and many others especially his friends in ASOR turn to history and archaeology for lessons? Because there are so many rich lessons to learn from.

In terms of the Old Testament? What did we learn from the two destructions of the Jerusalem Temple in 586 BC and 70 AD? That there was a creative spirit that would not take defeat on the ground to be the last word and the survivors edited and canonized the Bible as one way of dealing with the trauma, and developing private prayer as another way of dealing with it.

P. E. always saw that creative spirit at work in key moments of our past and would call them up to our attention to make a point about business, ethics, politics, or ASOR. History mattered and P. E. was a beacon for making history relevant. In times so overly focused on the present what with social media, cable new and the 24-hour news cycle, P. E. was always there to point out an historical precedent, and teach us something. In ASOR we often said our future lies in ruins, and for P. E. the mute stones of the past helped him and his archaeological fellows in ASOR [founded in 1900, and vibrant today as never before in large measure to P. E.'s largesse and vision], understand that a present shorn of its past is not one to last. P. E.'s legacy continues to be an inspiration for all of us today who seek to better understand ourselves and our future in light of the past.

APPENDIX D
The Rabbi Marshall T. Meyer Archive at Duke University

MY REMARKS AT THE dedication of the Marshall T. Meyers Human Rights Archive at Duke University,[1] Nasher Museum, March 16, 2009:

I want to thank Patrick Stawski and the individuals associated with the Human Rights Archives at Duke for making this event possible. As founder of the Center for Jewish Studies at Duke and now completing my fortieth year here, I am truly thrilled to be a part of this evening's activities honoring my late uncle, Rabbi Marshall T. Meyer.

This occasion is a very special one for me and our family: the Meyer/Meyers family. You see, my mother Shirlee, sister to Marshall Meyer, married a Meyers. When I was growing up in Norwich, Connecticut, we lived about a block away from Marshall's house on 16 Goldberg Ave., yes, you heard it correctly, "Goldberg Ave.," named after a very prominent local Jewish family. Our households were so intertwined our poor German shepherd, Prince, hardly knew where to go each day for food and attention. Uncle Marshall went away to Dartmouth in 1948 and was my principal babysitter, caregiver, you name it, along with his sister, my mom, and my grandmother Anita. This was another era but it served us well. And when Marshall was at Dartmouth, even as an eight year old I spent my vacations there, once even infecting a whole dorm (Wheeler) with mumps and they had me back the next year. I did the same when he went to JTS in NYC, spending my vacations with him there and visiting classes at the Seminary and Columbia and getting to know Rabbi Heschel and Marshall's other teachers. We also managed to go to the opera and all sorts of concerts, and I had the unique privilege of tending to Naomi when Marshall was too busy studying, and

1. See https://archives.lib.duke.edu/catalog/meyermarshall.

that was very special. In other words, Uncle Marshall and I were very close and my love of learning and especially for Jewish learning came from him. And as a child of a refugee German family whose father fled the Holocaust and who lost many relatives, I learned at an early age that we lived in a world in great need of repair and that the Jewish tradition offered one way to help make it a better place.

Rabbi Marshall T. Meyer celebration at the Nasher Museum, Duke University, March 16, 2009.

APPENDIX D: THE RABBI MARSHALL T. MEYER ARCHIVE

Marshall and Naomi went to Argentina in 1959 after he completed his rabbinic training and went on to start the Conservative Movement there, a legacy that lives on in the Seminario Rabbinico Latinoamericano, the Communidad Bet El, and synagogues over all of Latin America where ordained rabbis of his have taken over major congregations. It is not only a kind of modern Judaism that Marshall unleashed there and that we normally associate with America but also a true expression of prophetic Judaism that he took from his mentor, Rabbi Abraham Joshua Heschel, a towering figure in 20th century Jewish life who left his permanent mark on the Civil Rights Movement and the anti-War Movement in this country. Their vision of authentic Jewish life was infused with the imagination, moral grandeur, and spiritual vision of the prophets and the experience of the 1960s when Heschel and Martin Luther King marched hand in hand on the streets of Birmingham and Selma to show the world that all humanity was equal in the eyes of God and that the only way to express one's love of God was to ensure the love of all of one's fellow human beings regardless of race, gender, geography, or religious preference. Marshall brought that zeal of prophetic Judaism to Argentina and passed it on to his students and flock there and to New York when he returned to the Upper West Side and to B'nai Jeshurun (BJ) where two of his former rabbinical students who I have known for many years now hold sway in that congregation. BJ is where in 1840 Mordecai Manuel Noah declared that American Jews had an obligation to fight international anti-Semitism, in reference to the Damascus libel case that gripped America at the time, and help less privileged Jews all around the world. Marshall brought that kind of zeal to the Dirty War when he fought against the Junta and those improperly incarcerated like Jacobo Timmerman and Deborah Benchoam. For this he was honored by the later government of Argentina and by President Alfonsin with the Order of San Martin, and Alfonsin also put him on the national committee to examine this awful period in history as the only non-Argentinian.

His papers and wealth of material relating to this period of his life are now here at Duke University where they have been properly inventoried and now are available to all for examination. Naomi and our daughter Dina and Naomi and Marshall's daughter Anita spent innumerable hours organizing this material for FedEx and transfer to Special Collections, and we are so grateful to them and the whole Meyer family for allowing this material to be housed here. Carol and I have also established an archival collection here at Duke and people interested in the history of archeology in the Land of Israel or the study of women in Biblical society will have to come to the Rubenstein Library to find out about us as well. Patrick Stawski whose initiative it was for this celebration asked me to make a prayer or say something from the Jewish tradition that might make this day so very special, which it is. But let me simply quote the Ethics of the Fathers and the age-old saying attributed to Simon the Just: "The world is sustained on three pillars: (also in Hebrew) on Torah, on Service, and on deeds of loving kindness." And here I would emphasize deeds of loving kindness, which is really the basis for all human rights: the right of every individual to be treated with dignity and fairness by others, and the obligation each of us has to be our brother's and sister's keepers. And in the face of injustice, Marshall would have said in the words of the rabbis, "We have no right to be silent." And in a time or place when there are not those who can be authentic human beings in this regard, he would have said: "strive to be a real individual: *Sei a Mensch.*"

APPENDIX E

The Rabbi Abraham Joshua Heschel Archive at Duke University

My remarks at the dedication of the Abraham Joshua Heschel Archives and Exhibit,[1] Faith in Action, March 21, 2016:

Introduction to Susannah Heschel

Before introducing our main speaker in behalf of all the Rubenstein Library and Jewish studies faculty I want to thank Adrienne Krone, PhD candidate in Religion, for the fantastic work she has done in curating the Heschel exhibition and assisting in the process of identifying and cataloguing alongside Rachel Ariel, librarian, the Heschel archive. Adrienne please stand and let us give her a hearty round of applause. What an absolute honor it is for me to introduce to you Susannah Heschel on the occasion of the opening of the special exhibit in honor of her beloved, late father: *Faith in Action: In the Footsteps of Abraham Joshua Heschel From Europe on the Brink of World War II to Selma at the Height of the Civil Rights Movement.*

I know it may be hard for many of you to believe but I have had the pleasure of knowing Susannah since she was an infant when I first began visiting the Jewish Theological Seminary of American where my uncle, Rabbi Marshall Meyer, was her father's student and teaching assistant after graduating from Dartmouth College. In those year when my uncle was at the Seminary I also had the privilege of getting to know Rabbi Heschel as well whom I had the pleasure of later hosting at Dartmouth when he was a distinguished visitor there for a week in my senior year. So let me state at

1. See https://archives.lib.duke.edu/catalog/heschelabraham.

the outset, today's program may seem to you as a kind of love fest and I will admit straight away, that's what it is.

Faith in Action: In the Footsteps of Abraham Joshua Heschel

From Europe on the Brink of World War II to Selma at the Height of the Civil Rights Movement

Announcement of exhibit from the Rabbi Abraham Joshua Heschel Archive at Duke University, March 21, 2016.

Let me say just a few words about Professor Heschel before we get any farther. She is Eli Black Professor of Religion and Jewish Studies at Dartmouth College, how appropriate is that! She received her PhD from the University of Pennsylvania and taught at Southern Methodist University at the beginning of her professional career. She then was Abba Hillel Silver Professor of Jewish Studies at Case Western Reserve University for seven years before going to Dartmouth. She has also served as Martin Buber Visiting Professor at Johannes Gutenberg University in Mainz, Cape Town University in South Africa, and Princeton University. In the exhibit if you haven't noticed it already, under the heading "Heschel the Scholar," you will find a letter of Susannah's that she wrote as a sixth-grader at the Agnes Russell School in New York in response to the question: What is a professor? She wrote: "A professor is a person who studies hard. He [sic] will teach and usually write books. Sometimes he lectures. There are many kinds of professors: there are professors of philosophy, arithmetic, science, etc. A professor doesn't teach grade or high school. He teaches in college or universities. Professors have many jobs: teaching, writing, lecturing. I like professors. My father is a professor!" How sweet was that, writing her own job description as a child. How prescient she was!

Dr. Heschel was the Rockefeller Fellow at our own National Humanities Center in Durham and also recently was a fellow at the Wissenshaftskolleg in Berlin. She has also held major grants from the Carnegie, Ford, and Guggenheim foundations. Her scholarly work has focused on Jewish-Christian relations in Germany during the 19th and 20th century, the history of biblical scholarship, and the history of anti-Semitism. Her book *Abraham Geiger and the Jewish Jesus* won the national Jewish Book Award, and her more recent book, *The Aryan Jesus: Christian Theologians and the Bible in Nazi Germany*, not surprisingly, has spawned a healthy and robust discussion in many circles. She has also been an eloquent spokesperson on the subject of her father's writings and witness and they are reflected in her many articles, books, lectures, and TV appearances. Today's talk will focus in on aspects of the archive on display and her father's work in general. It will be followed by a dialogue with me.

But let me say something about how this treasure trove of Rabbi Heschel came to Duke. I believe the germ of the idea was planted when Susannah came down to speak at the dedication of the Rabbi Marshall T. Meyer archive, which at that time was the anchor of what I now like to call "The Jewish Human Rights Collection at Duke University," not an official title but nonetheless fitting. That was in 2009. I think both Susannah and I would agree that Marshall enjoyed a very special and precious relationship with Rabbi Heschel and in many ways ensured that Rabbi Heschel's legacy would be carried on worldwide as he did so wonderfully in Argentina and in Latin America and in New York at the end of this life, and of course through the hundreds of rabbis who studies with him in Buenos Aires and who are continuing in the Heschel-Meyer tradition. I call your attention to two letters of Rabbi Meyer on exhibit, his letter of condolence, and under Heschel the Scholar a letter dated April 12, 1965: "It is from you whom I have drunk so deeply as to receive refreshment and strength for the task that lies ahead." Marshall was still at Seminary when he wrote that. Let me close my opening remarks by first quoting from a letter that is not on display and that Marshall wrote to Rabbi Heschel on January 5, 1992, twenty years after Heschel's death. He wrote: "I bless your memory now and always and thank you each day of my life. I am convinced that human beings will be studying your words centuries hence. Your teachings and your love and your understanding mean more to me each day. I can only hope that you are somewhat pleased with what I have done under your inspiration. Certainly, my love for you has only grown through the years, As ever, your devoted student in love, Marshall." (MTM archive). How appropriate that these two rabbinic activists, mentor and disciple, are reunited here at Duke in the Rubenstein Library.

There is also the matter of ecumenicism and interfaith activities, and you will notice the influence of Rabbi Heschel on Vatican II with two items on display as well. I don't know if Susannah would agree with this but I see his interfaith activities arising out of his life-long love of biblical prophecy and the relationship between universalism and particularism that inheres in much of that legacy. And this he also passed on the to the 88 ordained rabbis who graduated from the Abraham Joshua Heschel Rabbinic School in Buenos Aires and many educators and cantors who still attend the Marshall Meyer Seminario Rabbinico Latinoamericano in Buenos Aires. Having visited there this past summer I can say that the Heschel influence still predominates, and it is where Pope Francis as a young priest, Father Bergoglio, visited and studied who today cites that experience as impressing upon him the importance of interfaith activities and social action, in his recent book with Rabbi Skorka, *Heaven and Earth*.

And finally, there is another scholar today who is in a similar way to Susannah and Marshall devoting his energies to calling attention to Rabbi Heschel's prophetic faith and social activism: "Heschel puts the stress on deeds, courage, sacrifice, and service to others," which is what the distinguished African American scholar, Cornell West, said recently when interviewed by the *Jewish Week* in regard to his book for Princeton University Press on Heschel's poetry, piety, and prophecy. West also said, "Part of my mission is to make the world safe for the legacy of Martin Luther King. And Heschel is one of the major figures who enables King ... Heschel is a bearer of that great spiritual moral revolution all the way back to Hebrew Scripture."

And now I have the great privilege and honor to present to you Susannah Heschel, dear friend and the direct bearer of her father's mantel, who in publishing many of her father's writings many of which are in our Duke collection, correctly entitled a book of his major essays, which also beautifully summarizes her father's legacy, "Moral Grandeur and Spiritual Audacity: Essays of Abraham Joshua Heschel." The short title pretty accurately sums up your father's life.

Susannah: Welcome back to Duke!

Index

Abraham Joshua Heschel Rabbinic
    School (Buenos Aires), 207
Adelman, Michael, 14–15
Adler, Cecile (cousin; née Padal), 76
Adler, Morris (cousin), 76
Agnon, S. Y., 57
Aharoni, Yohanan, 55, 58, 60
Akel family, 107
Albright, W. F., 55, 58, 184
Albright Institute of Archaeological
    Research (AIAR), 32, 72, 77,
    96–98, 100, 102–3, 109, 127, 129,
    131, 139, 141–43, 154, 160, 163,
    196–98
Alfonsin, Raúl, 202
al-Katib, Sana, 175
Altmann, Alexander, 42
American Academy in Rome, 154–55
American Center of Research (ACOR),
    142
American Jewish Museums, 197–98
American Palestine Exploration Society,
    185
Anchor Bible commentary, 84, 110, 122,
    140
Anglican International School, 102
Annenberg Foundation, 149
Annenberg Research Institute, 148–49.
    See also Dropsie College/
    University
Annenberg, Walter, 148–49
Arad. *See* Tel Arad (excavation)

Archaeological Institute of America
    (AIA), 145
Ariel, Rachel, 204
Arnold, Philip, 36
Assad, Mr., 102
Ashdod (excavation), 61, 109
ASOR, x, 32, 55, 60, 72, 74–75, 77, 87,
    98, 105, 109, 122–23, 127–28,
    130, 135, 140–46, 148–49, 154,
    185–86, 196–99
Association of Jewish Studies (AJS), 105
Aufbau, Die, 190
Aviam, Mordecai (Motti), 117
Avigad, Nachman, 45, 115
Aviram, Joseph, 129
Axelrod, Albert (Al), 42

Baker, Harold, 14–15, 72
Balouka, Marva, 132, 137–38
Bardo Museum (Tunisia), 125
Bar-Natan, Rachel, 132
Barras, Rabbi, 47
Becker, Fritz, 112
Beebe, Ms., 14
Benchoam, Deborah, 202
Ben Gurion, David, 54–55
Ben Tor, Amnon, 59
Berg, Alban, 187
Berger, Herbert, 168
Berger, Rivkah (Pukul), 132
Bertholdt, Fred, 21, 27, 32, 39–40
Bertholdt, Marjorie, 27
Beth El Synagogue, 167–68, 180–81

INDEX

Beth Jacob Hebrew School, 14–15, 18
Beth Jacob Synagogue, 7, 9–10, 14, 17–18, 23
Biblical Archaeologist (BA), 109, 122, 133–35, 141, 143–44
Bilgray, Albert, 97–98
Biran, Avraham, 93, 101
Bizet, Georges, 9
Björling, Jussi, 9, 14
Bland, Kalman (Kal), 94–95, 104, 111
Bloch, Ernest, 169–70, 180
Blue, John, 28
B'nai Jeshurun, 202
Bodemann, Michael, 64
Boston Area Seminar for International Students (BASIS), 63–64
Boston College Law School, 43
Boston University, 63, 145
Boyd, Bernard, 102
Brandeis University, x, 32, 37–43, 45–47, 53, 56, 61, 64, 74, 94, 170
Brettman, Estelle, 112–14
Brickner, Balfour, 119
Brickner, Doris, 112–14, 119
Brigham Young University, 154
Brooks, Patsy, 31
Brooks, Russ, 30–31
Brown University, 127–28, 145
Bruzelius, Caroline, 154–55
Buber, Martin, 53–54, 58, 152, 205
Bucaria, Nicolas, 154
Buckley, Kevin, 15
Bull, Robert Jehu, 73
Bulletin of the American Schools of Oriental Research (BASOR), 141–43
Burrus, Sean, 80
Bushell, Matt (cousin), 126

Camp B'nai B'rith, 32–34
Camp Judaea, 106
Camp Quinibaug, 17
Camp Ramah, 40
Camp Woodrest, 13
Cape Town University, 205
Carroll, Lucius, 14
Case Western Reserve University, 205

Center for Jewish Studies at the University of Pennsylvania. *See* Annenberg Research Institute and Dropsie College/University
Center for Theological Inquiry, 140
Channing, Steve, 181
Charlesworth, James H. (Jim), 83, 140
Chautauqua, 126, 135–36
Clapp-Channing, Nancy, 169
Clough, Jeff, 175
Coit, Mike, 41
Colafemmina, Cesare, 112–14
Combined Jewish Philanthropies of Greater Boston, 71
Communidad Bet El, 202
Comstock, Ms., 14
Cooper, James Fennimore, 14
Cooperative Program in Judaic Studies (Duke and UNC), 85, 94–95
Cornell University, 128
Crenshaw, James L., 111
Crete, 103
Cross, Carol, 66
Cross, Frank Moore, 53, 55–57, 64–65, 74–75, 83–84, 184, 196–97
Curland, Hanni. *See* Oppenheimer, Hanni
Custos Terra Sancta, 137
Cyprus American Archaeological Research Institute (CAARI), 142, 196

Dartmouth College, x, 10, 13, 21, 23–41, 46, 67, 162 192–95
David M. Rubenstein Rare Book & Manuscript Library, x, 162, 164, 182, 185, 203–4, 206–7
Davies, W. D., 83, 110
Dello Russo, Jessica, 114
Denk, Jackie, 82
Denk, Jeremy, 82
Denk, Joe, 82
Department of Antiquities. *See* Israel Antiquities Authority (IAA)
Dever, Norma, 96
Dever, William (Bill), 58, 96–98
Dickey, John Sloan, 25, 39

210

INDEX

Dionysos Mansion/Villa (Sepphoris), 134–35, 138
Dionysos mosaic (Sepphoris), 132, 136
Dorot Foundation, 128
Down Home: Jewish Life in North Carolina, 181
Drinan, Robert, SJ, 43–44
Dropsie College/University, 74, 98, 148–49
Dubilier, Karen, 113
Dubovsky, Peter, S.J., 159
Duke, John, 168
Duke Divinity School, 75, 83–84, 101, 163
Duke University, x, 32, 36, 74–76, 82–86, 89–90, 94–98, 100–101, 104, 106–7, 109–11, 113, 118–19, 121, 123, 125, 128, 136, 138–40, 145, 148–49, 151–54, 159, 163, 169–70, 174–75, 180, 182–85, 187, 192, 195, 200, 202, 207
   Alumni Office, 178
   Archives, 3, 162
   basketball, 18, 150
   Chapel, 106, 119–20, 169, 180
   Duke Engage, 195
   Duke in Berlin Program, 153
   Golf Course, 10, 174
   Graduate Faculty in Religion, 83, 110, 184
   graduates, 35, 119
   Hospital, 89, 174–76, 182
   Human Rights Archives, 200
   Library, x, 182
   Summer School, 85–86
du Voitel, Bruno, 187

Ebla/Tel Mardikh (excavation), 109
Edwards, Douglas, 87
Eisenberg, Lotta, 79
Eisenbraun, Jim, 123
Eisenbrauns, 123, 138
Emek Shaveh, 177
Emily M, 15
Evans, Eli, 181
Evans, Emanuel (Mutt), 85, 94–95
Evans, Sara, 85, 94

Ezrahi, Sidra 68
Ezrahi, Yaron, 68

Fatfut, 92
Feingold, Dave, 29–30
Fellner, Fritz, 37
Fentress, Elizabeth, 155
Fiano, Emanuel, 80
Finkelstein, Louis, 39
Fischer, Heinrich, 41
Fitz, Mike, 30–31, 33–35, 37
Flesher, Paul, x, 185
Fletcher, Martin, 132, 134
Foerster, Gideon, 59
Franchon, Patrick, 34
Francis, Pope (Jorge Mario Bergoglio), 207
Franz Schubert Conservatory. *See* Horak Conservatory
Friedl, Ernestine, 119
Free University of Berlin, 153
Freedman, David Noel, 77–78, 109, 122, 125
Freedman, Theodore (Ted), 47, 57
Frerichs, Ernest, 127
Friedman, Hillel, 40
Friedman, John, 171
Frieman, Jane (cousin; née Horwitz), 96, 191
Fritz, Volkmar, 56, 151
Frost, Robert, 39
Fuerstein, Amanda (cousin), 126
Fuerstein, Henry, 126
Fuerstein, Sidney, 126

Gager, John, 74, 140
Galilee, ix, 53, 55, 77–78, 88, 91, 123, 125, 132, 135
   Lower Galilee, x, 122, 185
   Sea of Galilee, 61, 79, 108
   Upper Galilee, x, 78, 84, 88, 115, 122–23, 171, 185
Gardener, Tommy, 33
Gehrig, Thomas, 175
German Archaeological School, 56
Gezer. *See* Tel Gezer (excavation)
Giorgi, Dieter, 152

INDEX

Gitin, Seymour (Sy), 139, 197
Glatzer, Nahum, 32, 37, 42–43
Glueck, Nelson, 55–56, 58, 72–73, 102, 196–97
Glueck School of Archaeology, 72
G & M Manufacturing Co., 5, 9–10, 12
Goldberg, Bev, 11, 13
Goldberg, Cook, 11, 13
Goldin, Judah, 83
Goldovsky, Boris, 43
Good Morning America, 119
Goodenough, Erwin, 37–38, 42–43, 46
Gopen, George, 170, 174
Gordon, Ben, 80
Gordon, Cyrus, 42
Gottesfield, Phillip, 5
Gottesman, Jane, 136
Gottesman, Sadie, 135
Grassi, Giovanna, 160
Green, Bobby, 179
Greenberg, Moshe, 45, 47
Greene, Henry, 180–82
Greenfield, Jonas, 102–3
Greyber, Daniel, 168
Groh, Dennis, 171
Gruber, Robin, 180
Gush Ḥalav (excavation), 78, 80, 107–8, 115

Hadassah Hospital, 103
Hagerman, Chuck, 28, 33
Halperin, Benjamin, 42
Halperin, David, 95
Hamilton College, 140
Hanks, John, 100–101, 107, 168–70
Hanson, Simon, 74
Haran, Menahem, 103
Harrington, Daniel (Dan), S.J., 65–66
Harris, Charles, 142–43, 146, 196
Hartman, David, 119
Harvard College, 197
Harvard Divinity School, 68, 77
Harvard Semitic Museum, 45, 58, 65, 88
Harvard University, 31–32, 37, 43, 45, 47, 53, 55, 58, 60–61, 63–77, 84, 88–89, 98, 128, 145, 152, 159, 184, 190, 193–94, 197

Near Eastern Languages and Literatures (NELL; Harvard), 65–66, 76
Haskalah (Jewish Enlightenment), 187
Heaton, Dan (uncle), 189
Heaton, Leni (aunt; née Meyerowitz), 7, 10, 62, 125, 188–90
Heaton, Tom (cousin), 189
Hebrew Immigrant Aid Society (HIAS), 191
Hebrew Union College (HUC), 27, 45, 49, 53, 55–56, 58, 60, 67–68, 72, 98, 142, 196–98
Hebrew University (Jerusalem), 45, 56–57, 101, 131–32, 134, 136–39
Heine, Heinrich, 36
Hell Gap, Wyoming (excavation), 60–61
Hendin, Dave, 80
Hendricks, Kate, 138
Herodium (excavation), 131, 134
Herzog, Fred, 75
Heschel, Abraham Joshua, 22–23, 32–34, 38–39, 162–64, 200, 202, 204–7
Heschel, Susannah, 22, 162–64, 204–7
Heyman, Albert, 180
Hillel: The Foundation for Jewish Campus Life, 27, 32–34, 38–39, 42–43, 46, 94, 197
Hillerbrand, Hans, 83
Hobbs, Marcus, 75–76
Hoffman, Stephen, 36
Homelands: Southern Jewish Identity in Durham and Chapel Hill, North Carolina, 180
Horak Conservatory, 35
Hunt, James B., Jr. (Jim), 95, 124
Hunt, Patrick, 171

Illinois Wesleyan University, 171
Immanuel Kant University, 7
Indiana University, 74, 94
International Catacomb Society, 114
Institute for European Studies (IES), 35–37
Institute of Christian Antiquity (Bari), 113
Ipke-Awujor, Kingsley, 63–64

INDEX

Isaac, Ephraim, 60
Isenberg, Shelly, 75–76
Israel Antiquities Authority (IAA), 77, 117, 137, 139, 154
Israel Embassy (Washington, DC), 171
Israel Museum, 57, 115, 134, 136
Irwin, James, 126
Itzkowitz, Yudah, 91

J Street, 177
Jacob Pfizenmayer (grandson), x, 159–60
Jaffe, Stephen, 170
James, Herbert, 26
Jenkins, Oli, 84
Jericho (excavation), 101, 131, 134
Jewish Community Center (JCC), 178, 182
Jewish Federation, 179
Jewish Heritage (Foundation) North Carolina (JHNC), 180–82
Jewish Museum (Berlin), 56
Jewish Museum (New York City), 197
Jewish National Fund (JNF), 115, 117, 132, 134
Jewish Studies Program, Duke, 94
Jewish Studies Program, Free University of Berlin, 153
Jewish Studies Program, University of Arizona, 97–98
Jewish Theological Seminary (JTS), 39, 57, 59, 67, 200
Jibrin, Omar, 72, 100, 102, 143
Johann Wolfgang Goethe University, Frankfurt, 151–53
Johns Hopkins University, 142–45
John Meyer of Norwich, 9, 15, 24
Johns, Christa, 83, 85
Johns, Dan, 83
Johns, Sheridan, 83
Joint Sepphoris Project (JSP), 102, 131, 138. See also Sepphoris (excavation)
Jones, Indiana, 120
Jones of New York, 15
Joukowsky, Artemis (Artie), 145
Joukowsky, Martha, 145
Judea Reform Congregation, 171, 181

Kando, 143
Kanael, Baruch, 74
Kaplan, Seymour, 149
Kastel, Dina, 97, 139
Katz, Gilbert (Gibby), 180–81
Katzenstein, Martin, 68
Katzir, Ephraim, 101
Kaufmann, Yehezkel, 66
Kazis, Israel, 43
Kemeny, John, 37
Kennedy, John F., 39
Kessner, Frau, 35
Khirbet Shemaʿ, 78, 80, 85–87, 92, 96
Khouri, Hayal, 108
Kindertransport, 181
King, Martin Luther, Jr., 202, 207
Koester, Helmut, 73
Kohl, Heinrich, 115
Kollek, Teddy, 129
Königsberger Operngesellschaft mbH, Die, 187
Koontz, Jason, 175–76
Korngold, Erich Wolfgang, 187
Kouneva, Penka, 170–71
Kraabel, A. Thomas (Tom), 73–74, 88, 92
Kravetz, Julius, 27–28, 32, 39
Krone, Adrienne, 204
Kunwald, Ernst, 7–8

Lacheman, Ernest, 47
Lacy, Corky, 83
Lakin, Martin, 76
Lambdin, Thomas, 65–66
Lance, H. Darrell, 58
Land, Edwin, 190
Land, Harry, 190
Landsberger, Henry, 181
Lanfer, Roy, 26
Langford, Thomas (Tommy), 75–76, 89, 102
La Verne University, 134
Lavi, Jamilla, 64
Lazarus, Mark, 107
Leeb, Joel, 172
Leeb, Susan, 123, 172
Lefkowitz, David, 107
Lehmann, Walther (Uncle Vacky), 8, 10, 189

INDEX

Leiden University, 159
Levine Jewish Community Center (Charlotte), 182
Levy, Leon, 127–28, 130
Lewandowski, Louis, 188
Lewandowski, Manfred, 188
L'Heureux, Georgie, 15
Lindsay, John, 76
Lindstrom Foundation for Archaeological Research and Development, 87
Lindstrom, Gary (Termite), 87–88, 107–8, 117
London Observer, 60
Lyons, Charlie (brother-in-law), 77, 92
Lyons, Harry (father-in-law), 47–49, 61
Lyons, Irene (mother-in-law), 47–49
Lyons, Max (uncle), 47–48

MacAllister, Chris, 198
MacAllister, Pershing Edwin (P. E.), 142–43, 146, 196, 198–99
Macht, Richard (Dick), 30, 34
Macht, Steve, 30, 34
Maltzman, Marshall, 22, 47
Marans, Jon, 35–36
Marcus, Elaine, 172
Marcus, Joel, 110
Marcus, Lee, 172
Marshall T. Meyer Seminario Rabbinico Latinoamericano, 202, 207
Martin, Dale, 152
Masada (excavation), 58–60, 74, 80, 127, 134, 160, 174
Mashkan, Josef, 25–36
McCarter, Kyle, 141–42
Meiron Excavation Project (MEP), 89, 96–97, 123, 139
Meironi, Eli, 92
Merrill, Robert, 9
Metropolitan Opera, 6, 13
Meyer, Anita (grandmother), 3–4, 8, 10–11, 16, 19, 21–22, 29, 46, 190, 200
Meyer, Anita (cousin), 160, 163, 202
Meyer, Arlene (aunt), 12, 30, 40, 49, 69–70, 83

Meyer, Emily (cousin), 70
Meyer, Gaby (cousin), 160, 163
Meyer, Isaac (Ike; grandfather), 3, 5, 8–11, 20–22, 190
Meyer, John (uncle), 5, 9–11, 30, 40, 48–49, 69–70, 82
Meyer, Lisa (cousin), 70, 126
Meyer, Marshall T. (uncle), 3, 6, 8–11, 13, 17–18, 21–22, 27, 29, 32, 40–41, 47, 57, 96, 106, 146, 162–63, 170, 193, 200–203, 206
Meyer, Naomi (aunt), 47, 160, 162–63 200, 202
Meyer, Robbie (cousin), 70, 96
Meyerowitz, Benno (aka Opa; grandfather), 7–8, 12–13, 187–91
Meyerowitz, Eva. *See* Oppenheimer, Eva
Meyerowitz, Felix (great uncle), 190
Meyerowitz, Käthe (aka Mutti or Oma; grandmother; née Supplee), 7, 13, 46, 187–91
Meyerowitz, Leni. *See* Heaton, Leni
Meyers, Carol (wife; née Lyons), ix–x, 12, 27, 43, 45–49, 55–71, 73–74, 76–77, 79–80, 82–83, 87, 89–90, 92, 96, 98, 102–4, 106, 108–11, 118–24, 127, 129–32, 134–41, 146–47, 149, 151–52, 157–60, 167, 169–70, 172–75, 178–79, 183–85, 196–97, 202
Meyers, Connie (sister), 5–6, 8–9, 11–15, 19, 30–31, 34, 40, 63–64, 89, 105, 146–48, 169
Meyers, Dina (daughter), ix, 12, 74, 89, 100, 102, 106, 124, 131, 140, 146, 148, 152, 159, 163, 167–68, 174, 176, 192, 202
Meyers, Eddie (uncle), 3, 189
Meyers, Julie (daughter), ix, 64, 71, 76–77, 82, 88, 100, 102, 106, 124, 126, 131, 140, 146, 149–50, 152, 159, 168
Meyers, Karl (father), 3–4, 6–7, 10–15, 19–20, 22, 24–26, 29–30, 40–41, 67, 69, 76, 105, 145–46, 187, 189–90, 193
Meyers, Mary Ann, 149

INDEX

Meyers, Shirlee (mother; née Meyer), 3–5, 7, 9–15, 20, 22, 24–25, 30, 40, 69–70, 76, 98–99, 105–6, 125, 146–48, 169, 190, 200
Mishkan Tefilah. *See* Temple Mishkan Tefilah
Moe, Dean, 73–74, 77, 79, 81
Molinoff, Perry, 31
Molinsky, Steve, 63, 66–67
"Mona Lisa of Galilee" mosaic (Sepphoris), 132–33
Morrison, Craig, O.Carm., 159
Moynihan, Liz, 130
Moynihan, Patrick, 130
Murphy, Roland E., O.Carm., 111, 159

Nabratein/Nevoraya (excavation), 92, 113, 115
Nagy, Rebecca, 124
Nasher Museum, 200
Nathans, Sydney, 180
National Defense Foreign Language Fellowship, 61
National Humanities Center, 206
National Park Authority of Israel (now Israel Nature and Parks Authority), 132
National Geographic Magazine, 135, 160
Near Eastern and Judaic Studies Department (NEJS; Brandeis), 37, 42
Near Eastern Archaeology, 144
Netzer, Ehud, 59, 101–2, 124, 131–32, 134–39
Neusner, Jacob, 39–40, 46
New York Times, 113, 190
Newman, Tom, 74
Noah, Mordecai Manuel, 202
Norman, Margaret, 43
North Carolina Museum of Art, 171
North Carolina Museum of History, 181–82
Norwich Free Academy (NFA), 8, 17–18, 20–21, 23, 25–26, 190
Norwich State Hospital, 191

Oppenheimer, Eva (aunt; née Meyerowitz), 6–8, 10, 13, 96, 188–90
Oppenheimer, Hanni (cousin), 10, 189–91
Oppenheimer, Kurt (uncle), 6–8, 10, 12–13, 19, 21, 24, 26, 36, 71, 96, 105, 189
Oppenheimer, Susie (cousin), 10, 12, 189, 191
Orlinsky, Harry, 68
Ornstein, Marilyn, 159, 172
Ornstein, Mr., 17
Ornstein, Peter, 159, 172
Osborn, Robert, 75
Oxford Centre for Postgraduate Hebrew Studies, 122
Oxford Centre for Hebrew and Jewish Studies, 122
Oxford Encyclopedia of Archaeology in the Near East, The, 144
Oxford University, 122–25, 151
Oxford University Press, 144

Panciera, Vic, 23
Paper, Herbert (Herb), 102–3
Peace Now, 177
Pearl, Moshe, 91
Pearl, Sara, 91
Pennsylvania State University Press, 123, 138
People magazine, 119–21
Petty, Olan, 85
Piccirillo, Michele, 137
Piva, John, 136
Pontifical Biblical Institute (PBI), Rome, 65, 137, 157–59
Princeton Theological Seminary, 140
Princeton University, 32, 56, 74–76, 140, 151, 205
Princeton University Press, 207
Puccini, Giacomo, 188

Queen Elizabeth House, Oxford, 122
Qumran, 36, 65, 67, 116

Rabin, Chaim, 58

INDEX

Rabinowitz, Israel, 9
Ravenwood, Marion, 120
Reed, Anne, 18
Reed, Jonathan (Jon), 134
Reed, Mr., 18
Reed, Mrs., 18
Richards, Kent, 53
Rogoff, Leonard (Len), 180–81
Romey, Kristin, 135, 160
Rosenstock-Huessy, Eugen, 21
Rosenzweig, Franz, 32
Ross, Donald, 10
Ross, Harold, 19
Ross, James (Jim), 32
Royal Dutch Academy of Sciences, 154
Royal Netherlands Institute in Rome, 154
Rutgers, Leonard, 152, 154–56
Rutty, Alexandro, 181
Ryder, Frank, 32

Sachar, Abram, 42–43
Safdie, Moshe, 197
Safinowitz, Leah, 16
Samfield, Isabel, 168
Sanders, E. P. (Ed), 84, 110
Sasson, Jack, 42
Sauer, James, 127, 141
Schäfer, Peter, 56
Scheuer, Joan, 198
Scheuer, Richard (Dick), 127, 143–44, 146, 196–98
Schewel, Steve, 180
Schiffman, Lawrence (Larry), 135
Schubert, Franz, 35
Schubert, Kurt, 36–37
Schubert, Ursula, 37
Schumann, Robert, 36
Schweitzer, Ada, 62
Scott, David, 83
Scott, James (Jim), 26–27
Scott, Jason, 83
Scott, Joshua, 83
Scott, Judy, 83
Scott-Craig, Pat, 21, 27, 29, 32
Scroggs, Robin, 38
Seabury-Western Theological Seminary, 143

Seger, Joe, 143
Seitenstettengasse synagogue, 35, 41
Sepphoris (excavation), x, 80, 122–24, 131–39, 141, 147, 152, 154, 160, 170–71, 174, 178, 185–86. *See also* Joint Sepphoris Project (JSP)
Seybolt, Larry, 23–24
Seymour, Thaddeus, 29–30
Shalev, Binny, 136–37
Shammai, 80, 92
Shanks, Hershel, 157
Shelkan, Gregor, 41–44, 68–69
Shennecossett Golf Course, 10, 23–24
Shiloh, Yigal, 128
Shenhav, Dodo, 137
Sigmund-Cerbu, Anton, 37
Silberstein, Dorothy (great aunt), 46
Silberstein, George (great uncle), 46
Silberstein, Larry, 68, 70
Simon the Just, 203
Skirball Cultural Center (Los Angeles), 197
Skorka, Abraham, 207
Smith, Benjamin (Ben), 169–70
Smith, Harmon, 75
Smith, Moody, 110
Smith, Patricia, 93
Smithsonian Institution, 53, 72, 74–75, 85
Society for the Protection of Nature (Israel), 117
Society of Biblical Literature (SBL), 53, 105
Southern Jewish Experience (New Orleans), 182
Southern Methodist University, 205
Speiser, Ephraim, 45, 47
Spigel, Chad, x, 185
Stager, Lawrence (Larry), 65, 128
Stahlman, Pablo, 163, 169
Stanford University, 171
Starke, Peter (uncle), 189
Stawski, Patrick, 163–64, 200, 203
Stern, Isaac, 170
Stern, Vera, 170
Strange, Carolyn, 145

INDEX

Strange, James F. (Jim), 73–74, 87–88, 92–93, 108, 119, 121, 123–24, 131, 135, 139, 145, 171
Strauss, Johann, 13
Strauss, Richard, 7, 31, 188
Strugnell, John, 65
Stuntz, David (Dave), 168–69
Suleiman, 107
Sulzer, Solomon, 35
Sykes, James A., 31

Talmon, Shemaryahu, 37–38, 42, 56–58
Talmon, Yonina, 57
Taylor, Ferebee, 95
Tel Arad (excavation), 55
Tel Gezer (excavation), 58, 60, 65, 67, 71, 73–74, 77, 88, 101, 197
Tel Beit Yerah (excavation), 61
Temple Mishkan Tefilah, 41–43, 61, 67, 71
    Hebrew High School, 43, 61–62, 68
Teringo, Robert, 135
Tetel, Joan, 170
Tetel, Mark, 107
Tfilinski, Nathaniel (Tiffy)), 77–78, 80, 115, 117
Thompson, Gough, 140, 143
Thompson, Robert, 65
Timmermann, Jacobo, 163, 202
Todd, Alan, 80
Triangle Jewish Chorale, 163, 168, 181
Trinity University (San Antonio), 185
Trotter, Gay, 110
Tunisia, 125
Tuschak, Peter, 37, 39, 41
Twersky, Isadore, 65, 70

Ulpan Etzion, 56–57, 151
Uncas, the Mohegan chief, 14
Ungerleider-Mayerson, Joy, 127–28, 143
United States Agency for International Development (USAID), 72
United Synagogue Youth (USY), 41
University of Alabama Press, 180
University of Arizona, 97–98
University of Bari, 112–14
University of Chicago, 21, 128

University of Florida, 74, 98
University of Frankfurt. *See* Johann Wolfgang Goethe University, Frankfurt
University of La Verne, 134
University of Michigan, 21, 102, 109, 123~%X
University of Minnesota, 74
University of North Carolina—Chapel Hill (UNC), 85, 94–95, 102, 104
University of Pennsylvania (Penn), 45, 47, 128, 149, 205
University of Utrecht, 154
University of Vienna, 31, 35
University of Wisconsin—Madison, 89, 98
University of Wyoming, 185

Vahl, Jessica, 80
Van Seters, John, 104
Vartoogian, Jack, 120–21
Venosa/Venusia (excavation), 112–14, 119, 154–56
Verdi, Giuseppe, 188
Vienna Staatsoper, 36
Vienna Volksoper, 35–36
Vilnay, Zev, 55–56

Watzinger, Carl, 115
Weiss, Zeev, 132, 134, 138–39
Wellesley College, 42–43, 45–47, 61, 89, 98, 106, 193
West, Cornell, 207
Westfeldt, Amy (niece), 64, 146, 149
Westfeldt, Connie. *See* Meyers, Connie (sister)
Westfeldt, Jennifer (niece), 146
Westfeldt, Pat (brother-in-law), 89
Wheaton College, 129
Wheelock, Eleazar, 194–95
White, Shelby, 127–28
Williams College, 146, 149
Wilmington Chorale, 170
Wissenschaftskolleg (Berlin), 206
Wolfson College, 122
Women's International Zionist Organization (WIZO), 102

Wood, Albert, 149
World Jewish Congress, 112–13, 155
Wright, Edward (Ed), 98
Wright, G. Ernest, 55–58, 61, 65, 69–70, 72–75, 83, 88, 98–99, 142, 184, 197
Wynkoop, Rodney, 169

Yadin, Yigal, 57–60, 127–28
Yadin, Yossi, 128
Yakim, 107
Yale New Haven Hospital, 104
Yale University, 32, 57, 145, 152, 194
Younger, John, 113
Yurka, Blanche, 27

Zak Davino (grandson), x
Zangenberg, Jürgen, 152–53, 158
Zevi, Tulia, 113, 155–56
Zias, Joe, 154–55
Zion, Leonard, 42
Zwelling, Jeremy, 41, 68

Ingram Content Group UK Ltd.
Milton Keynes UK
UKHW012307040423
419656UK00003B/34